LAROUSSE FRENCH HOME COOKING

Jacqueline Gérard and Madeleine Kamman

McGraw-Hill Book Company
New York   London   St. Louis
San Francisco   Toronto   Hamburg   Mexico

LA CUISINE by Jacqueline Gérard
Copyright © 1974 by Librairie Larousse, S. A., Paris
English translation copyright © 1980 by Librairie Larousse,
U.S.A., Inc.

Library of Congress Cataloging in Publication Data

Gérard, Jacqueline.
    Larousse French home cooking.

    Translation of La Cuisine de Jacqueline Gérard.
    Includes index.
    1. Cookery, French.   I. Kamman, Madeleine, joint
author. II. Title.
TX719.G4613   641.5944   80-14937
ISBN 0-07-023141-9

Editor-in-Chief:	Philip M. Rideout with Inez M. Krech
	and Jeanette Mall
Design:	BOOKGRAPHICS
Typography:	Edge Hill Typographics

CONTENTS

Dear Cook and Reader,

This collection of recipes was written for women by a woman, with the goal of simplifying your work, helping resolve your problems of meal preparation, and keeping meal times pleasant and relaxed for your whole family.

In this book you will find:

Traditional French recipes, presented in simple, detailed and direct terms, so you can continue, in an era all too dedicated to canned and packaged products, to enjoy the aroma of a real stew or the unequaled taste of a simple country pâté.

Quick, time-saving recipes; since many women are working and all women without exception chronically suffer from lack of time, more than half of the recipes presented here can be prepared in less than 30 minutes.

Modern and original recipes; the modern woman who likes to cook with a personal style and entertains friends will also find recipes with a new unexpected twist, that will, as time goes on, become classics.

Money-saving recipes; in our days of inflation, money-saving recipes are more than ever needed. It is necessary to learn how to utilize leftovers rather than letting them lose their vitamins on the refrigerator shelf.

This is a collection of some easy and some difficult recipes, none too difficult, however, for any woman to complete with all steps and techniques clearly explained.

It teaches how, starting from a basic recipe, one can develop many variations on an original theme.

It offers ideas for the presentation of dishes, hundreds of tips on how to purchase, choose and store ingredients, and how to prepare ahead to save time.

It explains how to use modern cooking implements, for in these days of speed and mechanical devices, one cannot continue cooking as grandmother used to.

You will not find in this book the highly technical terms of the professional cooks, since they are not a part of our everyday vocabulary. Being like you, a mother and a housewife, I think that plain, everyday language is best understood by everyone and will allow even the most inexperienced cook among you to prepare any recipe successfully on first try.

Jacqueline Gérard

Dear home cooks,

It is my pleasure to present the translation/adaptation of a French cookbook written by a woman for modern women and men.

During numerous years of teaching French cuisine in the United States, I have always regretted that French cuisine manuals, paraphrased or translated for English-speaking cooks, offered "chef's cuisine" with recipes carrying illustrious names of people long dead, cooking with pocketbooks fatter than ours, and producing extravagant waistlines. These manuals described cooking that reflected little of the numerous changes that have taken place in French home kitchens since the late 1950s.

In 1974 Larousse published this volume in France. It met with immediate success among younger working people and was a great seller in bookstores. The success of the book was due to the fact that Mme Gérard made the manual a mirror of her own preoccupations as a homemaker, mother and working professional woman. She was aware that French people were not about to give up their favorite ancestral dishes, so she minimized the work in them and presented new versions condensed to single pages; in earlier books these classics often covered several pages. She did not hesitate to leave options open to the cook, either to keep things simple or to complicate them according to the time available. She presented new ideas and time- and money-saving techniques. Anyone browsing through the book will realize that half of the recipes can be prepared in about half an hour. She also used modern ingredients and implements such as the blender, food processor and pressure cooker.

I agreed to translate and adapt Mme Gérard's book, because it is the first manual in three generations to present what we call in France *la cuisine du cœur*, the good old family fare, humbly prepared and without grandiloquent fanfares of snobbish complications.

Mme Gérard minimized technical language, but inevitably some remains. In order for you to understand fully particular techniques or to know how best to handle basic ingredients, I have prepared a glossary to explain any culinary word unknown to you.

I hope that this meeting between you and French home cooking will result in many happy, successful dishes on your dining table and many happy reunions of congenial family members and friends.

Madeleine M. Kamman

WEIGHTS AND MEASURES

When you measure with a spoon you obtain only an approximate weight since spoon capacities vary from country to country. The American soup spoon known as "tablespoon" (US TB) has a capacity of ½ ounce of liquid, while the European tablespoon (UK TB), used in the British Standards Institute (BSI) measuring system has a capacity of 1 ounce of liquid. A metric tablespoon also has a capacity of 1 ounce of liquid. In the recipes all three measures are given, American, British and metric, for ingredients measured by volume.

For oven use, temperatures are given in Fahrenheit, Celsius and Regulo (the system used on many British stoves), so that any American, British or Canadian cook can find the system she is accustomed to.

There are variations in weight, especially in ingredients such as *flour* (the starch content varies with the type of grain used; also the humidity of the day affects it; flour will weigh less on a cold dry day than it does on a hot humid day); *cheeses* (these vary with age; they lose moisture and consequently weight as they mature); *salt* (this varies also because of moisture content); *oils* (olive oil is heavier than corn oil, corn heavier than cottonseed, etc., because the density is varied).

To obtain a level tablespoon of a dry ingredient, fill the tablespoon so the ingredient is heaped above the rim; then level it off with the back of a knife blade or a spatula.

Some comparisons:
1 cup BSI = 10 fluid ounces; 1 cup US/AVP = 8 ounces
1 cup BSI flour = 4.5 to 5 ounces, depending on the flour; 1 cup US/AVP = 4 ounces
1 cup BSI sugar = 9 ounces sugar; 1 cup US/AVP = 8 ounces (½ pound)
1 cup BSI dried beans = 9 ounces dried beans; 1 cup US/AVP = 7 ounces
1 cup BSI Converted rice = 9.5 ounces rice; 1 cup US/AVP = 8 ounces

In both systems 1 average potato weighs 3 to 3½ ounces; 1 average apple weighs about 3½ ounces; 1 average carrot weighs about 3½ ounces; 1 average tomato weighs about 3 ounces.

Remember that vegetables bought fresh, in bulk, to be cleaned at home will yield only about one third of the original weight in prepared edible portions. Spinach: 2 pounds raw yields 10 ounces cooked and well drained. Peas: 2 pounds in pods yields 10 ounces shelled peas ready to cook. Beans: 2 pounds in pods yields 11 ounces shelled beans ready to cook.

Meats that are broiled or roasted lose one fifth of their initial weight during cooking.

Cooking times for meats are subject to variations from the times indicated here due to the volume of the meat, the shape of the roast, the age of the animal and, of course, your personal taste.

SOUPS
(Les Potages)

CHICKEN GIBLET BROTH AND SOUP
(Bouillon d'Abattis de Volailles)

Collect more giblets in a plastic bag and keep them frozen until you have enough to prepare a larger amount of broth. This broth can be frozen in its turn and kept in the freezer for later use in sauces and stews.

If you have made a dish of boiled beef, you can freeze any leftover beef broth in the same way.

■ Easy
   6 servings
   Inexpensive
   1 hour and 5 minutes, 45 minutes in pressure cooker
   Best season: year round

   giblets of 2 chickens
   4 small carrots
   3 small white turnips
   1 sprig of celery leaves
   2 sprigs of parsley
   marjoram
   basil
   salt and pepper
   water
   US ⅓ cup, UK 4 TB, Converted rice (60 g)
   dash of cayenne pepper
   US 2 TB, UK 1 TB, dry Madeira or dry vermouth (0.5 dl)
   chopped parsley

YOU CAN ALSO USE
duck or turkey giblets. If you use the liver it should be cleaned of all traces of bile. If you prefer, you may keep it for a small terrine. Note that the liver darkens the broth.

● Clean the giblets carefully.

● Peel and trim the vegetables. Wash them and cut them into large cubes.

● Put giblets, vegetables, parsley, and marjoram, basil, salt and pepper to taste in a large saucepan. Add 2 quarts water, bring to a boil, and simmer for 45 minutes. *In a pressure cooker use only 1½ quarts water and cook the soup for only 25 minutes.*

● Strain the broth into a clean saucepan; bring back to a boil. Keep vegetables and giblets hot.

● Add the rice to the boiling broth and let simmer until the rice is tender.

● Meanwhile cut giblets into small cubes; add them to the soup.

● Remove the broth from the heat and add cayenne and Madeira.

● Serve the soup sprinkled with some chopped parsley and serve the vegetables in a side plate, for guests to help themselves.

GARLIC SOUP
(Soupe à l'Ail)

You may wonder why only garlic and water without aromatics or bouillon cubes. This is the soup of the part of the Pyrénées known as Ariège (Capital Foix) and it is ancestrally prepared only with water and garlic. Your garlic is liable not to be as strong as the Ariègeois so do not hesitate to use even more than the recipe calls for.

- Easy
  6 servings
  Inexpensive
  25 minutes
  Best season: fall and winter

  1½ quarts water (1.5 L)
  10 large garlic cloves, or more
  US ½ cup, UK ⅓ cup, olive oil (1 generous dl)
  6 to 10 slices of French bread
  salt and pepper
  3 egg yolks

BE SURE TO
use olive oil; its fruity taste is necessary to the final flavor of the soup.

- Bring 1½ quarts water to a boil.
- Place the garlic cloves on a chopping board and crush them very well by squeezing each of them between the board and your knife blade and hitting the blade sharply with the side of your hand. Peel the garlic cloves.
- Heat the olive oil in a 2-quart saucepan and brown the garlic well, stirring often. The garlic should remain golden and not burn.
- Add the boiling water, cover, and let simmer for 15 minutes.
- Meanwhile, slice the French bread. Heat some more oil in a large frying pan and brown the bread slices in the oil, taking great care not to let them burn.
- Strain the broth so as to discard all traces of garlic. Season to your taste.
- Put the egg yolks in a soup tureen. Start beating them with a whisk while gradually adding a few tablespoons of the broth, stirring constantly.
- Serve piping hot. Offer the bread on a separate plate.

BASQUE COUNTRY BROTH
(Bouillon Basque)

A vegetable is said to be in "julienne" when it is cut into fine strips ⅙ to ¼ inch wide and about 2 inches long. Some vegetables can be processed in a food processor and turned into a "julienne" in a matter of minutes.

In a recipe like this one, cooked with bouillon as a base, you may of course use homemade bouillon, either of chicken (see p.12) or from any boiled beef dish, instead of using water and bouillon cubes.

- Easy
  6 servings
  Inexpensive
  25 minutes
  Best season: July through September

  4 or 5 green bell peppers
  1½ quarts water (1.5 L)
  4 large fresh tomatoes
  4 oz. raw ham (prosciutto type), in 1 thick slice (110 to 120 g)
  bouillon cubes or crystals as needed to your taste
  pepper
  chopped parsley

ABOUT YOUR INGREDIENTS
Choose the peppers smooth, shiny, unwrinkled and free of spots.

You can avoid the expense of buying prosciutto, if you prefer, by using any leftover meat finely diced; all meats will do, or even cold shellfish or fish fillets.

- Wash the bell peppers; cut open, remove all seeds and membranes, and cut into fine julienne.
- Bring the water to a boil.
- Meanwhile wash the tomatoes and remove the stems. As soon as the water boils, immerse tomatoes in it for 2 minutes and peel them. Cut them open, seed them, and cut them into small wedges. Add tomato wedges and the julienne of peppers to the boiling water. Let simmer for 10 minutes.
- Dice the ham very finely and add it to the simmering soup. Continue cooking for another 5 minutes.
- The soup although cooked will be bland, so add as much bouillon cubes or crystals as needed to bring it to your own taste. Check whether a pinch of ground black pepper is needed.
- Serve sprinkled generously with chopped fresh parsley.

ONION SOUP
(Soupe à l'Oignon)

No bouillon or bouillon cubes? Onions and aromatics are strong enough to flavor even plain water. Season very well.

- Relatively easy
  6 servings
  Inexpensive
  1 hour, 40 minutes in pressure cooker
  Best season: fall and winter

6 large onions
US 2 TB, UK 1 TB, oil of your choice (1 TB)
US 2 TB, UK 1 TB, butter (30 g)
1¾ quarts bouillon (fresh homemade,
  canned or made with cubes) (1.75 L)
1 sprig of thyme
½ bay leaf
salt and pepper
12 paper-thin slivers of French bread
5 oz. Gruyère cheese, cut into slivers
  (150 g)

ESSENTIAL
Your dish or bowls must be ovenproof; if you prefer, you can use individual bowls instead of a large casserole.

- Peel the onions and chop them coarsely by knife or in a food processor.
- Heat the mixture of oil and butter very well and add the onions. Cook them over medium-low heat until they have lost their moisture, then raise the heat and let them turn nice and golden, taking care to stir often so they do not burn and turn bitter.
- Add the bouillon, or water and cubes, and bring to a boil.
- Add to the pot the thyme, bay leaf, and a bit of salt and pepper only if needed. Cover the pot, reduce to a simmer, and cook for 30 minutes, *10 minutes in pressure cooker.*
- Meanwhile, toast the bread in a medium oven. In an ovenproof casserole, put alternate layers of bread and cheese, ending with a layer of cheese.
- Add the soup, either strained or with the onions left in, as you wish. Broil for about 10 minutes and serve piping hot.

CABBAGE SOUP
(Soupe au Chou)

This is truly a one-pot meal. Add more protein to the soup by serving with it a bowl of grated Swiss or Parmesan cheese. This is perfect for a Sunday night. To round out the meal, serve cheese and a plain green salad and a piece of fruit or a quickly prepared dessert.

■ Easy
6 servings
Inexpensive (also see advice)
2¼ hours
Best season: fall, winter, early spring

1 head of cabbage
6 to 8 carrots (1 lb. or 500 g)
4 white turnips (¾ lb. or 375 g)
1 very large onion
4 cloves
1 lb. slab bacon (500 g)
2½ to 3 quarts water (2.5 to 3 L)
salt
½ bay leaf
pepper
6 links of Italian sweet sausage
6 large potatoes
4 slices of light rye bread

- Clean and pare the vegetables. Leave the carrots whole; cut the turnips and the cabbage into 4 pieces each. Stick the onion with the cloves.
- Put the bacon in a suitable pot, cover it with cold water, bring to a boil, let blanch for 5 minutes, and drain.
- Bring 2½ quarts water to a boil in a 6-quart soup pot. Add the bacon, cabbage, carrots and turnips as well as the onion, a bit only of salt (mind the bacon), the bay leaf, and pepper to taste. Bring to a second boil, reduce to a simmer, and let cook for 1½ hours, *1 hour only in the pressure cooker.*
- Prick the sausages with a fork. Peel the potatoes and cut them into quarters. Add sausages and potatoes to pot and let cook for another 20 minutes, *10 minutes in the pressure cooker.*
- Now correct the seasoning; remove the onion and bay leaf. Cut bacon and sausages into slices; toast the bread.
- Put the bread into the tureen, add the soup and sliced meat, and serve.

CHOOSE WELL
The cabbage must be tight, with fresh outside leaves. Make sure that the cut of bacon contains at least 45 to 50% lean meat.

The Italian sausages can be replaced by any other of your choice.

LEEK AND POTATO SOUP
(Soupe aux Poireaux)

If any soup is too liquid after you have finished cooking it, a few teaspoons of instant mashed potato powder will thicken it immediately.

- Easy
  6 servings
  Inexpensive
  45 minutes
  Best season: August through May

  6 medium-size mealy potatoes
  4 large leeks or 6 smaller ones
  1½ quarts water (1.5 L)
  salt and pepper
  US ½ cup, UK 4 oz., milk (1 generous dl)
  US ⅓ cup, UK 3 oz., heavy cream (90 g)
  chopped parsley

CHOOSE YOUR POTATOES WELL
For a soup, the mealier and the starchier, the better.

- Peel the potatoes, wash them, and cut them into ½-inch cubes. Put the potatoes in a large saucepan.
- Pare the leeks of their dark green tops. Cut the leeks lengthwise into halves, leaving ½ inch still attached at the root. Wash carefully by letting water run between the folds. Cut the leeks across into 1-inch pieces. Add them and the water to the saucepan.
- Bring quickly to a boil. Turn the heat down and simmer for 25 minutes, *10 minutes in pressure cooker.* Add salt and pepper to taste.
- Purée the soup through a food mill placed over a bowl.
- Return the soup to the heat and add the milk. Reheat to the boiling point; correct the seasoning.
- Put the cream in the soup tureen. Season it lightly with a pinch each of salt and pepper, then add the soup and stir well. Sprinkle chopped parsley on the surface of the soup.

PUMPKIN OR SQUASH SOUP
(Soupe au Potiron)

Another method to fry bread: Butter the slices on both sides and fry in a preheated frying pan.

■ Easy
6 servings
Inexpensive
30 minutes
Best season: fall and winter

1½ lbs. pumpkin meat (750 g)
water
salt and pepper
US 3 TB, UK 1½ TB, cornstarch (1½ TB)
1½ quarts milk (1.5 L)
sweet spices of your choice (nutmeg, etc.)
6 thin slices of French bread
US 2 TB, UK 1 TB, oil (1 TB)
US 2 TB, UK 1 TB, butter (30 g)
4 oz. Parmesan cheese (125 g)

- Peel the pumpkin and cube it. Put the cubes in a saucepan, barely cover with water, and add a bit of salt and pepper. Cook over medium-low heat for 15 to 20 minutes.
- Purée the pumpkin through a food mill or in a blender. Return the purée to the saucepan.
- Put the cornstarch into a bowl and dilute it with 1 cup of the milk, cold.
- Mix the remainder of the milk with the puréed pumpkin and bring to a boil. Reduce to a simmer and add the mixture of milk and cornstarch, stirring until thickened. Add the sweet spices to your taste and let simmer for a few minutes.
- Brown the bread slices in the oil. Pour the soup into a tureen, mix in the raw butter, and float the bread croutons on top.
- Serve with a small bowl of Parmesan cheese on the side.

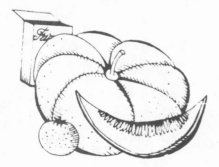

WOULD YOU ENJOY
this soup later in the year? Keep the pumpkin whole in a cool place or freeze the cooked meat in 1-pound packages.

You may use all other winter squashes such as butternut, Hubbard, acorn, etc. Adjust the cornstarch or even omit it, if the texture is thick enough without it.

PISTOU SOUP
(Soupe au Pistou)

Do you own a blender? If so, skip the additional olive oil of the aillade and purée basil and garlic in about 1 cup of the soup broth. Then mix into the bulk of the soup.

This soup is the glory of the summer Provençal cookery; should you have no basil, because it does not grow in your climate, add US 2 tablespoons, UK 1 tablespoon, dried basil to the soup as soon as it boils. Add mashed garlic cloves at the last minute. Tomatoes grown in northern climates are not as sweet as those ripened in the southern sunshine, so if you dwell in cool regions, replace some of the water by tomato juice.

You may also replace the potato by US 6 tablespoons, UK 3 tablespoons, small soup pasta.

- Medium difficult
  6 servings
  Inexpensive to expensive (see note on cheese)
  45 minutes, 25 minutes in pressure cooker
  Best season: July through October, when basil is plentiful

  ¾ lb. green beans (375 g)
  1 small zucchini (marrow or courgette)
  2 small leeks
  2 onions
  1 large potato
  3 large tomatoes
  US 6 TB, UK 3 TB, olive oil (3 TB)
  salt and pepper
  1¾ quarts water (1.75 L)
  5 oz. grated Parmesan cheese (150 g)

  AILLADE
  3 garlic cloves
  1 cup basil leaves, cleaned and dry (50 g)
  US 4 TB, UK 2 TB, olive oil (2 TB)

- String the beans and cut them into ½-inch pieces. Wash them quickly without soaking.
- Clean and pare the zucchini, leeks, onions and potato. Wash them well, cut them into small pieces. Cut the tomatoes after squeezing the seeds out of them.
- Heat the olive oil in a large saucepan. Add the onions and leeks and sauté them until golden.
- Add the green beans, zucchini, potato, tomatoes, salt and pepper to taste, and the water. Bring to a boil, reduce to a simmer, and cook covered for about 40 minutes, *15 minutes in pressure cooker.*

GARLIC PASTE (*Aillade*)
- Peel the garlic cloves. Chop them coarsely with the basil leaves. Pound them in a small bowl, adding the olive oil slowly until a paste results.
- Put the paste into a soup tureen and dissolve well with some of the broth. Pour in the remainder of the soup. Pass the cheese separately for guests to help themselves.

ABOUT PARMESAN CHEESE
The true Parmigiano-Reggiano makes this soup very expensive, so use domestic Parmesan and cut it with Swiss cheese to liven it up a bit.

VERMICELLI SOUP FROM THE JURA
(Soupe Franc-Comtoise au Vermicelle)

To toast vermicelli, use a thick enameled cast-iron pot; the heat is slower and more regular, which prevents scorching. This also applies when toasting any other pasta or rice.

- Easy
  **6 servings
  Inexpensive
  25 minutes
  Best season: fall and winter**

  **1¾ quarts water (1.75 L)
  3 small onions
  US 2 TB, UK 1 TB, butter (30 g)
  US 1 TB, UK ½ TB, oil (½ TB)
  US 1 cup, UK 1 scant cup, crushed
      uncooked Italian vermicelli (8 TB)
  2 garlic cloves, mashed
  salt and pepper
  good dash of nutmeg
  US ½ cup, UK ⅓ cup, heavy cream (1
      generous dl)
  US 2 TB, UK 1 TB, chopped parsley
  3 egg yolks**

- Bring the water to a boil. Peel and mince the onions finely with a knife or in a food processor.
- Heat the butter and oil very well in a thick pot. Add the onions and stir over medium heat until the butter has lost all its water and has become translucent.
- Add the uncooked vermicelli and keep stirring until it turns light golden. Meanwhile mash the garlic.
- Add the boiling water, salt and pepper to taste, garlic and nutmeg. Reduce the heat, cover, and let simmer for 10 minutes.
- Put the cream mixed with the chopped parsley and egg yolks at the bottom of the soup tureen. Whisk in about 1 cup of the soup very gradually, stirring constantly to prevent coagulation of the yolk, then gradually add the remainder of the soup, mixing very well. Correct the seasoning and serve. *Do not boil.*

YOU SHOULD KNOW THAT
oil added to butter allows it to heat at a higher degree without burning.

Vermicelli bought in spools must be crushed thoroughly before being used in this recipe.

CREAM OF LETTUCE SOUP
(Potage Crème de Laitue)

Are you in a hurry? Then peel the potatoes and quickly process them into fine strips in a food processor; they will cook faster.

- Easy
  **6 servings
  Inexpensive
  35 minutes
  Best season: summer and fall**

  **4 large potatoes
  2 large heads of soft-leaf lettuce (Boston, Bibb, Red, etc., not iceberg)
  1½ quarts water (1.5 L), cold
  1 bouillon cube (chicken or beef)
  salt and pepper
  2 egg yolks
  US ½ cup, UK 4 oz., heavy cream (1 generous dl)**

BE THRIFTY
In this soup, you can use all the dark green leaves that are too dark for salads, but are a good source of iron.

If you have a garden and lettuce heads that are slightly overgrown, use them to make the soup.

Of course, you can use any leftover bouillon or stock from a boiled dinner.

- Peel the potatoes, wash them, and cut them into ¼-inch cubes.
- Wash the lettuce heads carefully. Shake them to discard the excess water; remove the cores. Set aside 6 medium-size green leaves. Chop the remainder of the lettuce by hand or in a food processor.
- In a large pot put all together the chopped lettuce, potatoes, cold water, bouillon cube, and a pinch each of salt and pepper. Bring to a boil, turn down to a simmer, then let cook until the potatoes fall apart.
- Purée the soup through a food mill placed over a large mixing bowl. Re-heat well.
- Meanwhile, cut the reserved lettuce leaves into "chiffonnade" by rolling the leaves into cigars and cutting across the cigars at ¼-inch intervals with a knife or scissors. Put them into a soup tureen.
- Mix the egg yolks and cream well; whisk in about 1 cup of the soup. Pour this into the soup tureen and then gradually add the remainder of the soup, stirring well. Correct the seasoning.

WITH THE SAME METHOD
Swiss Chard Soup: Use the green leaves of Swiss chard; the soup will be very green and appetizing.

Parsley or Chervil Soup: Chop a large bundle of parsley or chervil leaves in a food processor and sauté them slowly in a pat of butter, before you add the potatoes and water.

CREAM OF SPINACH SOUP
(Potage Crème aux Épinards)

The soup becomes more substantial if you garnish it with slices of French bread fried in butter and oil. Use 1 slice per person.

Also, in all vegetable soups, remember that you can always replace the potatoes by bread slices. The heels of bread loaves are perfect for this use, and all breads (French, Italian, white, whole-grain or rye) may be used.

■ Easy
6 servings
Inexpensive
35 minutes
Best season: year around

1 lb. loose fresh spinach (500 g)
1 large onion
3 small potatoes
US 2 TB, UK 1 TB, oil (1 TB)
US 2 TB, UK 1 TB, butter (30 g)
pinch of nutmeg
salt and pepper
1½ quarts water (1.5 L)
US ¼ cup, UK 2 oz., heavy cream (50 g)

IF YOU ARE IN A RUSH
use two 10-inch boxes of frozen spinach and cook it with the potatoes.

- Clean the spinach. Wash the leaves in several waters to discard all traces of sand.
- Peel and chop the onion; peel the potatoes and cut into ⅓-inch cubes.
- In a large saucepan, heat the oil and butter. Add the potatoes and onion to the pan and brown both over high heat.
- Meanwhile reserve a small handful of spinach leaves and chop the remainder very well, either with a knife or in a food processor. Keep in a small bowl.
- As soon as the onions and potatoes are golden brown, add the spinach leaves, nutmeg, and salt and pepper to taste.
- Bring the water to a boil and add to the saucepan containing all the vegetables. Cover the pan and let simmer for about 20 minutes.
- Purée the soup through a food mill, or purée in a food processor.
- Reheat the soup to the boiling point and add the reserved spinach leaves.
- Turn the heat off and add the cream. Correct the seasoning and serve.

CREAM OF TURNIP SOUP
(Potage Crème de Navets)

Do you know that blanching under Step 2 is nothing more than your good old parboiling and that it should be done only with older vegetables? Skip this step with new spring and summer vegetables.

- Easy
  6 servings
  Inexpensive
  1 hour, 40 minutes in pressure cooker
  Best season: fall and winter

  12 average-size white turnips, or 2 small yellow turnips (rutabagas)
  US 2 TB, UK 1 TB, butter (30 g)
  US 2 TB, UK 1 TB, oil of your choice (30 g)
  3½ cups water (7.5 dl)
  a good pinch of ground or grated nutmeg
  salt and pepper
  2 cups milk (.5 L)
  6 slices of French bread
  chopped parsley
  heavy cream (optional)

- In a 2-quart pot bring 1 quart of water to a boil.

- Peel the turnips, cut them into ½-inch cubes, and add all to the boiling water. Bring back to a boil and let turnips blanch (see advice) for 5 minutes. Drain completely, discarding the water.

- Heat the butter and oil well. Add the turnips and stir so as to coat them well with the fats.

- Add 3½ cups water, the nutmeg, and salt and pepper to taste. Let cook until the turnips fall apart, 30 minutes, or *10 minutes in pressure cooker.*

- Purée the soup through a food mill placed over a bowl, or purée it in a blender. Mix the turnip purée with the milk, and bring back to a boil. Correct the seasoning and remove from the heat.

- Toast the slices of bread and put one in each plate. Sprinkle the soup with chopped parsley and ladle it over the bread.

- Pass a small bowl of heavy cream, lightly whipped, for guests to help themselves.

WITH THE SAME METHOD
Cream of Carrot Soup: Use 8 large carrots. Cook them in the 3½ cups of water without blanching them first. Add a couple of potatoes if you would prefer the soup a bit thicker.

ABOUT THE PRESSURE COOKER
Remember, when you cook in a pressure cooker, to add time for the utensil to reach the correct pressure, since the cooking starts only after it has been reached. Also, don't use the pressure cooker for items with a very short cooking time!

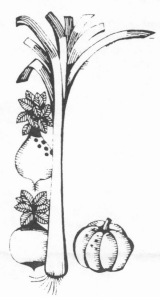

ASPARAGUS VELOUTÉ
(Velouté d'Asperges)

In winter you can prepare this soup with canned asparagus; there will be no need to recook them.

■ Easy
6 servings
Expensive
40 minutes
Best season: April to June

water for blanching the asparagus
1½ lbs. asparagus (750 g)
US 6 TB, UK 3 TB, butter (90 g)
US 6 TB, UK 3 TB, flour (50 g)
salt and pepper
nutmeg
3 cups milk, scalded (.75 L)
US ¼ cup, UK 2 TB, heavy cream (60 g)

BE THRIFTY
Use as much of the asparagus stem as possible; to do so, bend the asparagus from tip to root; it will break exactly where the fibers become too tough to be edible.

You may use the blender to purée the asparagus, but you will then have to strain the soup to discard the few fibers always present in asparagus.

- Heat a large pot of water. As soon as it boils add salt.
- While the water is heating, peel the asparagus, wash them, and cut them into 1-inch pieces.
- Blanch the asparagus pieces in the boiling salted water for 5 minutes. Remove the asparagus to a bowl. Save the water. Separate the asparagus tips and put them into another small bowl.
- In another large saucepan, melt the butter. When the foam starts receding, add the flour. Stir over low heat so as not to let the flour take on any color. Using a whisk, add a generous 2 cups of the asparagus blanching water and stir until the mixture boils. Add salt, pepper and a scrape or pinch of nutmeg.
- Add the asparagus pieces (not the tips), cover, and let simmer for 15 to 20 minutes.
- Purée the soup through a food mill and return to the heat. Add the scalded milk, mix well, and heat to serving temperature.
- Put the heavy cream and the asparagus tips into the soup tureen and pour the velouté over. Stir to homogenize, and correct final seasoning.

MUSHROOM VELOUTÉ
(Velouté de Champignons)

If more calories do not bother you, you may serve the soup accompanied by a small bowl of heavy and sour creams mixed in equal proportions and seasoned to your taste with salt, pepper and nutmeg.

- Medium difficult
  6 servings
  A bit expensive
  30 minutes
  Best season: October through May

  1 large onion (50 g)
  1½ quarts milk (1.5 L)
  US ½ cup, UK 4 oz., butter (120 g)
  US ½ cup, UK 2 oz., flour (60 g)
  salt and pepper
  1 lb. fresh mushrooms (500 g)

CHOOSE WELL
Good mushrooms are nice and white and their gills are tightly closed. Use any mushrooms on the day they are purchased.

- Peel the onion and chop it.
- Put the milk over medium heat to scald.
- Meanwhile heat the butter until the foam starts receding. Add the onion and cook until translucent.
- Add the flour and cook for 2 to 3 minutes, stirring once or twice.
- Off the heat, whisk in the milk in 2 additions until smooth. Return to the heat and bring to a boil, stirring constantly. Turn down to a simmer, add salt and pepper to taste, and let cook.
- While the light milk sauce cooks, wash the mushrooms quickly, pat them dry, and chop them into ¼-inch pieces, using either a knife or a food processor.
- Add the mushrooms to the simmering milk sauce and simmer for another 15 minutes.
- Using a slotted spoon remove and reserve about US ¼ cup, UK 2 tablespoons mushroom hash from the soup. Purée this through a food mill or in a blender. Adjust the seasoning; reheat well.
- Put the puréed mushrooms in a soup tureen and pour the hot soup over them.

WATERCRESS VELOUTÉ
(Velouté au Cresson)

If you prefer, you can replace the butter by the addition of 2 egg yolks mixed with about US ⅓ cup, UK 3 ounces, cream; or, if you want to avoid egg yolks, about US ½ cup, UK 4 ounces, evaporated milk.

■ Easy
 6 servings
 Inexpensive
 35 minutes
 Best season: year around

 **1 large or 2 small bunches of fresh
   watercress
 1½ quarts water (1.5 L)
 3 small potatoes
 salt and pepper
 US 4 TB, UK 2 TB, butter (60 g)
 6 small slices of French bread fried in half
   butter, half oil (optional)**

CHOOSE WELL
Watercress must be very fresh with shiny and waxy leaves.

- Wash the watercress very carefully.

- Separate the leaves and stems of the watercress. Chop the stems coarsely. Chop the leaves finely in a food processor or by knife as you prefer; reserve the leaves in a small bowl.

- Bring the water to a boil, add the chopped watercress stems and potatoes with a pinch of salt and pepper, and cook until the potatoes fall apart.

- Purée the soup through a food mill placed over another saucepan, or purée in a food processor. Reheat the soup until it boils again. Add the chopped watercress leaves and simmer for 4 minutes only. Turn the heat off and whisk in the butter.

- If you wish, brown the bread slices in a mixture of oil and butter and pour the soup over the obtained croutons.

VELOUTÉS OF DRIED LEGUMES
(Veloutés aux Légumes Secs)

Be thrifty. Do not hesitate to prepare this soup with any leftover baked beans that you may have and homemade broth or bouillon cube broth. Canned beans can also be used.

■ Easy
6 servings
Inexpensive
2½ hours, 1 hour in pressure cooker
Best season: fall and winter

7 oz. dried beans (200 to 210 g)
2 onions
bouquet garni
2 quarts water (2 scant L)
1 bouillon cube
salt and pepper
US ⅓ cup, UK 3 oz., heavy cream (1 scant dl)
chopped parsley

- Starting 24 hours ahead of time, soak the beans in plenty of cold water.
- At 2½ hours before dinner, peel and chop the onions. Tie parsley stems, bay leaf and thyme sprigs into a *bouquet garni* (see note below).
- Drain the beans. Put them in a large saucepan; add the water, chopped onions and *bouquet garni*. Bring to a boil slowly. As soon as the soup boils, reduce to a simmer and cook until the beans are tender and falling apart— about 2½ hours, *50 minutes in pressure cooker.*
- Remove the *bouquet garni*. Pour the beans and their cooking broth into a food mill and purée. You may purée in a blender if you prefer, but then you must strain the soup to discard the bean skins.
- Return the soup to the heat, bring back to a boil, and add the bouillon cube. Stir well and correct the final seasoning.

- Mix the heavy cream with a pinch of salt and pepper in the soup tureen and pour the soup over it. Mix well. Add chopped parsley.

WITH THE SAME METHOD
Esau Soup (Lentil Soup): Use dried lentils instead of dried beans. If you cook a blanched ¼-pound slab of bacon or 2 sausage links in the soup, it will taste better. Dice or slice meat in the finished soup as a garnish.

Moroccan Soup (Chick-pea Soup): Heat the contents of 1 can (16 oz. or .45 kg) of chick-peas in a pot. Purée as above and lighten to soup consistency by adding enough broth made with homemade chicken broth or bouillon cubes. Garnish with 1 bulb of fennel, very finely sliced by knife or food processor and added *raw* to the boiling soup.

Saint Germain Soup (Split-pea Soup): Prepare it with split peas soaked overnight and add also 1 large leek, white part only, finely chopped.

KNOW THESE SIMPLE FACTS
All legumes must start cooking in cold water or they never soften properly and completely.

A bouquet garni is a small bundle of parsley stems, a bay leaf, or part of it, and a sprig of thyme tied together. This bouquet garni must float freely in the pot during the cooking of a dish; it should not be wrapped in cheesecloth.

MUSSEL SOUP
(Soupe aux Moules)

Two possible additions: You may also pass a bowl of fresh cream to your guests and present some toasted bread rubbed with garlic.

■ Relatively easy
6 servings
Inexpensive
30 minutes
Best season: September to April

2 medium-size onions
4 sprigs of parsley
2 garlic cloves
thyme
1 bay leaf
1 bottle of dry white wine
3 quarts mussels
US 5 TB, UK 2½ TB, butter (75 g)
US 5 TB, UK 2½ TB, flour (40 g)
US 3 cups, UK 2 cups, water (.75 L)
chopped parsley

ABOUT MUSSELS
When scrubbing mussels, add a liberal amount of salt to any water they will come in contact with, or they will lose their natural tang.

- Peel the onions. Chop them finely as well as the parsley and the garlic. Crumble thyme and bay leaf finely.
- Pour the white wine into a gallon pot, add onions, parsley, garlic, thyme and bay leaf. Bring to a boil. Cover and simmer for 10 minutes.
- Meanwhile scrub the mussels and wash them in several baths of salted water.
- Add them to the pot containing the white wine. Cover and let cook over low heat, stirring several times, until all mussels have opened. Shell the mussels.
- Strain the cooking juices of the mussels through cheesecloth or filter paper.
- In another saucepan, melt the butter, add the flour and cook, stirring occasionally. Add the mussel cooking juices and the same amount of hot water. Bring to a boil, stirring, and turn down to simmer for 5 to 6 minutes.
- Return the mussels to the pot containing the soup. Correct the salt and pepper and add the parsley. Pour into the soup tureen.

SHRIMP VELOUTÉ
(Velouté de Crevettes)

A bit of budgeting: When you cook a fish in a court bouillon (see p. 295), strain the court-bouillon carefully and freeze it in jars. You can replace water or clam juice by that mixture in any soup of this kind.

- Relatively easy
  6 servings
  Medium expensive
  45 minutes, 35 minutes in pressure cooker
  Best season: year around

  1 lb. shrimps, cooked in the shells (500 g)
  3 cups water (.75 L)
  US 1 cup, UK 8 oz., clam juice (2.5 dl)
  US ½ cup, UK 4 oz., white wine (1 generous dl)
  1 large onion, chopped
  ½ bay leaf
  1 sprig of thyme
  2 cups milk (.5 L)
  US 3 TB, UK 1½ TB, butter (45 g)
  US 6 TB, UK 3 TB, flour (45 g)
  US ⅓ cup, UK 3 oz., tomato paste (90 g)
  salt and pepper
  cream, lightly whipped

- Shell the shrimps. Mix the shells with the water and liquefy in a blender.
- Turn the mixture into a saucepan. Add the clam juice and the white wine, the onion, bay leaf and thyme, and cook for 25 minutes, *15 minutes in pressure cooker.*
- Strain the mixture into a bowl.
- Scald the milk.
- Melt the butter in a saucepan, add the flour, and cook, stirring occasionally, without browning.
- Whisk the shellfish broth into the roux, then whisk in the hot milk. Stir well until the mixture comes to a boil. Add the tomato paste and simmer for 5 to 6 minutes.
- Meanwhile, cut the shrimps across in ¹⁄₆-inch slices. Add them to the soup just before serving and without reboiling. Correct the seasoning.
- Pass lightly whipped cream in a small bowl.

FOR THIS PREPARATION
No need to buy the largest size of shrimps; the medium-size or small ones have more taste.

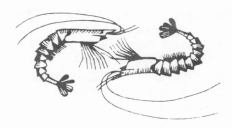

PROVENÇAL FISH SOUP
(Soupe de Poissons Provençale)

The fish used here are those preferred and well available in English-speaking countries. If you have access to the true Mediterranean fish, use a chapon (the name given to a large rascasse), 2 large whitings and several red mullets.

■ Relatively easy
6 servings
Medium expensive
1 hour
Best season: year around

**5 lbs. sole or flounder heads and bones
    (2.25 kg)
1½ quarts water (1.5 L)
3 large onions
a bundle of parsley stems
1 bay leaf
1 sprig of thyme
salt and pepper
12 garlic cloves
chopped parsley
US 4 TB, UK 2 TB, olive oil (50 g)
2 TB chopped fresh basil, or 1 TB dried
1 sprig of fresh rosemary, or 1 tsp. dried
1 tsp. fennel seeds
US ¼ cup, UK 2 TB, tomato paste (60 g)
4 medium-size potatoes
1 cup mayonnaise (see p. 62)
2 cups bread cubes
1 lb. medium-size raw shrimps, shelled
    (500 g)
½ lb. cubed monkfish (250 g)
½ lb. cubed halibut (250 g)
ground saffron**

● Put the fish heads and bones in a large pot, add the water, 1 chopped onion, the parsley stems, bay leaf, thyme, 1 teaspoon salt and pepper to taste.
● Bring quickly to a boil, turn the heat down, and simmer for 35 to 40 minutes. As the broth simmers, push down on the bones to break them up and release the flavor.
● Strain the broth well, pushing on the solids to press out all the flavorful broth.
● Peel and chop well the remaining onions and 11 garlic cloves. Chop enough parsley to obtain a good handful.
● Heat the olive oil. Add the above aromatics and cook until light brown.
● Add the basil, rosemary, fennel seeds, the fish broth and tomato paste, and simmer.
● Meanwhile peel the potatoes, cut into ½-inch cubes, and wash them.
● Add the potatoes to the broth and cook for 10 to 12 minutes.
● Meanwhile, crush and mash the last garlic clove and add it to the mayonnaise.
● Brown the bread cubes in some more olive oil and put them in a bowl.
● Bring the soup to a heavy boil. Add shrimps, monkfish and halibut cubes and saffron to taste; cover. Turn off the heat and remove to a counter. Let stand for 4 to 5 minutes.
● Serve the soup in a large soup or chowder bowl. Offer the garlic mayonnaise and bread croutons separately.

FIRST COURSES
(Les Hors-d'Œuvre)

MELON IN PORT
(Melon au Porto)

If your melons are ripe but not to be used until the next day, store them in a sealed plastic bag in the vegetable bin of the refrigerator.

■ Easy
6 servings
Affordable
5 minutes
Best season: the height of summer

3 small melons
Ruby Port

CHOOSE MELONS WELL
Remember that the smaller and heavier, the better. If you cannot choose the melon for yourself, tell your greengrocer when you plan to serve it.

- Cut each melon into halves across the natural marks on the rind.
- Empty the centers of all water, seeds and fibers until smooth.
- Add US 3 tablespoons, UK 1½ tablespoons, Port (1½ TB) to each cavity and roll the Port back and forth to spread the flavor of the wine over the whole cavity.
- Serve the melons set in crushed ice.
- Should the melons have to wait, refrigerate them covered with a plastic wrap to prevent the melon smell permeating the refrigerator.

GRATED CARROT SALAD
(Carottes Râpées)

About nutrition and time: Carrots are rich in iron and vitamins A, B, C. They are excellent for children and you should serve them often. To gain time, investigate one of those electric grating machines; they are worth their weight in gold.

■ Easy
   6 servings
   Inexpensive
   7 minutes
   Best season: late spring and summer

   6 medium-size carrots
   1 shallot
   salt and pepper
   US 2 TB, UK 1 TB, lemon juice (1 TB)
   US ⅓ cup, UK ¼ cup, oil (1 dl)
   chopped parsley

• Peel the carrots. Grate them or julienne them with any electric machine (Moulinette, food processor) to ⅛-inch strips.
• Peel the shallot and chop very fine. Put in a small bowl with salt and pepper to taste and the lemon juice. Mix well and gradually add the oil.
• Toss carrots into dressing. Transfer to a small salad boat and serve sprinkled with parsley.

WITH THE SAME METHOD
Any time you change the dressing, you will have a new salad, so improvise; here are a few ideas:

Grated Carrot Salad with Garlic and Herbs: Replace the shallot by a finely mashed garlic clove and chopped fresh herbs; the best herbs are mint, chervil, parsley, tarragon, chives, rosemary and savory.

Grated Carrot Salad with Anchovies: Dress the carrots with a little dressing made with vinegar to which you add 1 small white onion, chopped fine, 4 anchovy fillets, first carefully rinsed in water, then chopped, and capers.

Grated Carrot Salad with Cream: Dress with the juice of 1 lemon, salt, pepper and US ½ cup, UK ⅓ cup, heavy or sour cream.

Grated Carrot Salad with Raisins: Soak US ¼ cup, UK 1½ tablespoons, raisins in a little hot water for 15 minutes. Drain them and add them to the carrots. Make dressing with lemon juice, salt and pepper, oil and heavy cream.

A New Idea: Raw Red Beet Salad: Treat raw red beets as you would carrots; grate them and dress them in any of the dressings mentioned here; you will be surprised how delicious it is.

CHOOSE YOUR CARROTS WELL
The best are sold with their greens still on. Beware of large carrots in plastic bags especially through the winter; they are apt to be woody.

CELERIAC IN RÉMOULADE
(Céleri Rémoulade)

If you have time, do not hesitate to prepare this recipe ahead of time; the celery will be more flavorful and the salad keeps very well in the refrigerator.

You can also use commercial mayonnaise and add mustard and a dash of vinegar to obtain a quicker sauce.

■ Easy
  6 servings
  Inexpensive
  25 minutes
  Best season: fall and winter

  1 large or 2 small celeriac roots
  1 lemon
  water
  salt
  1 egg
  **US 2 TB, UK 1 TB, prepared Dijon
    mustard (1 TB)**
  US ⅔ cup, UK ½ cup, oil (2 scant dl)
  pepper
  leaves of 3 parsley sprigs

CHOOSE YOUR CELERIAC WELL
A good celery root feels heavier to the hand than it looks to the eye. It is hard and firm under the pressure of the finger.

- Peel the celeriac root(s) and pare of all woody material.
- Squeeze the lemon juice into a large bowl. Grate the celeriac and add grated portions immediately to the lemon juice, tossing well.
- Bring a pot of water to a boil. Add salt. Add the celeriac and let parboil for 1 minute. Remove celeriac with a slotted spoon and put in a bowl of cold water. Drain and pat dry in a tea towel.
- In the same water, cook the egg for 10 minutes. Remove the yolk to a small bowl, mash it finely with the mustard, add salt and pepper to taste, and whisk in the oil to obtain a mayonnaise-style dressing.
- Toss the celeriac into the dressing and put in a salad bowl.
- Chop parsley leaves and egg white semicoarsely and sprinkle on top of the salad.

MUSHROOM SALAD
(Champignons en Salade)

Do you know that when you peel mushrooms, you remove and discard their most flavorful and most nutritious part?

■ Easy
6 servings
Medium expensive
10 minutes
Best season: year around

¾ lb. fresh mushrooms (375 g)
1 large lemon
salt and pepper
US ½ cup, UK ⅓ cup, oil (1 generous dl)
chopped parsley or tarragon

- Cut the root end of the mushrooms. If they are very dirty, wash them quickly under running cold water. If they are not, wipe them clean with a tea towel. Do not peel them.
- Cut the mushrooms into ¼-inch-thick slices (½ cm) and put them on a small oval platter. Sprinkle them with the lemon juice.
- Sprinkle with salt and pepper and pour the oil over the mushrooms. Toss well. The mushrooms will soak up all their seasonings and no sauce will be left.
- Serve sprinkled with chopped parsley or tarragon.

CHOOSE YOUR MUSHROOMS WELL
Choose mushrooms small, white, round and firm with tightly closed gills.

To extract the maximum juice of a lemon, roll it several times on a table top, applying as much pressure as you can with the flat of your hand.

STUFFED TOMATOES AND VARIATIONS
(Tomates Farcies, Variantes)

Would you like a quick idea for a summer dinner? Double the proportions given here and serve with the dish a fine green salad dressed with cream, vinegar and chopped fresh herbs.

■ Easy
  6 servings
  Inexpensive
  30 minutes
  Best season: late summer when tomatoes are plentiful

  1 egg
  water
  6 medium-size tomatoes
  salt
  1 package (10 oz.) frozen mixed
    vegetables (285 g)
  1 can (6½ oz.) light tuna packed in oil
    (190 g)
  1 cup Mayonnaise (p. 62)
  pepper
  6 soft lettuce leaves

- Hard-boil the egg in boiling salted water for 10 minutes. Cool in cold water.
- Cut off the tops of the tomatoes, using a knife with a serrated blade. Using a teaspoon, empty the tomatoes completely without breaking the skin or the pulp of the shell.
- Salt the inside of the tomatoes lightly and turn them upside down on a plate to drain the water they will release.
- Boil the vegetables in boiling salted water for 3 minutes. Rinse under cold water and drain well.
- Mix gently vegetables, tuna and mayonnaise; correct the seasoning.

- Line a small round platter with the lettuce leaves. Arrange the tomatoes on top and fill them with the salad.
- Shell the egg and cut it into 6 slices. Set 1 slice of egg on each tomato.

WITH THE SAME METHOD
To use any leftover or on the contrary to present something a bit fancier, try these ideas:

Shellfish: Replace the tuna by shelled small shrimps, cooked mussels or crab.

Fish of any Kind: Replace the tuna by any leftover poached or baked fish, carefully cleaned and trimmed.

Meat: Replace the tuna by any cooked meat such as pork, veal, poultry, and add more mustard to the mayonnaise.

BE THRIFTY
Use light tuna instead of white tuna; it is less expensive and tastier.

TOMATOES WITH ROQUEFORT
(Tomates au Roquefort)

Is heavy cream too rich? Replace it by cottage cheese blended with a bit of milk until smooth, or even evaporated milk.

■ Easy
  6 servings
  Inexpensive
  20 minutes
  **Best season: late summer when tomatoes
    are plentiful**

1 egg
water
2 celery ribs
6 large tomatoes
**US ¼ cup, UK 2 TB, Roquefort cheese (2
  TB)**
**US 6 TB, UK ¼ cup, heavy cream (1 scant
  dl)**
salt and pepper
4 large soft lettuce leaves
a few sprigs of parsley

NO ROQUEFORT?
*Use any Blue cheese your area has to offer;
yes, that includes all cow's- and goat's-milk
cheeses.*

- Hard-boil the egg in boiling salted water for 10 minutes. Cool in cold water.
- Peel the celery ribs, wash them, and cut them into julienne pieces ⅙ inch thick and 1½ inches long.
- Cut the tomatoes crosswise into halves. Press out the water, using your index finger, and cut tomatoes into ¼-inch-thick slices.
- Shell the egg and mash the yolk with the Roquefort. Add the cream and pepper to taste. (Salt may not be necessary because of the salt level in the cheese.) Mix very well, using a whisk.
- Arrange lettuce leaves, then tomato slices on a round platter. Sprinkle the celery over the tomatoes and cover with the sauce.
- Chop together the hard-boiled egg white and parsley and sprinkle over the salad.

SUMMER VEGETABLES À LA GRECQUE
(Légumes d'Été à la Grecque)

Since this preparation is a bit time-consuming and since the vegetables keep well, it is practical to double or triple the recipe and store leftovers in sealable jars.

Cook the artichoke leaves and serve them at a family dinner with vinaigrette.

■ Easy
6 servings
Inexpensive
50 minutes, prepare ahead of time
Best season: the hot months

2 small celery ribs (from center of celery heart)
2 small zucchini (marrows or courgettes)
1 bulb of fennel
3 artichokes, uncooked
1½ lemons
US 1⅓ cups, UK 1¼ cups, dry white wine (3.5 dl)
1 sprig of thyme
1 bay leaf (Turkish)
5 peppercorns
ground coriander
salt
US ¼ cup, UK 1½ TB, olive oil (1½ TB)

- Peel the celery ribs and cut them into ¼-inch sticks, 1½ inches long.
- Wash the zucchini, do not peel them, and cut them into ½-inch slices.
- Clean the fennel bulb. Cut it lengthwise into halves, then across into ¼-inch strips.
- Remove the leaves of the artichokes and peel the bottoms as you would a potato. Rub immediately with lemon to prevent darkening. Cut bottoms into ⅓-inch-thick slices.
- Pour the white wine into a large saucepan; add thyme, bay leaf, 5 peppercorns, ground coriander to taste, a good amount of salt, ½ lemon cut into slices, and the oil. Bring to a boil and let simmer for 10 minutes.
- Add all the vegetables to the sauce and continue cooking for about 25 minutes.
- Pour vegetables into a salad bowl and let cool completely before serving. It is better to let them marinate in the sauce for 24 hours before serving.

WITH THE SAME METHOD
Mushrooms à la Grecque: Use 1 pound button mushrooms (500 g). Should they be a bit large, cut them lengthwise into halves. Discard the sandy stem and root end. Wash quickly without soaking. Cook for 10 minutes, following the basic recipe exactly.

Leeks à la Grecque: Clean 12 small leeks and trim so as to keep only the white part. Cook them as in the basic recipe for about 20 minutes. You may need a bit more wine as there will be more evaporation.

ABOUT OLIVE OIL
Olive oil is always more expensive especially if it is "cold-pressed" virgin oil. It is tastier, higher in vitamins and from the gastronomic angle always recommended for dishes of the Mediterranean or Southern French style.

ASPARAGUS IN HAM ROLLS
(Rouleaux de Jambon aux Asperges)

The best way to prepare asparagus: Hold stem end in right hand and tip end in the left hand. Bend until the asparagus breaks. The break happens exactly at the place where the stem becomes too tough to eat. Peel the asparagus with a small paring knife or vegetable peeler. Do not discard the stems; boil them and store them in the freezer until you have enough to prepare an Asparagus Velouté (see p. 24).

■ Easy
6 servings
Expensive
15 minutes
Best season: late March to June

2 eggs
6 soft lettuce leaves
12 jumbo asparagus or 24 smaller
    asparagus
water
US 1½ tsp., UK 1 tsp., dry mustard (1 tsp.)
US 1 TB, UK 1½ tsp., vinegar (1½ tsp.)
salt and pepper
US ⅔ cup, UK ½ cup, oil (2 scant dl)
6 slices of boiled ham
a few sprigs of fresh parsley

- Hard-boil 1 egg and cool it in cold water.
- Arrange some lettuce leaves on a platter. Peel the asparagus (see advice).
- Cook the asparagus in boiling salted water for 3 to 7 minutes, depending on size.
- Prepare the mayonnaise with the raw egg yolk, the mustard, vinegar, and salt and pepper to taste. Mix very well in a bowl and gradually whisk in the oil (see method under Mayonnaise, p. 62).
- Beat the egg white with a pinch of salt until it can carry the weight of a raw egg in its shell. Mix one quarter of it into the mayonnaise, folding with a small rubber spatula. Then fold in the remainder.
- Place the slices of ham flat on a board. Spread each with mayonnaise. Place 2 asparagus on each slice of ham, and roll into a cigar, letting the asparagus show at both ends of the ham.
- Arrange the ham rolls on the lettuce leaves.
- Chop the hard-boiled egg yolk, the hard-boiled egg white and the parsley and mix them. Sprinkle the mixture over the ham rolls.

WITH THE SAME METHOD
You can save money by preparing the following:

Ham Roll with Vegetable Salad: Replace the asparagus by a package of frozen mixed vegetables. Cook in boiling water, drain carefully, and pat dry in cloth or paper towels before adding the mayonnaise to them. Roll mixture into ham slices.

YOU CAN USE ANY ASPARAGUS
Fresh ones in season, white or green, frozen green asparagus or canned white asparagus. The latter are extremely expensive and less tasty than the green ones.

POTATO AND HAM SALAD
(Salade de Pommes de Terre au Jambon)

When boiling potatoes, always add a few more for a dish of home fries.

■ Easy
  6 servings
  Medium expensive
  35 minutes
  **Best season: with new potatoes at the
    beginning of summer**

  4 to 5 potatoes
  salt
  US ¼ cup, UK 2 TB, white wine (2 TB)
  1 sweet red pepper
  6 oz. boiled ham in 1 piece (180 g)
  6 sour pickles
  **US 2 TB, UK 1 TB, prepared Dijon
    mustard (1 TB)**
  US ¼ cup, UK 2 TB, vinegar (2 TB)
  US ¾ cup, UK ⅔ cup, oil (2 dl)
  pepper
  **chopped fresh parsley or snipped fresh
    chives**

ABOUT POTATOES
*Use very waxy potatoes that do not break
after cooking.*

- Wash the potatoes; do not peel them. Put them in cold water, bring to a boil, add salt, and simmer for 20 to 30 minutes, depending on size.
- Peel the potatoes while they are hot; slice them and sprinkle them with the white wine.
- Cut the red pepper into ¼-inch julienne.
- Cut the ham also into ¼-inch julienne.
- Chop the pickles coarsely.
- Prepare the vinaigrette by mixing together well mustard, vinegar, oil, and salt and pepper to taste.
- Mix all the ingredients and sprinkle with the chopped parsley or chives. Let cool completely before serving.

WITH THE SAME METHOD
Using the potato salad as a base, you can vary this first course as follows:

Seafood and Potato Salad: To the potatoes add 6 ounces shelled small shrimps, 2 dozen shelled cooked black mussels, and some chopped parsley.

Tuna Salad: To the potatoes add 1 can (6½ oz.) oil-packed tuna, 2 hard-boiled eggs, chopped, and some snipped fresh chives.

TROPICAL FRUIT SALAD
(Salade Exotique)

Bananas darken extremely fast; they must be prepared last and immediately sprinkled with lemon juice.

■ Easy
6 servings
Medium expensive
10 minutes
Best season: year around

2 small grapefruits
2 large avocados or 3 smaller ones
2 large bananas
juice of 1½ lemons
US 6 TB, UK 3 TB, heavy cream (3 TB)
salt
sweet paprika
6 lettuce leaves (optional)

- Peel the grapefruits so as to expose the flesh completely. Separate the sections by passing the blade of the knife between pulp and membrane. Let the slices fall into a strainer placed over a bowl.
- Cut the avocados into halves, remove the pits, and lift the meat, using a teaspoon and shaping pieces as regular as possible.
- Peel the bananas, cut them into slightly slanted slices, and toss them immediately with some lemon juice.
- Prepare a simple sauce by mixing well together the cream, remaining lemon juice and salt to taste.
- Toss the fruit delicately into the sauce and serve sprinkled with sweet paprika. Serve either in glasses or on lettuce leaves.

SHRIMPS IN AVOCADOS
(Avocats aux Crevettes)

Is shrimp too expensive? You can gain volume and buy less by cutting them lengthwise into halves.

- Easy
  6 servings
  Medium expensive
  5 minutes
  Best season: summer

DRESSING
US 2 TB, UK 1 TB, lemon juice (1 TB)
salt and pepper
US 1/3 cup, UK 1/4 cup, oil (1 dl)
US 2 TB, UK 1 TB, heavy cream (1 TB)

**1/2 lb. shelled medium-size shrimps or
    prawns, cooked (250 g)**
a few soft-leaf lettuce leaves
3 avocados
red pepper flakes

- *Prepare the dressing:* Put the lemon juice in a bowl; add salt and pepper to taste. Gradually stir in the oil, then the heavy cream. Mix well.
- Put the shrimps to marinate in the dressing.
- Arrange the lettuce leaves on a platter and cut the avocados into halves. Remove the pits and skins. Cut a little bit of the pulp away at the thickest round part of the fruit, so the fruit can sit on the platter without bobbling.
- Fill the centers of each fruit half with the shrimps and dressing and sprinkle with a few red pepper flakes. Present the avocados on the lettuce leaves.

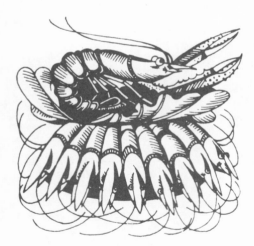

CHOOSE THE AVOCADOS WELL
They should be spotless and with an undamaged skin. Test their ripeness as you would that of a pear: the meat gives in gently when pressed with the tip of a finger. The best avocados are those that you buy green and ripen at home in a brown paper bag.

CRAB-MEAT COCKTAIL
(Cocktail de Crabe)

No clam juice at your fingertips? To prepare the sauce you have a number of solutions: Use some of the cooking water of the crab if you use fresh crabs; use the canning liquid of the crab if you use canned crab meat; and if you use frozen crab, shell it, then boil the shell in a little water for 5 minutes and lighten the sauce with that water.

■ Easy
  6 servings
  Expensive
  25 minutes
  Best season: year around

1 small zucchini (marrow or courgette)
salt, very little
¾ lb. best available crab meat, fresh,
    frozen or canned (375 g)
1 egg yolk
1 lemon, cut into 6 slices, ⅛ inch thick
US 2 TB, UK 1 TB, tomato paste
pepper
US ¼ cup, UK 1½ TB, heavy cream (1½
    TB)
US ¼ cup, UK 1½ TB, clam juice (1½ TB)
cayenne pepper
18 cooked shrimps
1 red bell pepper
1 green bell pepper

ARE YOU USING FRESH CRAB?
*Then add 30 to 45 minutes to your work time
for cooking and shelling.*

• Cut the zucchini into ⅛-inch-thick slices, using an ordinary slicer or a knife. Cut each slice into ⅛-inch strips. To gain time you can cut several slices piled on top of each other at once.

• Sprinkle the zucchini with a bit of salt and let stand for 10 minutes.

• Pick over the crab meat and discard all cartilages. Pull the crab meat apart into large shreds.

• Put the egg yolk, a dash of lemon juice (use the ends of the lemons for this), and the tomato paste in a small bowl and mix well. Add pepper to taste and gradually add the heavy cream. The sauce will be thick; lighten it with the clam juice. Correct the salt and pepper seasoning only after the sauce is finished. Add last a tiny sprinkle of cayenne.

• Drain, rinse, and pat dry the zucchini strips, and mix them into the crab meat. Add the sauce and mix delicately. Correct the final seasoning. Spoon salad into 6 champagne cups, cover with plastic wrap, and refrigerate.

• Before serving straddle 3 shrimps and 1 lemon slice on the edge of each glass. Cut six 1-inch circles out of the meat of the red and green pepper and decorate the top of the crab-meat salad with the circles of color.

CRAB-MEAT GRATIN
(Gratin au Crabe)

Would you prefer individual presentation dishes? Then divide the finished mixture into 6 ramekins or scallop shells made of glass or porcelain or natural shell, and top each shell or dish with one sixth of the Gruyère.

■ Relatively easy
6 servings
Expensive
30 minutes
Best season: year around

1 can (13 oz.) or 2 cans (6 ½ oz. each) crab meat (375 g)
US ⅔ cup, UK ½ cup, milk (2 scant dl)
½ lb. mushrooms (250 g)
US ¼ cup, UK 2 TB, butter (60 g)
salt and pepper
US 2 TB, UK 1 TB, flour (15 g)
pinch of cayenne pepper
US 2 TB, UK 1 TB, tomato paste (1 TB)
US ½ cup, UK 4 TB, grated Gruyère cheese (4 TB)

WOULD YOU PREFER
another type of crab? Use frozen crab defrosted before using, or cook 2 fresh crabs, but then you will have to shell and pick them over, which requires more time.

- Open the crab meat. Drain the canning juices into a cup and add the milk.
- Separate the lumps of crab meat and reserve them on a plate.
- Wipe the mushrooms, remove the dried stem ends, and wash only if extremely dirty. Slice the mushrooms. Heat half of the butter in a frying pan. Add the mushrooms, salt and pepper. Toss the vegetables in the hot butter, then cover to extract the juices. When the mushrooms float in their own juices, drain juices into the cup containing the mixture of milk and crab juices.
- Heat the remainder of the butter in a saucepan and add the flour. Cook for 3 to 4 minutes. Whisk the mixture of juices and milk into the roux and bring to a boil. Stir constantly. Add a bit of salt. (Not too much should be necessary.) Add black pepper and a pinch of cayenne pepper. Let simmer for 5 minutes.
- Add the tomato paste, the crab meat and the mushrooms. Reheat well.
- Empty the mixture into a fireproof dish. Sprinkle with the Gruyère cheese and broil for a few minutes, or until the cheese turns golden. Serve piping hot.

CROQUE-MONSIEUR

Not only the cheese can be varied but also the meat: ham can be replaced by any luncheon meat, any cold meat left over from a roast and sliced, and even sliced cooked frankfurters.

■ Easy
6 servings
Medium expensive
15 minutes
Best season: year around

6 slices of boiled ham
6 slices of white bread, ⅓ inch thick
6 oz. Gruyère cheese (180 g)
US 2 TB, UK 1 TB, butter (1 TB)
coarsely cracked pepper

- Preheat the broiler.
- Recut the ham so it fits the size of the bread slices. Cut the Gruyère cheese the same way.
- Spread a thin layer of butter on each slice of bread, then put on the ham slice, coarsely cracked pepper and the cheese. Brush the cheese with the remainder of the butter.
- Broil until the Gruyère is melted and golden. Serve immediately.

ABOUT WHITE BREAD
This recipe needs thick slices of bread. Melba toast thin bread breaks while cooking.

WITH THE SAME METHOD
For large appetites prepare:

Giant Croque-Monsieur: Prepare the same sandwich but use 3 times as much bread, ham and cheese to obtain several layers. Bake at 350°F., 185°C. or 5 to 6 Regulo, for 15 minutes, then broil the top for 1 or 2 minutes.

Croque-Monsieur en Papillote: To prevent making the oven dirty and to keep the appetizers warm if they have to wait, wrap the sandwiches in aluminum foil and bake them in 350°F., 185°C. or 5 to 6 Regulo oven for 10 minutes.

Panfried Croque-Monsieur: Cover the cheese with a second slice of buttered bread (the buttered side is down in contact with the cheese) and cook in a frying pan in a mixture of 75% butter and 25% oil. Turn over as soon as the first side is golden. Finish the cooking on the other side.

Diverse Variations: You can try all kinds of different French, English and American cheeses. Among the best are Edam, processed Gruyère portions, Port-Salut, Caerphilly, Pyrénées cheese and Munster cheese.

CRÊPES FILLED WITH CHEESE
(Crêpes Fourrées au Fromage)

You can double this recipe if you want to. Prepare a second dish of crêpes, wrap it in foil, and freeze it for another day. Do not defrost it. Put it all frozen in the oven; bake at 350°F. for 15 minutes with the foil on, then remove the foil and bake for another 15 to 20 minutes.

■ Relatively easy
6 servings
Thrift recipe
45 minutes
Best season: fall and winter

CRÊPE BATTER
US ½ cup, UK 2 oz., sifted flour (60 g)
salt
1 large egg
US ½ cup, UK scant ½ cup, milk (1 generous dl)
US 2 TB, UK 1 TB, oil (1 TB)

SAUCE
US ¼ cup, UK 2 TB, butter (60 g)
US 3 TB, UK 1½ TB, flour (30 g)
US 1½ cups, UK 1 generous cup, milk, scalded (.25 L)
salt, pepper, nutmeg
6 oz. Gruyère cheese, grated (180 g)
butter for baking dish

CRÊPE BATTER
• Sift the flour into a bowl and make a well in the center. Add salt and egg in the well. Gradually mix the flour with the egg, using a whisk. As soon as the batter becomes stiff, gradually add the milk. Stir well until the batter is very smooth. Let the batter stand while you prepare the sauce. If you have time, let batter rest for a full 30 minutes. Strain the batter into a pitcher or a measuring cup with a spout.

SAUCE
• Melt the butter in a heavy saucepan. Add the flour, and cook for 3 to 4 minutes. Add the hot milk in 2 additions, stirring well with the whisk. Bring back to a boil. Add salt, pepper and nutmeg to taste; simmer for 2 to 3 minutes. Add half of the cheese, stir well, and remove sauce from the heat.

TO COOK THE CRÊPES
• Heat a crêpe pan over medium-high heat. Add the oil to the pan, swish it around. Pour it and whisk it into the crêpe batter. Homogenize well.

• Leaving the crêpe pan over the burner, lift it forward at a 45-degree angle. Pour enough batter into the lip of the pan to fill it by two thirds. Slowly tilt the pan backwards, back and forth to allow the batter to cover the whole bottom of the pan. Cook for 1 minute. Turn over and cook for 1 minute more on the second side.

• As soon as a crêpe is ready, start another one. While this second crêpe is cooking, spread a ¼-inch-thick layer of sauce over the surface of the first one. Roll into a cigar and repeat until you have made and filled 12 crêpes.

• Lightly butter a baking dish and arrange the filled crêpes in it. Sprinkle the crêpes with the remaining cheese. Slide under the broiler just long enough to melt the cheese and brown it lightly. Serve immediately.

WITH THE SAME METHOD
You can replace the cheese in the sauce by other ingredients to obtain the following variations:

Crêpes Filled with Minced Beef or Other Meat: Add to the sauce US ¼ cup, UK 2 tablespoons, tomato paste (2 TB) and finely minced cooked beef, pork, veal or poultry.

Crêpes Filled with Mushrooms: Mix into the sauce ¾ pound mushrooms (375 g), sliced and precooked in a little butter with a dash of lemon juice.

Crêpes Filled with Shellfish: Add to the sauce some shelled mussels, some shelled shrimps and, if you have it, some flaked cooked fish. Enrich the sauce with a little heavy cream.

ANY CRÊPE BATTER LEFT OVER?
Store it in a tightly closed jar in the refrigerator; it will keep for 2 days at least.

CHEESE FRITTERS
(Beignets au Fromage)

For a change, you can use half Gruyère, half ham, making sure that the ham is chopped extremely fine. Also many other cheeses can be used: Cheddar, Jarlsberg, Fontina, mozzarella.

■ Somewhat difficult
6 servings
Medium expensive
30 minutes
Best season: fall and winter

10 oz. Gruyère cheese (285 g)
salt
pepper
6 egg whites
a few tablespoons of flour for dusting
oil bath

WORKING WITH EGG WHITES
This is a good recipe to use extra egg whites. The texture of beaten egg whites is extremely important. The way to check it by using a raw egg is the only true safe method. If the egg falls and sinks into the foam by more than ¼ inch, the foam is too soft. But if the egg sits high on top, you have beaten too much and the foam, then too dry, will not bend well to your folding.

• Grate the Gruyère cheese.

• Add a pinch each of salt and pepper to the egg whites and beat them until their bulk can carry the weight of a raw egg in its shell.

• Sprinkle the Gruyère over the whites and fold cheese in until the mixture is homogenous.

• Heat the oil bath. While the bath is heating, sprinkle some flour on a plate and with 2 spoons shape little balls of cheese mixture that you will roll in the flour.

• When the oil bath is hot, let 4 to 5 balls slide into the bath at once but no more. Turn them over if they do not bob over by themselves.

• When the fritters are golden, lift them out of the bath with a slotted spoon and put them on several layers of crumbled paper toweling.

• Present them on a plate lined with a folded white linen napkin. Serve piping hot.

QUICHE LORRAINE

In Lorraine the old country women used to make this quiche, also known as galette, with bread dough. The pie made with pastry is a little more refined but not as authentic. Cooking it first on the bottom rack eliminates the need to prebake the shell.

■ Relatively easy
  6 servings
  Medium expensive
  50 minutes to 1 hour
  Best season: fall and winter

For a pie plate of porcelain or black metal approximately 12 inches in diameter:

PASTRY
US 1½ cups, UK 6 oz., flour (180 g)
US ½ cup, UK 4 oz., butter (100 g)
salt, a large pinch
US ⅓ cup, UK 3 TB, water (3 TB)

FILLING
3 eggs
salt and pepper
US 1½ cups, UK 1¼ cups, light cream (3.5 dl)
6 oz. thick-sliced smoked bacon (180 g)
6 oz. diced ham (180 g)
a bit of grated Gruyère cheese (optional)

PASTRY
• Put the flour on the countertop and make a well in the center. Add the cold butter, cut into large chunks, and the salt and mix together with the finger-tips. Then add the water and mix to-gether into a ball. Flatten the ball of dough on the table top, pressing nut-size pieces of the dough with the heel of your hand. Gather into a ball again and repeat the operation a second time. The dough will not stick to the table anymore. Flatten it to form a cake ½ inch thick. Let it rest for 30 minutes, preferably in the refrigerator.

• Preheat oven to 375°F., 200°C. or 5 to 6 Regulo.

FILLING
• In a bowl mix together the eggs, salt and pepper to taste, and light cream, and beat until homogenous.

• Flour the table or countertop lightly and roll out the pastry ⅛ inch thick. Transfer the pastry to the lightly greased pie plate.

• Cut the slices of bacon into 1-inch pieces and sauté them lightly until golden but not crisp. Add the ham to the pan and sauté for 1 or 2 more min-utes. Transfer to a bowl. Cool the fat in the pan.

• Brush a bit of bacon fat on the bottom of the pastry. Add bacon and ham and push down lightly to allow them both to stick into the fat and not come float-ing to the top as you pour the custard over them.

• Bake on the bottom rack of the oven for 15 minutes. If you wish the pie sprin-kled with the grated cheese, add it be-fore baking. Raise the quiche to the upper rack of the oven and finish bak-ing for another 15 to 20 minutes.

PISSALADIÈRE
(The traditional onion pizza from Nice)

Would you like to peel onions without crying? Cut a plastic bag open at both ends and peel inside of it, or peel onions close to a working burner of your stove. The heat "swallows up" the fumes.

- A bit difficult
  6 servings
  Medium expensive
  1 hour
  Best season: summer to late fall, when the tomatoes are plentiful

  1 generous pound onions (500 g)
  US ⅔ cup, UK ½ cup, olive oil (2 scant dl)
  20 oil-cured black olives
  3 medium-size tomatoes
  US 1½ TB, UK ¾ TB, cornstarch (¾ TB)
  US ⅔ cup, UK ½ cup, milk (2 scant dl)
  1 egg
  2 cans (2 oz. each) flat anchovy fillets
  1½ tsp. butter to butter pie pan
  ½ lb. pie pastry, or 1 package (½ lb.) frozen pastry (227 g)

- Peel the onions and slice them finely with a knife or in a food processor.
- Heat the oil in a large saucepan. Lightly brown the onions, stirring well, then cover and reduce heat. Let cook for 30 minutes, or until onions are soft and like a purée.
- Pit the olives. Cut the tomatoes into thin slices.
- Preheat oven to 400°F., 220°C. or 6 Regulo.
- Dilute the cornstarch with US ¼ cup, UK 2 tablespoons, cold milk (2 TB).

- Heat the remainder of the milk. Add the mixture of starch and cold milk to the hot milk, stirring until thickened. Add the onions, then remove from the heat.
- Beat the egg well; add it, whisking, to the pan of onions. Correct the seasoning; do not oversalt: olives and anchovies are very salty.
- Rinse the anchovy fillets.
- Butter lightly a 10-inch pie plate preferably made of porcelain or black metal.
- Roll out the pastry to ⅛-inch thickness and fit it into the prepared plate.
- Empty the onion mixture into the pastry and arrange on top the rinsed anchovy fillets, the olives and the tomato slices.
- Bake on the bottom rack of the oven for 15 minutes, then raise the pie to the upper rack and continue baking for another 15 to 20 minutes.
- Serve the tart warm or cold.

PASTRY
Prepared and frozen pastry can be found in any market. If you prefer making it yourself, see opposite page under Quiche Lorraine.

CHEESE SOUFFLÉ
(Soufflé au Fromage)

Short of time? Prepare the soufflé the day before or several days before and freeze it. When you are ready to bake it, thaw at room temperature for 15 minutes, then bake it for 1 hour and 15 minutes at the temperatures in the basic recipe.

- Medium difficult
  6 servings
  Affordable
  50 to 60 minutes
  Best season: fall and winter

  US 4 TB, UK 2 TB, butter (60 g)
  US 3 TB, UK 1½ TB, flour (25 g)
  US 1 cup, UK 1 scant cup, milk (2.5 dl)
  salt and pepper
  freshly grated nutmeg
  6 oz. grated Gruyère cheese (180 g)
  6 eggs

- Preheat oven to 325°F., 165°C. or 4 to 5 Regulo.

- Butter a 6-cup soufflé mold.

- In a 2-quart saucepan melt and heat the butter. Add the flour and cook, stirring occasionally, for 3 to 5 minutes. Meanwhile, scald the milk.

- Add the scalding milk at once and continue whisking quickly until the mixture thickens and boils. Add a pinch of salt and pepper and nutmeg to taste.

- Remove the pan from the heat. Mix in the grated cheese. Add the egg yolks one by one, beating well after each addition. Let cool.

- Beat the egg whites until they are stiff enough to carry the weight of a raw egg without the egg sinking into the foam by more than ¼ inch. Add one quarter of the egg whites to the sauce base, stirring well. Fold the remainder of the whites into the base, cutting at the center of the bulk of batter and bringing the sauce from the bottom to the top, until the batter is homogenous.

- Spoon the batter into the prepared soufflé mold, building it in 2 or 3 even layers of spoonfuls. The dish should not be more than three quarters full.

- Bake in the preheated oven for 35 to 40 minutes. Do not open the oven during the first 20 minutes of baking.

WITH THE SAME METHOD

Asparagus Soufflé: Scrape the pulp of 1 pound cooked asparagus after you cut them lengthwise into halves. Purée pulp in a blender and add it to the sauce base instead of the cheese.

Crab Soufflé: Replace the Gruyère by the contents of 1 can (6½ oz. or 195 g) of crab meat, using the canning juices to replace some of the milk. Pick the crab meat over very well and chop it finely.

Ham Soufflé: Replace the Gruyère by 6 ounces (180 g) of finely chopped cooked ham, or use half ham, half Gruyère.

Tuna Soufflé: Replace the Gruyère by the contents of 1 can (6½ oz. or 195 g) of white tuna, well chopped. Watch the salt, you will need very little.

Meat Soufflé: Chop finely 6 ounces (180 g) of leftovers of any of these meats: veal, poultry, rabbit, pork. Add a good pinch of tarragon to the sauce base.

ABOUT SALT
The saltiness of Gruyère varies considerably, so be careful of how much salt you add. Also, you can vary the cheeses; think of Edam or Cheddar; they make good cheese soufflés.

CHEESE TART
(Tarte au Fromage)

Would you like a "souffléed tart"? Then beat 2 egg whites and fold them into the cheese base.

Also think of using diverse types of Swiss cheeses such as Emmentaler, Sbrinz or Appenzeller. Add a tablespoon or so of crumbled Blue, Roquefort or Stilton; it does wonders.

■ A bit difficult
6 servings
Medium expensive
1 hour
Best season: fall and winter

For a 10-inch pie plate

PASTRY
US 1½ cups, UK 6 oz., flour (180 g)
US ½ cup, UK 4 oz., butter (120 g)
large pinch of salt
US 4 TB, UK 2 TB, water (2 TB)

FILLING
US 3 TB, UK 1½ TB, cornstarch (1½ TB)
US 1 cup, UK 1 scant cup, milk (2.5 dl)
salt and pepper
2 oz. grated Gruyère cheese (60 g)
3 eggs
2 oz. slivers of Gruyère cheese (60 g)

PASTRY
• Put the flour on the table or countertop and make a well in the center. Add cold butter in chunks, and the salt. Mix well with fingertips. Add water and gather into a ball. Flatten the ball of dough on the table top, pushing nut-size pieces of the dough with the heel of your hand. Gather into a ball again and repeat the operation a second time. The dough will not stick to the table any more. Flatten it into a cake ½ inch thick and let it rest for 30 minutes, preferably in the refrigerator.
• Preheat oven to 375°F., 200°C. or 5 to 6 Regulo.

FILLING
• Put the cornstarch into a saucepan. Add a bit of milk to dissolve it, then add the remainder of the milk. Bring to a boil over medium heat, stirring constantly until it thickens. Add salt lightly and pepper generously. Remove the pan from the heat and add the grated cheese; stir well. Let cool for 5 minutes. Then add the eggs, one by one, beating well after each addition.
• Roll out the pastry ⅛ inch thick and fit it into the buttered pie plate. Pour the filling into the plate. Cover with the slivers of Gruyère.
• Bake on the bottom shelf of the oven for 15 to 20 minutes, then finish baking on the top shelf.
• Let cool a bit before serving.

WITH THE SAME METHOD
Ham and Cheese Tart: When the pastry is in the plate, sprinkle it with any type of ham (cooked, prosciutto, etc.), before adding the cheese filling and baking.

Meat and Cheese Tart: A good way to use your leftover meats or poultry. Dice them finely, sprinkle them on the bottom of the pastry, and pour the filling over.

CHOOSE YOUR PAN WELL
The best type for all quiches and savory pies is a fireproof white china dish. Unmolding is no problem since it is unnecessary. The dish looks good enough to come to the table.

BURGUNDY CHEESECAKE
(Gougère Bourguignonne)

For a nourishing family dinner in the Burgundy manner, serve a soup first and a nice salad of many vegetables with the gougère. The gougère is the ancestral cheesecake of Burgundy vintners. It is still quite often offered to visitors of cellars and vine estates of this French province.

- Medium difficult
  6 servings
  Medium expensive
  1 hour
  Best season: fall and winter

  US 1 generous cup, UK 1 cup, water (.25 L)
  US ½ cup, UK 4 oz., butter (120 g)
  salt
  US 1 cup, UK 4 oz., flour (125 g)
  4 eggs
  5 oz. Gruyère cheese (150 g)
  pepper
  freshly grated nutmeg
  1 egg yolk
  US 2 TB, UK 1 TB, milk (1 TB)

NUTMEG
It can be bought whole, to be grated as needed, or already grated. The first solution is the best and tastiest. Nutmeg complements well all white sauce and cheese dishes.

- Preheat oven to 375°F., 200°C. or 5 to 6 Regulo.
- Place water, the butter cut into small cubes, and a bit of salt in a large saucepan. Bring to a boil. As soon as the water foams up, remove it from the heat and add the flour at once. Stir well to make a ball of dough. Return to the heat for 1 or 2 minutes, stirring constantly. The dough will roll free and without sticking to the pot.
- Remove pan again from the heat and do not return to the heat again. Add 1 egg, and stir energetically until homogenous. Repeat with the other 3 eggs.
- Cut the Gruyère cheese into ¼-inch cubes. Add three quarters of the Gruyère to the pot, along with pepper to taste and several gratings of nutmeg.
- Butter a baking sheet. Drop spoonfuls of batter onto the baking sheet, forming a crown. The spoonfuls will bond together as they bake.
- Beat the egg yolk with the milk and brush it on top of the cake, then sprinkle with the remaining diced cheese.
- Bake on the middle shelf of the oven for 30 minutes. Let gougère cool a bit before serving.

SAUCES

(Les Sauces)

ADVICE FOR GOOD SAUCE-MAKING

DID YOU KNOW THAT

A *roux* is a mixture of flour and butter cooked on top of the stove.

A *roux blanc* (white roux) is cooked for a few minutes only and is used to thicken white sauces.

A *roux brun* (brown roux) is cooked longer and should turn light hazelnut brown. It is used to thicken brown sauces.

A *bouquet garni* consists of parsley stems, ½ bay leaf, 1 sprig of thyme tied together.

TO PREPARE GOOD SAUCES YOU SHOULD HAVE

Good saucepans, the thicker, the better; a wooden spoon so as not to burn your hand; a small wire sauce whisk that breaks lumps even before they form and is your key to a smooth texture.

BÉCHAMEL SAUCE
(Sauce Béchamel et variantes)

The small sauce whisk is your best friend; it allows you, as you move it very quickly across the bottom of the saucepan, to add scalding milk to the roux without making lumps and to save time since the sauce will come to a boil so much faster.

- Easy
  30 minutes
  Warm sauce

  1 large onion, chopped
  US 6 TB, UK 3 TB, butter (90 g)
  US 6 TB, UK 3 TB, flour (45 g)
  1 quart milk (1 L)
  ½ bay leaf
  1 sprig of thyme
  salt and pepper

- Chop the onion finely.
- Heat the butter, add the onion, and sauté until translucent. Add the flour and cook over medium heat, stirring occasionally, for 5 to 6 minutes.
- Meanwhile, scald the milk; when scalded, pour half of the milk into the pot and whisk to prevent lumps from forming. Add remainder of the milk, stir until smooth, and bring to a boil. Add bay leaf and thyme.
- Reduce heat to a simmer and let sauce cook for no more than 10 minutes.
- Strain into a bowl; correct the seasoning. The sauce can be used with eggs and various vegetables.
- Béchamel is a basic sauce used to build a good number of other sauces such as the following variations.

WITH THE SAME METHOD
Aurore Sauce: Add US 3 tablespoons, UK 1½ tablespoons, tomato paste (1½ TB) to each 1½ cups of finished Béchamel. Serve especially with hard-boiled eggs.

Curry Sauce: When preparing the roux, add to the flour US 1½ tablespoons, UK 2 teaspoons, fresh curry powder and cook together to lock the taste of the curry into the sauce. Add a bit of cream to the finished sauce. Serve over rice, pasta, young lamb, poultry.

Dieppe Sauce: Mix by volume two thirds Béchamel with one third fish broth (left over from soup on p. 30) or even clam juice. Garnish with cooked tiny shrimps, mushrooms and a dash of cream.

Vegetable Sauce: Prepare the Béchamel using half milk, half water used for cooking vegetables (asparagus, cauliflower, etc.) or half juices (mushroom). Remove the sauce from the heat and quickly whisk in 1 egg yolk or 2 tablespoons of cream.

Mornay Sauce: Add some grated Swiss or Parmesan cheese to Béchamel, or use half of each cheese. Mornay sauce is used on eggs, some fish, asparagus, cauliflower, lambs' brains, etc.

Sauce for Fish: Prepare the Béchamel using half milk, half well-strained fish cooking court-bouillon (see p. 295), and add a bit of cream.

CONSISTENCY AND USE
The consistency of the basic sauce is medium. For a thick sauce usable for soufflés, use twice as much onion, flour and butter.

The recipe yields 1 quart. Freeze whatever is unused and defrost in a hot water bath.

WHITE SAUCE
(Sauce Blanche)

A bit of history of cooking: This sauce is a shortcut to the Classic Velouté Sauce.

■ Easy
35 to 40 minutes
Warm sauce

US 4 TB, UK 2 TB, butter (60 g)
4 chicken wings or necks, chopped
2 chicken gizzards, sliced
1 large onion, chopped
US 6 TB, UK 3 TB, flour (45 g)
1 quart hot water (1 L)
1 bay leaf
1 sprig of thyme
salt and pepper

- Melt the butter in a saucepan. Add the chicken wings and gizzards and brown all around until golden. Remove them to a plate.
- To the same butter, add the onion and sauté until translucent. Add the flour and cook lightly for 3 to 4 minutes.
- Add half of the hot water and whisk well, then add remaining water and bring to a boil, stirring. Return the chicken wings and gizzards to the pot. Add bay leaf and thyme and simmer for 30 minutes.
- Strain the sauce into a bowl. This sauce can be used on eggs and some fish, or can be mixed with rice or pasta.
- Most of the time this sauce is not used by itself but in combination with other ingredients to obtain a derivative.

WITH THE SAME METHOD
Cream Sauce: When the sauce is done take any amount you need and reduce for 5 or 6 minutes, then add a few tablespoons of heavy cream.

Vegetable Sauce: Remove the chicken wings. Keep the gizzards and make the sauce using the cooking water of vegetables (cauliflower, asparagus).

Mustard Sauce: To each cup of white sauce add US 1 tablespoon, UK ½ tablespoon, strong prepared Dijon mustard (½ TB). Whisk well.

Poulette Sauce: To each cup of basic hot sauce add 1 egg yolk mixed with 1 teaspoon lemon juice and chopped parsley. Use with carrots, potatoes, pasta, rice, brains, sweetbreads, etc.

White-Wine Sauce: Prepare the basic sauce using half water, half wine. This sauce is good with potatoes, sausage of any kind, and some fish.

CONSISTENCY AND USE
The consistency of the basic sauce is medium. Look for modifications of the thickness in the variations.

The recipe yields 1 quart. Freeze any unused quantity in a jar and defrost in a double boiler.

SIMPLE MUSHROOM SAUCE
(Sauce aux Champignons)

Would you like more sauce? Add 4 ounces water or, better, bouillon, and increase the cornstarch by ½ teaspoon.

■ Easy
Medium expensive
6 servings
20 minutes
Warm sauce

½ lb. fresh mushrooms (250 g)
US 4 TB, UK 2 TB, butter (60 g)
salt and pepper
4 shallots, chopped
US ½ cup, UK ⅓ cup, dry white wine (1 generous dl)
lemon juice
US ½ cup, UK ⅓ cup, heavy cream (75 to 80 g)
1 tsp. cornstarch
chopped parsley or tarragon

TO SERVE WITH
poached fish, broiled fish, roast chicken parts, panfried steaks, sautéed sea scallops, skewered sea scallops, fish.

- Cut the root end of each mushroom. Wash the mushrooms very quickly *only* if they are very sandy. If not, wipe them with a cloth or tea towel and slice them thinly.

- Heat the butter in a frying pan; add the mushrooms. Toss them in the butter, salt and pepper them, and add the chopped shallots. Cover the pan, reduce the heat, and let the mushrooms lose all their juices. Empty the juices obtained into a bowl.

- To the mushrooms still in the pan, add the white wine and a drop or so of lemon juice, and let juices evaporate almost completely over high heat. Return the mushroom juices to the pan and keep warm over low heat.

- Mix the heavy cream with the cornstarch and pour into the frying pan; let the mixture thicken while you mix very well. Add chopped fresh parsley or, if preferred, chopped tarragon. Correct seasoning and serve.

BROWN SAUCE
(Sauce Brune)

Keep trimmings of steaks, veal chops or shanks frozen in plastic bags, together with any veal bones from chops and shanks. Pack in 1 bag just enough for 1 recipe of brown sauce, and freeze. Trimmings may have gristle and connective tissue, but no fat.

- Easy
1 hour
Warm sauce

US 4 TB, UK TB, butter (60 g)
a handful of steak or beef stew trimmings,
    fat free
1 small veal bone
2 small onions
US 4 TB, UK 2 TB, flour (30 g)
1½ quarts boiling water (1.5 L)
US ½ cup, UK ⅓ cup, dry white wine (1
    generous dl)
US 1 TB, UK ½ TB, tomato paste (½ TB)
½ bay leaf
1 sprig of thyme
1 small beef bouillon cube

- In a 2-quart saucepot, heat the butter well. Brown the beef trimmings and veal bone well until very brown.
- Meanwhile, chop the onions.
- Remove browned meats to a plate. Add the onions to the pot and brown well. Add the flour and cook with the onions for 8 to 10 minutes.
- Using your sauce whisk, add half of the boiling water to the saucepan, whisking well. Then add the remainder. Return the meat trimmings and veal bone to the pot.
- Bring back to a boil and add white wine, tomato paste, bay leaf, thyme and bouillon cube.
- Let cook, uncovered, over medium heat for 40 to 45 minutes or longer. By the time the sauce is done you should have 3 to 4 cups left.
- Strain the sauce into a bowl. Cool at room temperature. If you want to defatten the sauce completely, refriger-

ate it overnight and lift off the fat that will have hardened completely on the surface.

WITH THE SAME METHOD
Please correct salt and pepper in all sauces before serving.

Shallot Sauce: Use 2 large or 3 smaller shallots per cup of brown sauce. Chop them finely, sauté them lightly, and simmer them with the basic sauce for 10 minutes. Excellent on boiled beef.

White-Wine Matelote Sauce: Mix 1 chopped onion, 12 chopped mushrooms, a small *bouquet garni* (p. 293), and US ½ cup, UK ⅓ cup, dry white wine (1 generous dl) and cook until the wine has evaporated. Remove the *bouquet garni* and add mixture to 1 cup brown sauce. Simmer together for 5 minutes. Good for fish and some red meats.

Pickle Sauce: Cook 3 finely chopped shallots in 1 cup brown sauce. Add 6 finely sliced midget sour pickles with a dash of their pickling vinegar. For boiled beef.

Portuguese Sauce: To 1 cup of finished brown sauce add US 2 tablespoons, UK 1 tablespoon, dry Madeira and US 1 tablespoon, UK ½ tablespoon, tomato paste. For chicken, beef steaks, broiled steaks, etc.

Robert Sauce: Mix 1 chopped onion, 2 chopped shallots, US ½ cup, UK ⅓ cup, dry white wine (1 generous dl). Reduce until almost dry. Add 1 cup brown sauce and US 2 tablespoons, UK 1 tablespoon, prepared Dijon mustard after adding US

2 tablespoons, UK 1 tablespoon, tomato paste and simmering for 5 minutes. Add finally a handful of chopped fresh herbs of your choice and a few drops of lemon juice.

CONSISTENCY AND USE
The brown sauce is never used as prepared

in the basic recipe, but rather with other ingredients added to change its noncommittal taste.

The texture of a brown sauce is always rather thin; this is why the basic recipe contains little flour.

Freeze in jars any portion of the sauce unused.

RAVIGOTE SAUCE
(Sauce Ravigote)

No fresh tarragon or chervil? Add the same dried herbs to the vinegar before reducing it with the shallots, and use only chopped fresh parsley at the end.

■ Medium easy
6 servings
Inexpensive
30 minutes
Warm sauce

3 shallots
US 1 TB, UK ½ TB, snipped chives (½ TB)
US ½ cup, UK ⅓ cup, vinegar (1 generous dl)
US 1½ cups, UK 1⅓ cups, bouillon (3.5 dl)
US 2 TB, UK 1 TB, butter (30 g)
US 2 TB, UK 1 TB, flour (15 g)
salt and pepper
tarragon, chervil and parsley
2 egg yolks

TO SERVE WITH
broiled beef, boiled or poached poultry, broiled pork, leftover pork or beef roast slowly reheated in the sauce; hard- or soft-boiled eggs.

- Peel and chop the shallots and mix them with the chives.
- Put these and the vinegar in a small pot and reduce, uncovered, over medium heat, until about US 2 tablespoons, UK 1 tablespoon, is left. Strain the vinegar into the bouillon.
- Heat the butter in the same small pot and add the flour. Cook until the roux takes on a light golden color, then whisk in the hot bouillon and bring back to a boil, whisking until the sauce has thickened. Add salt if needed and pepper to taste.
- Chop enough tarragon, chervil and parsley to have US 1 tablespoon, UK ½ tablespoon, of each. Reserve.
- Place egg yolks in a bowl. Whisk in about one third of the hot sauce, then reverse the process and whisk the mixture into the bulk of the sauce. Stir until you can see 1 bubble appear at the surface of the sauce. Turn the heat off and add the herbs. Correct the final seasoning.

DRY VERMOUTH SAUCE
(Sauce au Vermouth Blanc)

The best dry vermouth comes from Italy and France. This is white wine in which wormwood and absinthe have been steeped, hence its little bitter edge.

■ Easy
6 servings
Medium expensive
25 minutes
Warm sauce

2 small onions
3 small shallots
US 2 TB, UK 1 TB, olive oil (1 TB)
US 1½ TB, UK ¾ TB, flour (11 g)
US 1 cup, UK 1 scant cup, bouillon (2.5 dl)
US 2 TB, UK 1 TB, tomato paste (1 TB)
salt and pepper
large pinch of cayenne pepper
dash of lemon juice
US ¼ cup, UK 2 TB, dry vermouth (2 TB)

- Peel onions and shallots and chop very finely.
- Heat the olive oil and add onions and shallots. Let them turn golden, but do not overbrown to prevent bitterness.
- Add the flour and let cook for 4 minutes. Add the bouillon all at once, whisking with a small wire whisk. The sauce will thicken instantly. Bring it to a boil.
- Add tomato paste, salt and pepper to taste, cayenne pepper, lemon juice and two thirds of the vermouth. Simmer for 12 minutes. Stir often.
- Just before serving add remaining vermouth. Correct the seasoning and serve.

SERVE WITH
broiled meats, kidneys, fondue bourguignonne, leftover roast pork or beef gently reheated in the sauce.

FRESH TOMATO SAUCE
(Sauce Tomate)

To obtain a fresh tomato soup, all you need to do is add 2 cups bouillon.

■ Easy
6 servings
Warm sauce
**Best season: August to October with fresh
   sun-ripened tomatoes**

1 sprig of thyme
small bundle of parsley stems
½ bay leaf
1 large onion
2 garlic cloves
1½ lbs. fresh tomatoes (750 g)
salt and pepper
US 2 TB, UK 1 TB, butter (30 g)
US 1 TB, UK ½ TB, cornstarch (½ TB)
water

- Tie the thyme sprig, parsley stems and bay leaf into a *bouquet garni* (see p. 293).
- Peel and chop onion and garlic.
- Wash the tomatoes, cut them into quarters, and press well into a bowl to extract seeds and water.
- Put *bouquet garni*, onion, garlic, tomatoes, and salt and pepper to taste in a saucepan and bring to a boil. Reduce the heat and cook over medium heat for 20 minutes.
- Remove the *bouquet garni* and purée the sauce through a food mill.

- Put the sauce back over heat and add the butter.
- Dissolve the cornstarch in a bit of cold water and add it to the simmering sauce. Stir well until thickened. Correct seasoning.

WITH THE SAME METHOD
Winter Tomato Sauce: Proceed the same way and use the same ingredients, but replace fresh tomatoes by tomato paste. You will need one 6-ounce can of paste; dilute it with 18 ounces water (.5 L). Let simmer uncovered until reduced to about 2 cups.

Provençale Sauce: Use the same ingredients as in the basic recipe but omit the butter and start by sautéing onion, garlic and tomato in olive oil. When using diluted tomato paste, brown only the onion and garlic.

SERVE WITH
pasta, rice, potatoes, cauliflower, cooked meats such as boiled beef or boiled shoulder of ham, leftovers of roast beef, broiled meats.

MAYONNAISE AND VARIATIONS
(Sauce Mayonnaise et variantes)

About that seasoning: More pepper? Add it directly to the finished sauce. More salt? Dissolve it in the hot water before adding it to the sauce.

■ Easy
Cold sauce
5 minutes by hand, 3 minutes by electric mixer

1 egg yolk
2 tsp. prepared Dijon mustard
¼ tsp. salt
⅛ tsp. white pepper
US 1 TB, UK ½ TB, vinegar, heated
US ⅔ cup, UK ½ cup, oil of your choice (2 scant dl)
US 1 TB, UK ½ TB, hot water

- Made with the exact quantity of each ingredient mentioned here, the mayonnaise will be exactly seasoned as it should be.
- Put egg yolk and mustard in a small round bowl. Add salt and pepper, then the hot vinegar. Let stand for 1 minute. Mix well.
- Measure the oil in a measuring cup. Gradually pour oil into yolk mixture, mixing very fast with hand whisk or with the electric mixer on medium high speed. Add very little oil at a time at the beginning, then increase the quantity added as soon as the sauce has started to thicken.
- Finally, whisk in the hot water, which will prevent any leftover from "bleeding" droplets of oil on standing.
- Any leftover mayonnaise will keep in the refrigerator for 1 week.

WITH THE SAME METHOD
Aïoli: Mash very well from 1 to 4 garlic cloves, according to your taste, and add to mayonnaise. Excellent with poached cod or haddock, boiled beef, cold leg of lamb.

Lemon Mayonnaise: Replace the vinegar by lemon juice when making the mayonnaise. You may need more salt.

Pickle Mayonnaise: Chop finely several midget sour pickles and add to finished mayonnaise.

Mediterranean Mayonnaise: Replace salt in the mayonnaise by garlic salt. Add to the finished sauce a tablespoon or so of tomato paste and 1 generous teaspoon of strong anise spirit such as French Pernod or Pastis, or Greek Ouzo. For fondue bourguignonne, cold lamb, broiled fish, barbecued meats and fish.

Mousseline Mayonnaise: Beat the white of the egg used to make the mayonnaise and salt it a bit. Fold it into the finished mayonnaise. To cut calories somewhat!

Roquefort Mayonnaise: Mash 1 scant tablespoon Roquefort cheese very finely with a fork or the tip of a knife blade and add as much as your taste dictates to the basic mayonnaise. Watch the salt; you will need less. For all vegetable salads.

Pink Mayonnaise: Add 1 to 2 tablespoons tomato paste to finished mayonnaise.

Green Mayonnaise: Chop any green fresh herbs that you have or like and add to the finished mayonnaise. Chives, tarragon and parsley are a winning combination.

PLEASE READ CAREFULLY
All the ingredients for a mayonnaise should be at the same temperature, so keep them all at room temperature for 30 minutes before you start.

HOLLANDAISE SAUCE
(Sauce Hollandaise)

Sorry! These sauces do not freeze, but leftovers of them can be added to soups instead of yolks and cream.

- Said to be difficult but *is not*
  25 minutes
  6 servings
  Warm sauce

  US ⅓ cup, UK ¼ cup, water (1 scant dl)
  juice of ⅓ lemon
  salt and pepper
  ½ lb. unsalted **butter (250 g)**
  3 egg yolks
  cold salted water

- Put water, lemon juice, ¼ teaspoon salt, and pepper to taste in a saucepan. Cook over medium heat until US 2 tablespoons, UK 1 tablespoon, liquid is left.

- Meanwhile, melt the butter and keep it no more than lukewarm.

- Remove the saucepan from the heat. Add the egg yolks, one at a time, stirring very fast and very well with your whisk. Continue whisking until the yolks form a heavy foam full of millions of air bubbles and until you can see the bottom of the pan for a split second at a time.

- Gradually add the melted butter, bit by bit. You will see the sauce thicken as you add it.

- Heat a pot of water on the stove and keep the pot containing the sauce immersed in it until serving time. The water bath should remain at 140°F. and never boil. If the sauce becomes dangerously thick while it waits, add cold salted water. The thickening is due to the evaporation of the liquids on standing.

- If the sauce shows puddles of butter at the edges of the pan, add as much cold salted water as needed, stirring, until the smooth texture comes back; it will.

WITH THE SAME METHOD
Béarnaise Sauce: Cook together 2 ounces each (US 4 TB, UK 2 TB, .75 dl) white wine and vinegar to which you have added 3 chopped shallots and 1 mashed garlic clove, as well as 1 teaspoon each of dried tarragon and parsley. When reduced to US 2 tablespoons, UK 1 tablespoon, add the yolks and proceed exactly as described above for Hollandaise. Strain the sauce after cooking it and add chopped fresh parsley or tarragon. For broiled fish, beef, lamb, white meat of chicken.

Mousseline Sauce: Whip US ⅓ cup, UK ¼ cup, seasoned heavy cream not too stiff. Fold cream into the basic hollandaise and use on the same preparations as the latter.

YOU NEED THE FOLLOWING IMPLEMENTS
a thick-bottomed 2-quart saucepan, enameled cast iron or aluminum-clad stainless steel;
your wire sauce whisk.

Please have fun! This sauce is a pleasure to prepare and is excellent on all poached or broiled fish, all sautéed shellfish, asparagus and cauliflower.

WALNUT SAUCE FROM ALBI
(Sauce Albigeoise)

This sauce will separate quite rapidly on standing if hand whisked, but will stay together longer if prepared in a food processor or a blender.

No Roquefort? Try Stilton, Danish Blue or any of the many French Blues existing; remember to adjust to their salt content, which varies.

■ Relatively easy
5 minutes
Cold sauce

US ⅓ cup, UK ¼ cup, shelled walnuts (4 TB)
US 2 TB, UK 1 TB, fresh Roquefort cheese (1 TB)
1 tsp. lemon juice
US ⅔ cup, UK ½ cup, oil of your choice (1.75 dl)
pepper from the mill

- Chop the nuts as finely as possible in a food processor or with a knife.
- Crumble the Roquefort cheese and mash into the walnuts, using a fork. Transfer mixture to a small bowl.
- Lighten the texture of the mixture with the lemon juice.
- Gradually beat in the oil either with a hand whisk or with an electric mixer at slow speed.
- Correct the seasoning.

THIS SAUCE CAN BE SERVED WITH
hot red meats, broiled meats, barbecued meats, fondue bourguignonne, etc., or with cold roast beef, cold leg of lamb, cold shoulder of lamb.

VINAIGRETTE
(Oil and Vinegar Dressing)

- Easy
  1 minute
  Cold sauce

  Use by volume and in any quantity you
    need:
  ¼ vinegar
  salt and pepper
  ¾ oil of your choice

  US ¼ cup, UK 1½ to 2 TB, dressing will
    dress a salad for 6 persons.

- Mix vinegar, salt and pepper in a bowl
  and gradually add the oil.
- Pour into a jar and shake very well
  every time you want to use the dressing.
- Keeps very well in the refrigerator.

WITH THE SAME METHOD
Blue Cheese or Roquefort Dressing: Mash
US 1 tablespoon, UK ½ tablespoon,
cheese for each 6 servings; add vinegar,
pepper and oil. No salt may be necessary. If needed, add very sparingly.

Lemon Vinaigrette: Replace vinegar by
lemon juice. The dressing is best balanced when using the juice of 1 lemon
for US ⅔ cup, UK ½ cup, oil (2 scant dl).
Olive oil is best here.

Caper Vinaigrette: Use capers whole and
pickles finely chopped and use a little
less vinegar. US 2 tablespoons, UK 1
tablespoon, each of capers or pickles
will do for 6 persons.

Shallot Vinaigrette: Add 1 finely chopped
shallot to each cup of vinaigrette.

Herb Vinaigrette: Chop any fine fresh
herbs of your choice and add as much as
you like.

Mustard Vinaigrette: Add mustard to vinegar before adding oil; use a little less
vinegar to compensate for the acidity of
the mustard.

Hard-Boiled Egg Vinaigrette: Prepare the
vinaigrette and add finely chopped egg
yolk. You can also mix the chopped yolk
with pickles and capers.

Provençale Vinaigrette: Prepare a basic
vinaigrette. Add US ¼ cup, UK 1½ tablespoons, yogurt with chopped chives
and parsley to taste and a good pinch of
mild paprika to each cup of vinaigrette.
Good with cold fish, broiled fish and
boiled potatoes.

THERE IS MORE THAN VEGETABLE OIL
For a treat and a change of taste try corn,
olive, walnut, sesame seed, safflower, cot-
tonseed or peanut oils, alone or in combina-
tion. The taste will vary every time.

Oils keep very well as long as they are stored
in a dark cupboard.

MAÎTRE d'HÔTEL BUTTER
(Beurre Maître d'Hôtel)

Maître d'hôtel butter in bulk: You can prepare as much of this "compound" butter as you desire, shape it, and freeze it. To use, dip a knife blade into very hot water and cut slices as you need them. Also, parsley is not the only herb you can use; try any fresh herbs growing in your garden (mint, tarragon, basil, etc.) and of course finely chopped onions, garlic and shallots, alone or in combinations.

- Easy
  5 minutes
  May be used cold or warm

  ½ lb. butter, unsalted or salted to your taste (250 g)
  lemon juice
  salt and pepper
  US ¼ cup, UK 2 TB, finely chopped parsley (2 TB)

COLD MAÎTRE d'HÔTEL BUTTER

- Remove the butter from the refrigerator and let it stand until flexible.

- When the butter is soft, but not oily, mash it with a fork or whip it with an electric mixer.

- Add lemon juice and salt and pepper to your taste and mix well so the juice is absorbed by the butter.

- Finally add the parsley.

- Shape the butter into a log. Cool in the refrigerator. Then lift from the plate and roll into clear plastic wrap. Keep cold. Cut slices as thin or as thick as you desire.

WARM MAÎTRE d'HÔTEL BUTTER

- Use pats of cold maître d'hôtel butter as follows:
  Heat about US 2 tablespoons, UK 1 tablespoon water, bouillon or fresh court-bouillon (p. 295) in a small pan, or in the frying pan that you just used to cook a piece of meat. Remove the pan from the heat and swirl in the pat of butter, using your small whisk. The butter will melt and foam. Pour over the meat or fish.

SERVE WITH
broiled red meats, broiled or poached fish, boiled vegetables, especially green beans. Also, on rice, cereals in pilaf, pasta.

EGGS
(Les Œufs)

HOW THE FRENCH USE EGGS

In France, eggs are not served for breakfast, but are appropriate for lunch and dinner. They played an important role in the nutrition of poor peasants during past centuries. You will find here eggs accompanied by all kinds of other foods readily available on a farm or in a city household of very modest means. To this day France retains its love for eggs that it inherited from its Gallo-Roman past, and she uses them with as much flair as do her Italian neighbors. As you will see from the recipes, a mother will not hesitate to cook up a "big mess" of eggs, whichwill be enthusiastically devoured by the family circle.

Use large eggs weighing each 2 ounces. Two eggs provide ample protein for a dinner or lunch.

PROVENÇAL STYLE EGGS
(Œufs à la Provençale)

Garlic and parsley chopped finely together are known in French culinary terms as persillade.

■ Easy
6 servings
Thrift recipe
30 minutes
**Best season: year around, but best in
    summer with sun-ripened tomatoes**

**6 tomatoes
1 large garlic clove
several sprigs of parsley
US 3 TB, UK 1½ TB, oil (1½ TB)
salt and pepper
12 rashers of thin-sliced bacon
12 large eggs
US 2 TB, UK 1 TB, butter (30 g)**

THE COOKING OF BACON
*In French cuisine bacon is not as completely
cooked as it often is in the United States.
Like the Italians, the French like their bacon
light golden and still soft under the thin
crust.*

CLEAN EGGS ARE A MUST
*Shells are porous and bacteria can invade
and contaminate your nutritious eggs by in-
filtrating through those pores.*

- Wash and dry the tomatoes. Remove the stem ends. Cut them crosswise into halves.
- Peel the garlic; chop it with the parsley (see advice).
- Heat the oil in a large skillet and in it fry the tomatoes, cut side down first. Let cook for a few minutes, then turn over. Sprinkle with salt and pepper to taste and the chopped garlic and parsley. Turn the heat down and let cook for a few minutes longer.
- In another skillet, slowly cook the slices of bacon until light golden on both sides. Do not overcrisp for the true French taste. Remove to a warm platter.
- Break 6 eggs into the skillet in which the bacon was cooked. Let eggs cook until the white is set and the yolk still liquid. Season with salt and pepper.
- Remove the tomatoes to the platter and arrange them around the bacon. Keep warm. Put the butter in the skillet in which the tomatoes were cooked, and break the other 6 eggs into it. Cook exactly as you did the first 6 eggs. Season with salt and pepper.
- Using a spatula, remove the cooked eggs to the serving platter, placing them over the slices of bacon. Serve promptly.

SCRAMBLED EGGS WITH CROUTONS
(Œufs Brouillés aux Croûtons)

About "bain marie": Marie indeed existed. Her name was Maria de Cleofa. She was an Italian woman alchemist of the 14th century who used the hot water bath so much in her experiments that it became Ban Maria.

- Relatively easy
  6 servings
  Thrift recipe
  15 minutes
  Best season: year around

  12 eggs
  US 6 TB, UK 3 TB, light or heavy cream (3 TB)
  6 slices of white bread, ⅓ inch thick
  US 6 TB, UK 3 TB, oil (3 TB)
  US 6 TB, UK 3 TB, butter (3 TB)
  salt and pepper
  tomato sauce or ketchup (optional)

- Break 10 eggs into a bowl. Add 2 tablespoons cream of your choice and beat very well with a fork, just to blend well.

- Break 2 eggs into a second smaller bowl and beat well.

- Remove crusts from the slices of white bread and cut slices into ⅓-inch cubes.

- Heat the oil in a skillet and fry the croutons, stirring constantly, until golden; the cubes must be golden and crispy. As soon as this stage is reached, drain the bread onto several layers of crumpled paper towels. Keep warm, at the open edge of a low oven with the door ajar.

- Melt the butter in a saucepan and twist the pan in all directions to butter the sides well. Pour the 10 eggs and cream through a strainer into the pan. If you are using a thick enameled cast-iron pan, cook the eggs over direct very low heat. If you are using a thin aluminum or stainless-steel pan, immerse it in a pan of hot water to make a *bain marie*. Put the hot-water bath over medium heat. In both cases stir or whisk, covering all sides of the pan constantly to prevent thickening of the eggs in any part of the pan.

- Toward the end of the cooking add the remainder of the cream, remove the pan from the heat, and add the last 2 eggs, and salt and pepper to taste. Whisk very well. This method guarantees immediate stopping of the hardening of the eggs and keeps the eggs nice and mellow.

- Add the croutons to the scrambled eggs and serve with a small bowl of tomato sauce or ketchup.

WITH THE SAME METHOD
You can vary the recipe with all kinds of ingredients added to the eggs. Always garnish the platter with a few croutons or slices of bread fried in oil or butter.

Scrambled Eggs with Mushrooms: Replace the small cubes of bread with a small can of mushrooms or, better, ½ pound mushrooms cooked for a few minutes in butter with a dash of lemon juice, salt and pepper.

Scrambled Eggs with Fines Herbes: Chop parsley, chives, chervil and tarragon and, if you have them, a few leaves of sorrel. Add them to the beaten eggs before cooking. You need at least a teacup full of herbs.

Scrambled Eggs and Ham: Replace the cubes of bread by 3½ ounces of ham, cut into small pieces.

Scrambled Eggs with Chicken: Replace the cubes of bread by 3½ ounces of cooked chicken, finely chopped.

CODDLED EGGS AND HAM
(Œufs Cocotte au Jambon)

No ramekins or custard cups? Try muffin tins. Also, you can use these eggs as a first course and serve 1 ramekin per person. Used as a main course, you will need two.

■ Easy
  6 servings
  Thrift recipe
  20 minutes
  Best season: year around

  US 4 TB, UK 2 TB, butter (2 TB)
  5 oz. cooked ham (150 g)
  salt and pepper
  6 eggs
  a kettle full of boiling water

  You must have either fireproof ramekins
    or custard cups.

● Preheat oven to 425°F., 250°C. or 7 to 8 Regulo.

● Butter the baking dishes with half of the butter. Cut the ham into small cubes; divide cubes into 6 equal parts and put 1 part into each dish.

● Sprinkle a little salt and pepper into each dish and break an egg into it. Top with a small piece of butter.

● Put the baking dishes into a roasting pan and pour in enough boiling water to reach two thirds of the way up the dishes.

● Bake in the preheated oven for 6 to 7 minutes; the white must be cooked but the yolk remain liquid. Take the eggs out of the oven and serve them immediately for, if you wait, the yolk will continue cooking.

WITH THE SAME METHOD
Replace the ham by other ingredients and you will have new recipes. Here are a few examples but you can imagine many others:

Coddled Eggs with Shrimps: Chop 6 ounces shelled raw shrimps coarsely. Add a portion of them to each ramekin, plus a generous tablespoon of cream, a bit of salt and pepper.

Coddled Eggs with Mushrooms: Clean and chop 6 ounces mushrooms (180 g) of any style or breed. Chop them, cook them in a bit of butter for 5 minutes, and add salt, pepper and a dash of lemon juice. Add an equal portion of them to each ramekin.

DO YOU KNOW THAT
a very fresh egg has, when broken onto a plate, a bright yellow and bulging yolk with the white appearing all bunched up tightly around the yolk? An egg with the white spreading on the plate is not that fresh.

BOILED EGGS OF ALL KINDS
(Œufs à la Coque)

A good trick: French country lore has an amazing way to tell how an egg can be judged as fresh: it consists in touching both ends of the egg with the tip of the tongue; the rounded end should feel lukewarm and the tip end cold!

Use 1 or 2 eggs per person. Young children and older persons will need only one, adults will need two. Also, adapt the number of eggs served per person to the opulence of your menu.

FRESHNESS IS IMPORTANT
Since in this type of preparation the eggs are served in their shells, use fancy fresh quality, grade AA eggs.

EGG STORAGE
Keep eggs stored in their carton and refrigerated; they will keep longer.

- For these preparations, there must be enough water in the saucepan to cover the eggs completely and generously.
- If you cook several eggs at once, they must be immersed at once in the pot to obtain the same degree of cooking. To achieve this easily, put the eggs in a strainer; you will have no problem removing the eggs from the water.
- The cooking time starts after the water has come back to a boil.
- Remove the eggs from the water as soon as the cooking time is up so they do not continue cooking.
- If you're afraid that the eggs will overcook from the accumulated heat in their mass, rinse them under cold water for 1 minute. This will not affect their texture but effectively cools their mass lightly enough to prevent quick hardening.

SOFT-BOILED EGGS
- The white must be milky and the yolk liquid. There are two methods:
  1. Immerse the raw eggs in salted cold water. Set the pan over medium heat and as soon as the water boils the eggs are cooked.
  2. Immerse the eggs in boiling salted water, bring the water back to a boil, and boil the eggs for 3 minutes.
- In France soft-boiled eggs are eaten from a small egg cup. One dips small buttered sticks of bread into the yolk. In other countries one empties the egg into a cup.

"MOLLET" EGGS
- The white is firm and the yolk is still liquid, but less liquid than in a soft-boiled egg.
- Cooking time: 6 minutes in salted boiling water. In this case the passing of the eggs under running water after the eggs are cooked is a must or the yolk will turn hard very quickly from accumulated heat in the mass of the egg.
- "Mollet" eggs are eaten the same way as soft-boiled eggs, but often they replace poached eggs in culinary preparations because they are easier to prepare for the home cook.

HARD-BOILED EGGS
- Both white and yolk must be firm.
- There are two cooking methods:
  1. Immerse the eggs in cold salted water. Bring to a boil, and boil for 8 minutes.
  2. Add the eggs to boiling salted water, and bring the water back to a boil. Boil eggs for 10 minutes, then immerse them in cold water, so a layer of steam builds between the shell and the white to make the peeling easier. Also, the cold water bath stops the cooking.

HARD-BOILED EGGS AU GRATIN
(Œufs Durs au Gratin)

Room temperature is the temperature at which eggs are best handled for culinary preparations, so take them out of the refrigerator early.

■ Easy
6 servings
Thrift recipe
25 minutes
Best season: year around

12 eggs
US 2¼ cups, UK 2 cups, milk (.5 L)
US 3 TB, UK 1½ TB, butter (45 g)
US 3 TB, UK 1½ TB, flour (20 g)
salt and pepper
nutmeg
US ⅔ cup, UK ½ cup, grated Gruyère cheese (120 g)
US 3 TB, UK 1½ TB, heavy cream (45 g)

- Hard-boil the eggs in salted boiling water for 10 minutes (see p. 72).
- Scald the milk.
- In another saucepan, prepare a white roux with butter and flour. Add the scalding milk, using a whisk, and bring back to a boil. Add salt, pepper and nutmeg to taste. Simmer for no more than 10 minutes.
- Add two thirds of the finely grated Gruyère cheese. Remove from the heat as soon as the cheese starts melting. Stir until smooth and add the cream. Correct the seasoning.
- As soon as the eggs are cooked, immerse them in cold water, peel them, cut them lengthwise into halves, and put them yolk side up in a lightly buttered long fireproof baking dish.
- Cover with the sauce and sprinkle with the remainder of the Gruyère. Let brown under the broiler for a few minutes.

WITH THE SAME METHOD
Eggs au Gratin with Mushrooms: Add to the sauce 4 ounces canned mushrooms or ½ pound fresh mushrooms sautéed in butter with salt, pepper and a dash of lemon juice.

Eggs au Gratin with Cauliflower: Same recipe, but set the eggs on a bed of cauliflowerets blanched in boiling salted water until almost soft.

Eggs au Gratin with Spinach: Prepare the same recipe, but set the eggs on a bed of cooked spinach leaves.

Eggs au Gratin with Mussels: Add about 1 teacup full of shelled cooked mussels to the sauce. Part of the milk can be replaced by some mussel juices, very well strained to discard sand.

Eggs au Gratin with Fish: Add to the sauce 5 ounces (150 g) of cooked flaked fish of your choice.

POACHED EGGS IN ASPIC
(Œufs en Gelée)

For this recipe you need 6 individual 1-cup molds or custard cups. If you do not own any, use teacups. You can also use "mollets" eggs or hard-boiled eggs, but you will then need oval molds.

- A bit difficult
  6 servings
  Thrift recipe
  30 minutes, but must be prepared a day ahead
  Best season: year around

  3 cups canned jellied consommé, or 3 cups homemade bouillon with 1½ envelopes unflavored gelatin
  large pot of water
  salt
  US ½ cup, UK ⅓ cup, vinegar (1 generous dl)
  6 eggs
  herb leaves, olives, or 1 tomato for cutouts to decorate molds
  3 slices of boiled ham, cut lengthwise into halves
  6 lettuce leaves

TO MAKE THE ASPIC BETTER AND STRONGER
add US 2 tablespoons, UK 1 tablespoon, dry Port or Madeira (1 TB) after aspic has cooled.

Prepare the aspic jelly:
- If you are using canned consommé, let it come to room temperature.
- If you are using homemade bouillon with gelatin added, heat half of the bouillon, sprinkle the gelatin over the cold bouillon, stir well; then add the hot bouillon and reheat the mixture, stirring until gelatin has completely dissolved.
- Rinse the molds with cold water. Pour about ¼ inch of jelly into each dish and refrigerate so it can become firm.
- Meanwhile, heat 2 quarts of water in a saucepan; add salt and vinegar. Bring to a boil and turn down to a bare simmer. Break the eggs, one at a time, into a cup and let slide into the bath. Let the eggs cook for 3 to 4 minutes.
- With a slotted spoon lift the eggs out of the bath; rinse them in a bath of cold salted water and drain on crumpled paper towels.
- Take the prepared molds out of the refrigerator and decorate the bottom with sprigs of herbs or cutouts of olives or tomatoes.
- Roll each egg in a strip of ham and put 1 egg into each mold. Fill the molds with the remainder of the jelly. Refrigerate overnight.
- To unmold, dip the molds into hot water for 1 second and turn them over onto a platter lined with lettuce leaves.

BAKED EGGS WITH HAM
(Œufs au Jambon au Four)

Do you know that you can safely turn off the oven after the eggs have been baking for about 3 minutes? The heat they will have absorbed will be sufficient to cook them through.

This method is well adapted to use small amounts of leftovers.

■ Easy
6 servings
Thrift recipe
20 minutes
Best season: year around

several sprigs of parsley
3 slices of ham
6 eggs
US 6 TB, UK 3 TB, heavy cream (3 TB)
salt and pepper
US 4 TB, UK 2 TB, butter (60 g)

- Preheat oven to 375°F., 200°C. or 5 to 6 Regulo.
- Wash, dry, and chop the parsley. Chop the ham.
- Break the eggs into a bowl, add the cream, parsley, ham, some salt (not too much), and pepper to taste. Beat as you would an omelet.
- Butter a 1-quart baking dish and pour the mixture into it.
- Bake in the preheated oven for 10 minutes.

WITH THE SAME METHOD
Baked Eggs and Vegetables: Replace the ham by any leftover vegetable, which you must drain extremely well and chop finely before adding to the eggs.

Baked Eggs with Fish: Replace the ham by 3 to 5 ounces (150 g) of flaked cooked fish.

Eggs with Meat: Replace the ham with 3 to 5 ounces (150 g) of chopped cooked meat; any leftover meat will do.

EGG STORAGE
Keep eggs stored in their carton and refrigerated; they will keep longer.

BAKED EGGS AND POTATOES
(Œufs au Four)

Would you like to save heating the oven? Then use a large-size electric frying pan. The whole cooking can be done in it from start to finish. Put the lid on with the vent closed to melt the cheese.

- Easy
  6 servings
  Thrift recipe
  40 minutes
  Best season: year around

  4 potatoes, preferably the waxy type
  5 oz. fresh pork brisket (150 g)
  US ¼ cup, UK 2 TB, oil (2 TB)
  US 2 TB, UK 1 TB, butter (1 TB)
  12 eggs
  US ½ cup, UK ¼ cup, heavy cream (4 TB)
  ½ lb. Gruyère cheese, cut into slivers (250 g)
  salt and pepper

ABOUT THE CHEESE
Use any Swiss-style cheese available to you: Emmental, American Swiss, Sbrinz, Appenzeller, Austrian or Finnish Swiss-type cheese or Port-du-Salut will do very well here. The star would be an Italian Fontina.

- Peel the potatoes, wash them, dry them well, and cut them into thin slices.
- Cut the fresh pork brisket into small sticks ⅓ x 1 inch (in French, *lardons*).
- Heat the oil and butter in a skillet and add the pork brisket *lardons*. Sauté them until light golden on all sides.
- Add the potatoes to the mixture of pork and fat and let the potatoes brown well on one side. Turn them over and brown them on the other side. (The turning over is best done by sliding the potatoes onto a plate, then inverting them back into the skillet.) Reduce the heat to complete the cooking of the potatoes, but keep them uncovered all through the cooking.
- While the potatoes cook, preheat oven to 375°F., 200°C. or 5 to 6 Regulo. Empty the potatoes and pork into a baking dish. Break the eggs over the potatoes, cover the eggs with the cream and the cheese slivers, and pepper well but do not salt too much because of the saltiness of the cheese.
- Bake in the preheated oven for 10 minutes. Serve immediately.

EGGS IN RED-WINE SAUCE
(Œufs en Meurette)

There is no need to use an expensive wine in this recipe, but the meurette being a specialty sauce of Burgundy, you will want to use a good-quality Burgundy.

If you prefer, instead of the fried bread, you can serve boiled potatoes or boiled rice.

- A bit difficult
  6 servings
  Medium expensive
  45 minutes
  Best season: fall and winter

  6 slices of French bread
  US ¼ cup, UK 2 TB, oil (2 TB)
  3 onions
  2 garlic cloves
  1 bottle of red wine, Burgundy or Côtes du Rhône
  ½ bay leaf
  2 sprigs of thyme
  2 sprigs of parsley, chopped
  salt and pepper
  12 eggs
  US 1½ TB, UK ¾ TB, flour (12 g)
  US 2 TB, UK 1 TB, butter (30 g)

A VERSATILE DISH
to be used as a first course or as a main course. Use 1 egg per person in the first case and 2 eggs in the second case.

- Fry the slices of bread in the oil.
- Peel the onions and the garlic; chop them coarsely.
- Pour the red wine into a saucepan, add the onions, garlic, bay leaf, thyme, parsley, and salt and pepper to taste. Bring to a boil. As soon as the mixture boils, reduce the heat; cover the saucepan and simmer gently for 30 minutes.
- Strain the sauce into another saucepan and set the saucepan over heat.
- Cook 2 eggs at a time proceeding this way: Break the egg into a cup and slide it into the wine sauce. Adjust the heat so the sauce barely simmers. Let cook for 3 to 4 minutes, bringing the egg white over the yolk with the slotted spoon. Drain the eggs and deposit each egg on a slice of fried bread.
- Mix the flour and butter well together, using a fork. Whisk into the simmering sauce. Stop cooking as soon as the sauce has come to a boil and thickened.
- Correct the seasoning and pour over the eggs. Serve immediately.

EGGS IN RATATOUILLE
(Œufs à la Ratatouille)

No ratatouille? Go to an Italian grocery store and purchase a large can of caponata.

■ Easy
  6 servings
  Thrift recipe
  20 minutes
  **Best season: late summer when squashes
    and tomatoes are plentiful**

  a few sprigs of parsley
  2 to 3 cups leftover Ratatouille (see p. 232)
  12 eggs
  salt and pepper

WOULD YOU RATHER
*bake the dish? Then preheat your oven to
375°F., 200°C. or 6 Regulo, and bake for 5
minutes; turn off the oven.*

● Chop the parsley
● Reheat the ratatouille in a small
  saucepan and let the water it may still
  contain evaporate.
● Empty the ratatouille into a fireproof
  dish or skillet.
● With a spoon make holes in the
  ratatouille and break an egg into each
  hole.
● Cover with aluminum foil and keep
  covered until the eggs are set. The
  ratatouille should not boil.
● Remove from the heat and uncover as
  soon as the egg whites are coagulated.
  You can cook the eggs longer if you
  wish both the white and the yolks to be
  more solid. Season them lightly.
● Sprinkle with the chopped parsley.

SOUFFLÉED EGGS
(Œufs Soufflés)

Another way to check whether egg whites are ready to use and whipped enough is to look at the mass of white on the beater. It should stand in stiff peaks.

- Relatively easy
  6 servings
  Thrift recipe
  25 minutes
  Best season: year around

12 eggs
US 1 cup, UK 8 oz., heavy cream (225 g)
salt and pepper

UNLESS
you have a gall bladder condition or a tendency to high cholesterol, do not hesitate to use eggs every day. They are a good cheap source of protein.

- Preheat oven to 375°F., 200°C. or 5 to 6 Regulo.
- Butter a fireproof baking dish.
- Separate the egg whites from the yolks, dropping the whites into a bowl and keeping each yolk in a half-shell.
- Add a pinch of salt to the whites and beat them stiff or until they can carry an uncooked egg in its shell. (An electric mixer would be a help.) The uncooked egg should not sink into the foam by more than ½ inch.
- Empty the whites into 1 or 2 baking dishes. Fold the unwhipped cream into the egg whites.
- Using a spoon, make 12 holes in the bulk of the whites. Sprinkle salt and pepper into each hole and into each hole drop 1 egg yolk.
- Bake for 10 minutes and serve immediately.

LORRAINE OMELET
(Omelette Lorraine)

To lighten an omelet and give it volume, beat one quarter of the whites into a good solid foam and fold this into the other eggs and egg yolks, already well beaten. Keep the heat high and the butter plentiful.

■ Relatively easy
6 servings
Thrift recipe
25 minutes
Best season: preferably fall and winter

3 small waxy potatoes
6 oz. slab bacon (180 g)
US 2 TB, UK 1 TB, oil (1 TB)
12 eggs
US ¼ cup, UK 2 TB, milk (2 TB)
salt and pepper
US 6 TB, UK 3 TB, butter (90 g)

IS THE IDEA OF SEVERAL OMELETS BOTHERING YOU?
Please do not worry about time; with a properly heated pan each omelet will cook in barely 1 minute.

- Peel the potatoes, wash them, dry them, and cut them into ⅓-inch cubes.
- Cut the bacon into ⅓-inch cubes.
- Put the bacon in a cold frying pan. Let it cook until barely golden. Add the oil and the potatoes and cook until the potatoes are done and golden all around.
- Beat the eggs, adding milk, and salt and pepper to taste.
- When the potatoes are done divide them into 3 portions. With each portion: prepare a 4-egg omelet to serve 2 persons, adding the potato-bacon mixture directly to the egg batter. Use US 2 tablespoons, UK 1 tablespoon, butter (1 TB) each time to cook the omelet.
- Slide the omelet into the lip on the pan. Fold over and invert onto a plate.

OMELET PANS
Good omelet pans are made of cast iron and used only for making omelets. An omelet pan is a small lifetime investment; it gets washed only once in its lifetime, just after it has been bought; otherwise it is wiped with paper towels. It is sterile because of the very high heat it is subjected to.

MUSHROOM OMELET
(Omelette aux Champignons)

Are you short of eggs? Do as the women of the French Auvergne did in times of food shortages: Dilute a couple of tablespoons of flour with ½ cup of milk and replace 2 eggs by this mixture.

- Relatively easy
  6 servings
  Medium expensive
  25 minutes
  Best season: year around

½ lb. mushrooms (250 g)
US ¼ lb., UK ¼ lb., butter (125 g)
dash of lemon juice
salt and pepper
US ¼ cup, UK 2 TB, heavy cream (2 TB)
12 eggs
US ½ cup, UK ⅓ cup, milk (1 generous dl)

- Cut the stem ends of the mushrooms. Wash them only if they are very dirty, otherwise wipe them clean with a tea towel and slice them thinly.
- To a small saucepan add US 1 tablespoon, UK ½ tablespoon, butter (½ TB) and the mushrooms. Add a drop of lemon juice and salt and pepper to taste. Cook covered for 5 minutes.
- Add the cream to the mushrooms and let cook together until the cream and mushroom juices have cooked down to coating consistency.
- Beat the eggs and the milk together in a large bowl. Add a pinch of salt and pepper.
- Prepare three 4-egg omelets as follows: Heat US 2 tablespoons, UK 1 tablespoon, butter each time in an omelet pan. Heat the pan until the butter turns brown. Pour one third of the egg batter into the pan. Using a fork, beat the eggs as if they were still in the bowl, gathering all the portions of already cooked egg toward the center of the pan. Shake the pan on the stove burner back and forth. Slide the omelet forward into the lip of the pan,

add one third of the mushrooms, and fold the top of the omelet over the mushrooms.
- Invert the omelet on a plate. Repeat with the remaining egg batter.

WITH THE SAME METHOD
The variety of garnishes for omelets is endless. Here are a few:

Fines Herbes Omelet: Add to the omelet batter any fresh herb finely chopped. If you use dried herbs, either crumble them very finely or revive them in a bit of hot water before using them.

Cheese Omelet: Add 2 tablespoons cheese for an omelet for 2 persons. The only cheeses that can be mixed into the batter are the dry, finely grated Italian cheeses (Parmesan, Romano, etc.). All cheeses with a relatively high moisture content (Gruyère, Edam, Cheddar) should be spooned between the folds of the omelet and allowed to melt in its heat. These cheeses will often cause an omelet to ooze water when cooking.

Ham Omelet: Chop 1 or 2 slices of boiled ham and add to the batter.

Tomato Omelet: Cook 1 tomato, peeled and seeded, per person, in a bit of oil. Add chopped onion, chopped garlic, salt and pepper. Cook uncovered to evaporate the juices and stuff into the omelet as was done with the mushrooms.

Tuna Omelet: Prepare some tomatoes as for the Tomato Omelet and add to them 1 can (3½ oz.) tuna (100 g), finely flaked. Use to stuff 3 omelets, each of them made with 4 eggs.

PIPÉRADE
(Pipérade)

About pipérade: This is the most popular egg dish of the French part of the Basque Country. The ham used in France is Bayonne ham. Any leftovers of pipérade can be served the next day with a vinaigrette (p. 65) flavored with chives.

■ A bit difficult
  6 servings
  Medium expensive
  45 minutes
  **Best season: late summer when tomatoes
    and peppers are plentiful**

  3 onions
  6 tomatoes
  3 green bell peppers
  2 garlic cloves
  6 slices of raw mountain ham (prosciutto)
  US ½ cup, UK ¼ cup, oil (4 TB)
  salt and pepper
  9 eggs

A NICE DECORATION
How about a few bread croutons cut into triangles and fried in the oil before you fry the ham?

- Peel and chop the onions.
- Immerse the tomatoes in boiling water for 1 minute. Peel them, seed them, chop them coarsely.
- Cut the bell peppers into ⅓-inch strips. Peel and mash the garlic.
- Cut the ham into ⅓-inch strips. Heat the oil and sauté the ham in the hot oil for 1 minute. Remove it to a plate.
- Replace the ham in the pan by the onions and let those sauté gently without coloring. Add the tomatoes, peppers and garlic. Let cook uncovered until all the vegetable juices have evaporated. Reduce the heat to very low.
- Beat the eggs as you would for an omelet. Pour them into the panful of vegetables. Stir constantly to prevent coagulation of the eggs; they should turn into a thickish cream. If your pan is made of aluminum or stainless steel, this operation will be best done over a hot water bath. Correct the seasoning.
- Pour onto a platter and top with the ham.

FISH AND SHELLFISH
(Les Poissons, les Crustacés, les Coquillages)

EXPERIMENT WITH UNFAMILIAR SPECIES

In France, fish is not always served as the main course, but more often than not as a hot first course. You will find that these recipes are excellent main courses for family dining as well as for pleasant entertaining.

Whenever you can, bake a fish with its head on; its flavor will be better and you will be able to enjoy two choice morsels: the cheeks. Why discard them when they are really the best-tasting part of the fish? Oh! but those poor eyes staring at every one from the plate! Simply cover them with a slice of lemon and a sprig of parsley, and no one will notice them.

As the species of fish that have been popular in our English-speaking countries disappear slowly for diverse reasons, other species are becoming better known and more used; think of tilefish, monkfish or anglerfish, pollock. You will find them more available in your markets. The recipes given here will help you to prepare them well and give another dimension to your fish cookery. The French have used all these "new" fish for several centuries.

BROILED WHOLE FISH
(Poissons Grillés)

Any leftover cooked fish can be used as part of a mixed salad.

■ Easy
Adapt number of fish to number of guests
From cheap to expensive
25 minutes
Best season: Use the best that each season
has to offer.

1 or several fish, approximately 2 lbs. (1
kg)
salt and pepper
oil
sauce of your choice (see text)

FISH TO USE
You can use turbot, brill, small striped bass,
gray sole, flounder, plaice, larger sand dab,
small salmon, trout or salmon trout.

- Have the fish dressed by the fish market, the tail and fins cut off but the head left on.
- Preheat the broiler.
- Wash the fish, dry it with paper towels, season with salt and pepper, then oil the side that will be broiled first.
- Put the fish in a special fish broiler basket, or, if you do not own one, on a cake rack placed over a jelly-roll pan and also oiled.
- Broil the fish 4 inches from the source of heat for 5 minutes, then move the pan to a lower rack, 6 inches from source of heat, for another 3 minutes. Place a second oiled rack over the fish; grasping both racks, turn the fish over. Broil on the second side close to the source of heat for 2 minutes and 6 inches from the source of heat for no more than 4 minutes. Remove the top rack.
- To transfer to a serving platter, place the platter upside down over the fish, grasp platter and rack at once, and turn over; remove the rack.
- All the broiled fish indicated here are very tasty fish which deserve a plain but delicious sauce. Use either noisette butter and lemon juice (p. 95), Béarnaise Sauce (p. 63) or Mousseline Mayonnaise (p. 62).

FILLETS OF FRESH COD OR SCROD BASQUE STYLE
(Filets de Cabillaud Basquaise)

Are you using frozen fish? Do not defrost it, but put it all frozen on the vegetable bed and bake for 10 to 15 minutes longer. Also, why don't you accompany the fish with buttered noodles or spaghetti instead of the same old potatoes?

- Easy
  6 servings
  Medium expensive
  25 minutes
  Best season: summer and early fall for best tomatoes; year around with canned tomatoes (see note below)

  4 large shallots
  4 large tomatoes
  1½ lbs. fillets of cod or scrod (750 g)
  salt and pepper
  ½ lb. fresh mushrooms (250 g)
  US 1½ cups, UK 1⅓ cups, dry white wine (3.5 dl)
  US 2 TB, UK 1 TB, oil (1 TB)
  US 2 TB, UK 1 TB, butter (1 TB)
  chopped parsley

ABOUT THOSE TOMATOES
If fresh sun-ripened tomatoes are not in season, use 6 canned pear-shaped tomatoes with about US ⅓ cup, UK ¼ cup, canning juices (1 scant dl). The best canned pear-shaped tomatoes are from the Mediterranean basin, so check the label.

- Preheat oven to 325°F., 200°C. or 5 Regulo.
- Peel the shallots and chop them finely.
- Wash the tomatoes, cut them into quarters, remove all seeds. If you prefer the tomatoes skinless, you can peel them; immerse them in boiling water for 2 minutes before cutting them.
- Put the tomatoes and shallots in a 2-quart baking dish. Add the fillets of fish and sprinkle with salt and pepper.
- Remove the stem end of the mushrooms. Wash them only if they are very dirty, otherwise wipe them with a tea towel. Cut them into halves or quarters depending on their size and put them around the fish.
- Pour the white wine over the fish, also add the oil, and dot the fish with small pieces of butter.
- Bake for 15 to 20 minutes, depending on the thickness of the fillets. While baking, baste the fish 2 or 3 times with the juices in the dish.
- Remove fish from the oven and serve it in the baking dish. Sprinkle well with chopped parsley.

SALT COD AU GRATIN
(Morue au Gratin)

French cod fishermen are mostly from Brittany and they are called Terre-Neuvas because their fishing grounds are close to Iceland and Newfoundland (Terre Neuve in French). They prepare the salt cod on board ship and have a saying "salt for preserving is not salt for cooking." What they mean is that after soaking, the cod should be almost bland and salt-free and require a bit more salt.

■ Easy
  6 servings
  Thrift recipe
  1 hour
  **Best season: fall and winter months, and
     early spring**

1½ lbs. fillets of salt cod (750 g)
8 small potatoes for baking
5 large onions
US 4 TB, UK 2 TB, butter (60 g)
salt and pepper
1 tsp. dried thyme
US 1 cup, UK 1 scant cup, water (2.5 dl)
**US ½ cup, UK ⅓ cup, heavy cream (1
     generous dl)**

YOU MAY WANT TO BUY
*a whole side of salt cod; it will taste better,
but your soaking time will be 24 hours.*

- The day before, or at least 12 hours before cooking, put the cod to soak in plenty of cold water. Change the water at least 6 times.
- The day you plan to serve, preheat oven to 375°F., 200°C. or 5 to 6 Regulo.
- Peel the potatoes. Wash them; cut them into thin slices.
- Drain the cod, cut it into small pieces, remove all bones.
- Peel onions and cut into thin slices.
- Butter a 2-quart baking dish heavily with half of the butter and arrange the ingredients in it as follows: 1 layer of potatoes, 1 layer of cod, 1 layer of onions, and so on. End with a layer of potatoes.
- Salt lightly and pepper reasonably. Sprinkle the thyme and remaining butter cut into small pieces over all and add the water.
- Bake in the preheated oven for 40 minutes.
- Just before serving, pour the cream evenly over the whole surface of the dish.

HERRINGS MARINATED IN WHITE WINE
(Harengs Marinés au Vin Blanc)

About baking dishes: Avoid any metal with the exception of stainless steel because of chemical reactions with the vinegar. The best baking dishes are those of white or brown ovenproof porcelain.

■ Easy
6 servings
Thrift recipe
30 minutes (to be prepared a day ahead)
Best season: in the spring when herring is running

6 herrings
US 1 TB, UK ½ TB, oil (½ TB)
½ tsp. dried thyme
¼ bay leaf, crumbled
1 tsp. crumbled dried tarragon
1 tsp. crumbled dried chervil
1 TB chopped parsley
3 cloves
3 shallots, finely minced
1 onion, finely minced
salt and pepper
US 1½ cups, UK 1¼ cups, dry white wine (.35 L)
US ⅔ cup, UK ½ cup, vinegar (2 scant dl)
US 1 cup, UK ¾ cup, water (2.5 L)

- Preheat oven to 400°F., 220°C. or 7 Regulo.
- Have the fish store remove the heads of the herrings and dress and scale them.
- Arrange the herrings head to tail in a lightly oiled baking dish.
- On top of the fish arrange the spices and aromatics and sprinkle with salt and pepper.
- Heat the wine, vinegar and water until boiling. Pour this mixture over the fish. Bake in the preheated oven for 10 minutes.
- Remove from the oven; let cool. Cover with plastic wrap and refrigerate.
- To serve, remove the cold fish to a country-style deep dish; discard all aromatics, and strain the broth over the fish.

OTHER TYPES OF FISH
to use for this preparation include mackerel fillets, smelts, ocean perch fillets, or large whiting fillets.

MACKERELS EN PAPILLOTE
(Maquereaux en Papillote)

No tinker mackerels? Try smelts, small red mullets, small ocean perch, butterfish, steaks of any white fish, even rainbow or brook trout. Yes, you can cook this also on your barbecue.

- Easy
  6 servings
  Thrift recipe
  30 minutes
  Best season: the spring when small mackerels run heavily

  12 tinker (small) mackerels
  oil of your choice
  1 jar Dijon mustard
  salt and pepper
  2 bay leaves
  1 tsp. crumbled dried thyme
  12 small boiling potatoes (optional)
  butter, lemon juice and parsley (optional)

CHOOSE YOUR FISH WELL
Large mackerels are too fat for this presentation. Tinkers (4 to 6 oz.), baby mackerels, are perfect, delicious and soft as butter.

- Preheat oven to 425°F., 250°C. or 7 Regulo.
- Have the fish store dress the fish for you. Rinse them carefully under running cold water. Pat dry with paper towels.
- Prepare 6 aluminum foil sheets 17 x 13 inches and brush each with oil at the center.
- Brush each fish with prepared Dijon mustard. Salt and pepper lightly and add a tiny piece of bay leaf and a few leaves of thyme.
- Enclose 2 fish in each sheet of foil; use drugstore wrap, which will seal it well.
- Put the packages of fish on one of the oven racks and bake for 15 to 20 minutes.
- Serve 1 *papillote* per person and let each person open his own.
- For an accompaniment you may want to boil a few potatoes in their jackets and prepare a Maître d'Hôtel butter with butter, lemon juice, chopped parsley, salt and pepper.

WITH THE SAME METHOD
Haddock Steaks en Papillote: Spread each steak with a compound butter made of lemon juice, parsley, salt, pepper and butter creamed all together. You will need US 1½ tablespoons, UK ¾ tablespoon, butter (25 g) per person. The other ingredients will be according to your personal taste. Bake for 15 minutes.

MONKFISH IN WHITE-WINE SAUCE
(Lotte au Vin Blanc)

If you plan on serving rice, do not hesitate to double the quantity of sauce. The rice is delicious covered with this sauce.

- Relatively easy
  6 servings
  A bit expensive
  35 minutes
  Best season: year around

  2½ lbs. fillets of monkfish (anglerfish), trimmed well (1 heavy kg)
  US 1½ cups, UK 1¼ cups, dry white wine (3.5 dl)
  2 onions, chopped fine
  1 shallot, chopped fine
  1 garlic clove, chopped fine
  1 sprig of thyme
  ½ bay leaf
  1 bunch of parsley stems, chopped
  US ⅔ cup, UK ½ cup, water or bouillon (2 scant dl)
  US ½ cup, UK ⅓ cup, clam juice (1 generous dl)
  US 1 TB, UK ½ TB, cornstarch (½ TB)
  US 4 TB, UK 2 TB, heavy cream (2 TB)
  lemon juice
  chopped parsley

- Wash the fish; cut it into 1-inch cubes.

- Put the wine, onions, shallot, garlic, thyme, bay leaf and parsley stems in a pot. Reduce by half.

- Add to the pot the water or bouillon and clam juice, and bring back to a boil.

- Add all the fish. Bring to a second boil. Remove the pot from the heat immediately, cover, and let stand off the heat for 5 minutes. The fish will then be cooked. Transfer it to a deep country-style dish. Discard all traces of aromatics on the fish.

- Bring the cooking juices of the fish back to a simmer. Dilute the cornstarch with a few drops of cold water or clam juice and add to the simmering liquid. It will thicken immediately. Let simmer for 5 minutes, then strain into a clean pot. Add the cream, lemon juice to taste and chopped parsley. Pour over the fish.

FISH AND MUSHROOM GRATIN IN SHELLS
(Coquilles de Poisson Gratinées)

Would you like to make this dish more plentiful? Use a 2-quart baking dish. Add enough cooked rice, hot and well buttered, to serve 6 persons, and arrange the fish and its sauce on top. Broil until the top is golden.

- Easy
  6 servings
  Thrift recipe
  25 minutes
  Best season: year around

  5 oz. fresh mushrooms (150 g)
  US 3 TB, UK 1½ TB, butter (1½ TB)
  salt and pepper
  lemon juice
  US 1⅓ cups, UK 1¼ cups, milk (1 generous .25 L)
  US 2 TB, UK 1 TB, flour (1 TB)
  1½ lbs. cooked, cleaned fish (750 g)
  US ½ cup, UK ⅓ cup, grated Gruyère cheese (4 TB)

TO BE QUICK AND ORGANIZED
When you buy fish to poach in court-bouillon, always buy twice as much as needed and cook it all. This will give you fish ready to be prepared quickly with this simple but good recipe.

- Cut the stem end of the mushrooms; wipe them clean with a tea towel. Wash them only if they are very dirty. Slice them thinly.
- Melt a small piece of butter in a saucepan. As soon as it is hot, add the mushrooms. Season them with salt and pepper and add a dash of lemon juice. Cook, covered, for 6 to 7 minutes.
- Scald the milk.
- In another pot, prepare a roux with the rest of the butter and the flour. Add the scalding milk, using a whisk, and bring to a boil. Reduce the heat and simmer for 5 minutes.
- Add the mushrooms and their cooking juices to the sauce. Simmer for another 5 minutes and add the fish.
- Divide this mixture into 6 shells for coquilles Saint-Jacques, or other shallow individual baking dishes. Cover with the grated Gruyère cheese. Slide under the broiler until the tops are golden.

POLLOCK IN TOMATO SAUCE
(Lieu Noir à la Tomate)

Any starch will be good to absorb that good sauce; try rice (p. 206), potatoes, spaghetti, tagliatelle and even wheat as is done in the Middle East.

■ Easy
  6 servings
  Medium expensive
  40 minutes
  Best season: year around

  6 tomatoes
  4 large onions
  1 green pepper
  1 red pepper
  fresh parsley, chopped fine
  **fresh tarragon, chopped fine, or
    crumbled dried tarragon**
  1 bay leaf
  1 sprig of thyme
  salt and pepper
  US ⅓ cup, UK ¼ cup, oil (1 scant dl)
  **2½ lbs. pollock, in 2 large pieces (1 heavy
    kg)**

YOUR CHOICE OF FISH AND OIL
Pollock is easier to find, but tilefish is what you really need for this good dish. Use olive oil and you may think that you are in Portugal. As a matter of fact tilefish is always available in Portuguese neighborhoods.

● Wash the tomatoes. If you want them skinless and have time, immerse them in boiling water for 1 minute, then peel them. Press out the seeds, cut flesh into cubes, and put into a 3-quart sauteuse pan.

● Peel the onions; chop both the onions, the green and red peppers and all the herbs. Add to the saucepan containing the tomatoes; add also the bay leaf, thyme, salt and pepper to taste and the oil.

● Wash the fish carefully and put it on the bed of vegetables. Cover.

● Put the sauteuse over medium high heat. As soon as the vegetable mixture boils, reduce the heat and let cook very slowly for about 20 minutes. Remove the fish to a platter. Keep warm.

● Strain the sauce through a coarse strainer to discard the pepper skins and aromatics; return sauce to the stove. Turn the heat to high and reduce the sauce well. Remove the skin and bones of the fish. Pour the sauce over the fish. It will be very smooth because of the emulsion of oil in it.

RED SNAPPER IN LEMON SAUCE
(Daurade au Citron)

Would you like a complete meal? Then add 1 small potato per person, peeled and diced, to the dish. Add also a bit more white wine and a small cup of bouillon. If you have no wine, a little bouillon and the juice of another lemon can substitute.

- ■ Easy
  6 servings
  Medium expensive
  40 minutes
  Best season: year around

  2 red snappers, about 2 lbs. each (1 kg each)
  1 lemon
  1 carrot, sliced thinly
  ½ bay leaf, crumbled
  1 sprig of thyme, crumbled
  fresh chopped tarragon or crumbled dried tarragon
  chopped parsley
  salt and pepper
  US ⅓ cup, UK ¼ cup, dry white wine (1dl)

- ● Preheat oven to 375°F., 200°C. or 6 Regulo.
- ● Wash the fish carefully and blot it dry with paper towels.
- ● Cut the lemon lengthwise into halves, then across into thin slivers. Cut a few indentations into one side of each fish and insert a sliver of lemon into each cut.
- ● Butter a 2-quart baking dish. Set the fish in that dish. Peel the carrot; slice it paper-thin. Arrange slices around the fish together with the crumbled bay leaf and thyme, and tarragon and parsley to taste. Sprinkle with salt and pepper and finally pour in the wine.
- ● Bake in the preheated oven for 30 to 35 minutes. At regular intervals, baste the fish with the juices in the dish.
- ● Serve in the baking dish.

OTHER FISH
The same recipe is excellent prepared with red ocean perch, sea bass, striped bass, grey mullet or large pompano.

BROILED SALMON WITH TARRAGON
(Saumon Grillé à l'Estragon)

Ideal for barbecueing; it is easier to control the cooking and all smells disappear into the fresh air!

■ Difficult
6 servings
Expensive to very expensive
30 minutes
Best season: whenever the salmon runs in your area; seasons vary with the climate.

6 salmon steaks
approximately US 1 cup, UK 1 scant cup, oil (3 dl)
salt and pepper
1 egg, separated
juice of ½ lemon
1 tsp. prepared mustard
chopped fresh tarragon or dried tarragon
soft-type lettuce leaves
boiled potatoes for garnish

SALMON
- Preheat the broiler or start the barbecue fire.
- Wipe salmon steaks dry without washing them. Brush them with some of the oil, and salt and pepper them lightly.
- Put the steaks on a broiler pan and broil 6 inches from the source of heat for 3 to 4 minutes on each side. Do not apply high initial heat or the salmon will overcook on the outside and remain raw in the center. The salmon is done when you can see the meat starting to loosen from the bone.

SAUCE
- Place the egg yolk, lemon juice, mustard, and salt and pepper to taste in a small bowl. Whip very well and gradually add the remainder of the oil (see Mayonnaise, p. 62). Wash and chop the tarragon if fresh, or revive it in a few drops of hot water if dried, and add to the mayonnaise. Last, beat the egg white and fold it into the tarragon sauce.
- Present the salmon on a bed of lettuce on a small platter, and surround with some boiled potatoes. Present the sauce in a boat.

WITH THE SAME METHOD
Broiled Fresh Tuna: The preparation is identical but since the piece will be very large, you will need 2 meat spatulas to turn it over.

OTHER FISH
Try salmon trout steaks, swordfish steak, or halibut steak.

SKATE IN BROWN BUTTER
(Raie au Beurre Noir)

Brown butter is not black butter. It is essential to cook the butter only until brown, not black. This butter is known as "Noisette Butter" because as the solids in the butter cook they acquire a faint taste and smell of hazelnut. When the solids burn, the taste is bad and the butter is no longer very digestible.

- Relatively easy
  6 servings
  Medium expensive
  20 minutes
  Best season: fall, winter, early spring

  2½ lbs. skate (1.25 kg)
  3 quarts water (3 L)
  juice of 2 lemons
  salt
  US 1½ TB, UK ¾ TB, salt (¾ TB)
  US ½ cup, UK 4 oz., butter (120 g)
  US 3 TB, UK 1½ TB, vinegar (1½ TB)
  US 4 TB, UK 2 TB, small capers (2 TB)
  pepper
  chopped parsley

SKATE IS HIGHLY PERISHABLE
Skate develops strong smells and off-flavors if not used on the same day as bought.

- Cut the skate into 6 pieces approximately 6½ ounces each. Wash the pieces very well.

- Bring 3 quarts of water to a boil; add the juice of 2 lemons and about 1 large tablespoon salt.

- Add the skate to the boiling water; bring water back to a boil. Remove the pot from the heat, cover it, and let stand for 6 minutes.

- Meanwhile, put the butter in a frying pan and heat it until it turns golden brown and smells of hazelnuts. Remove from the heat; add the vinegar and capers. Season with salt and pepper.

- Remove the skin and bones of the skate by sliding the blade of a knife between meat and bones. Arrange fish on a serving platter, pour the sauce over, and serve sprinkled with parsley.

FILLETS OF SOLE MEUNIÈRE
(Filets de Sole Meunière)

As a vegetable try a few steamed potatoes; they can absorb any excess butter on your plate.

■ Easy
6 servings
Expensive
20 minutes
Best season: year around

10 double fillets of sole (see note below)
salt and pepper
flour
US ½ cup, UK 4 oz., butter (120 g)
chopped parsley
juice of 1 lemon

ABOUT FILLETS OF SOLE
They come in different styles:
*   *double, or one side of a fish made of 2 fillets;*
*   *single, one side of a fish cut through the center lengthwise to yield 2 single fillets.*
A portion consists of 1 double for men and 1½ singles for women and children.

* Wash the fillets well. Dry them with paper towels. Cut them lengthwise into halves, then each half again into halves crosswise.
* Salt and pepper the fillets, then flour them.
* Heat US 6 tablespoons, UK 3 tablespoons, butter (90 g) until it turns golden (see note on noisette butter, p. 95). Add the fillets and brown well on one side, turn over, brown on the second side.
* Remove cooked fillets to a heated platter and sprinkle with parsley.
* To the cooking butter of the fish add the remainder of the uncooked butter. Let it turn *noisette* brown, then add the lemon juice and mix well. Pour over the fish and serve immediately.

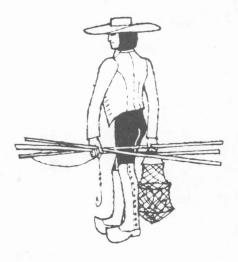

FILLETS OF LEMON OR GRAY SOLE MAÎTRE d'HÔTEL
(Filets de Limande Pochés Maître d' Hôtel)

Another way to prepare maître d'hôtel butter: Cream the butter, salt and pepper it, then add the lemon juice and parsley. Shape this into a log 1 inch in diameter and freeze it. You can cut slices of it and use it as needed on broiled fish steaks.

■ Easy
6 servings
Medium expensive
40 minutes
Best season: year around

1½ lbs. fillets of lemon sole (large) or gray sole (smaller) (750 g)
1 large onion
1 small carrot
salt and pepper
US ½ cup, UK ⅓ cup, dry white wine (1 generous dl)
US ½ cup, UK ⅓ cup, water or clam juice (1 generous dl)
juice of 1 lemon
US ½ cup, UK 4 oz., butter, preferably unsalted (120 g)
chopped parsley

THIS COOKING METHOD
is a type of poaching; it can also be used for small whole fish such as trout and for all kinds of fish steaks.

- Wash the fillets of fish.
- Preheat oven to 350°F, 200°C. or 5 Regulo.
- Butter a baking dish lightly.
- Chop the onion and the carrot rather small. Add them to the dish. Fold the smaller fillets in half lengthwise. Salt and pepper them and put them in the dish. Larger fillets will stay in one piece. Add wine and water or clam juice.
- Cover the fish with a buttered parchment or baking paper. Bake for 20 minutes.
- Remove the fish to a hot platter; keep warm.
- Strain the cooking juices into a 1-quart saucepan and cook down to no more than US ¼ cup, UK 2 tablespoons. Add the lemon juice. Keep boiling as you add the butter, tablespoon by tablespoon, using a whisk. Add the parsley; correct the seasoning.
- Spoon the sauce over the fillets.

BAKED SOLES
(Soles au Four)

If you can locate smaller fish, count 1 fish per person and cook in the same manner, putting 3 soles in each dish. Remove only the top skin of each fish and let guests remove the fillets themselves as they eat dinner.

- Relatively easy
  6 servings
  Expensive
  30 minutes
  Best season: year around

  2 gray soles, 2 to 3 lbs. each (1 to 1½ kg each)
  US ½ cup, UK 4 oz., butter (120 g)
  ½ lb. mushrooms (250 g)
  salt and pepper
  3 lemons, slice 1, juice 2
  chopped parsley

THIS RECIPE CAN BE USED FOR
gray sole and all types of flounders, plaice, sand dabs, pompano. Of course if you are in an area where Dover sole is available, it remains the best even though the most expensive.

- Have the fish market dress the fish, cut the tail and the fins. Wash the fish, dry it. Fold the fish head to tail, pushing hard until the back bone breaks.
- Preheat oven to 375°F., 200°C. or 5 Regulo.
- Butter 2 large gratin dishes with a bit of the butter. Put a sole in each dish. Add the mushrooms, sliced, salt and pepper to taste, the lemon juice and chopped parsley, arranging mushrooms and parsley around the fish and using half of each ingredient in each dish. Put 3 lemon slices on top of each fish.
- Put one baking dish on the left side of the top rack and the second one on the right side of the bottom rack. Bake for 20 minutes.
- Remove the mushrooms from the dishes to a colander or strainer placed over a bowl. Skin and fillet the soles and put them in a deep serving dish. Empty the cooking juices into a 1½-quart saucepan.
- Reduce the cooking juices to approximately US 3 tablespoons, UK 1½ tablespoons. Using a whisk, quickly whisk in the rest of the butter, tablespoon by tablespoon. Correct the seasoning and add the reserved mushrooms. Reheat well and pour over the fish.

STRIPED BASS WITH FENNEL
(Loup ou Bar au Fenouil)

No anise liqueur? Replace it by the same amount of whisky, brandy or Cognac. But the anise-flavored liqueur is truly better. It was imported all through the Mediterranean by the Ancient Greeks who roved the sea and established colonies on all its coasts. In Marseille to this day Pastis is still the favorite liqueur and a first cousin to the Greek Ouzo.

■ A bit difficult
6 servings
Quite expensive
50 minutes
Best season: excellent for the hot weather

1 striped bass, 3 lbs. (1.5 kg)
US 4 TB, UK 2 TB, olive oil (2 TB)
2 oz. fennel seeds (60 g)
2 garlic cloves
US 3 TB, UK 1½ TB, butter (45 g)
Pastis, Pernod, Ouzo or any unsweetened
    anise or fennel spirit of your choice
salt and pepper

YOU SHOULD KNOW
that a loup in France is not always a wolf, but the name given on the southern coasts to the sea bass known as bar on the northern coasts; that if you cannot locate a bass, red snapper, ocean perch, large whiting, small haddock and pompano can be prepared the same way.

- Have the fish store dress and scale the fish very well. Wash it well, letting clear fresh water run through the body cavity to flush all blood away. Dry very well.

- Heat the olive oil in a small pan and add 1 tablespoon fennel seeds. Let steep for about 15 minutes.

- Mash the garlic cloves. Add to them 2 teaspoons fennel seeds and the butter. Cream together; when well creamed add 1 teaspoon of the liqueur of your choice, and salt and pepper well.

- Spread this butter into the cavity of the fish.

- Brush the fish well with some of the fennel-flavored olive oil. Cut 3 indentations about ¼ inch deep into the skin of the fish at a 45-degree angle and spaced about 1¼ inches from one another on each side of the fish.

- Preheat the oven broiler or your barbecue grill. If using the barbecue, throw a handful of fennel seeds on the white coals just before you broil the fish. Set the fish on a broiler rack.

- Broil the fish about 4 inches from the source of heat or from the coals, for 10 to 12 minutes on each side.

- Transfer fish to a serving platter. Heat 1 ounce of the chosen anise/fennel liqueur in a small pot; ignite it in the pot. Pour the flaming liqueur over the fish at the dining room table; it is a very effective sight.

POT-ROASTED TUNA
(Thon à la Cocotte)

Marinate tuna in the wine and vegetables, if you have the time before cooking it, for 1 to 2 hours. To brown the fish, pat it very dry with a towel.

■ Easy
  6 servings
  Quite expensive
  1¼ hours
  Best season: whenever you can locate fresh tuna

  3 onions
  3 carrots
  1 lemon
  US ½ cup, UK ⅓ cup, oil, preferably olive (1 generous dl)
  2 lbs. fresh tuna in one piece (1 kg)
  thyme
  ½ bay leaf
  chopped parsley
  ½ quart dry white wine (.5 L)
  salt and pepper

ANY LEFTOVERS
Use them as you would canned tuna in a mixed salad.

- Peel onions and carrots; cut them into slices ¹/₆ inch thick.

- Peel the lemon to the flesh, removing every trace of white pith, then cut it into slices ⅛ inch thick. Remove the pits, which would give the sauce a bitter taste.

- Heat the oil in a braising pot known as a *cocotte* (see note on p. 173).

- Wash and dry the tuna. Brown it on both sides in the *cocotte*, then remove it to a plate.

- At the bottom of the *cocotte* put half of the onions, carrots and lemon. Set the piece of tuna on the vegetables; cover it with the remainder of the vegetables. Add thyme, bay leaf, parsley and white wine. Season with salt and pepper. Cover the pot and let cook slowly for about 45 minutes.

- For a vegetable, serve mashed potatoes or rice and spinach.

BREADED FILLETS OF WHITING
(Colin Pané à l'Anglaise)

Why brush the egg on the fillets? Because it is essential to obtain a very thin coating which will crisp fast and let the heat go fast to the center of the fillet; at the same time, the breading is not thick enough to absorb the mixture of fats in the frying pan. Keep the initial heat nice and high, then turn it down just as soon as both sides of the fish are seared. Also, if you brush the egg mixture on meat or fish instead of dipping, you avoid the unpleasant experience of breading your own fingertips.

- A bit difficult
  6 servings
  Prices vary with season and location
  20 minutes
  Best season: year around

  2 eggs
  salt and pepper
  1 tsp. oil
  US 2 to 3 TB, UK 1 to 1½ TB, flour (15 to 25 g), approximately
  US ½ cup, UK 4 TB, fresh or dry bread crumbs, approximately
  6 medium-size fillets of whiting
  US ¼ cup, UK 2 TB, oil (2 TB)
  US 5 TB, UK 2½ TB, butter (2½ TB)
  2 cups tomato sauce of your choice, homemade or canned
  herbs

OTHER NAMES, OTHER FISH
Whiting is to be found easily in all Italian neighborhoods under the name of merluzzo. If there is no whiting, you can use sole, flounder, plaice, sand dab or monkfish, cut into ⅓-inch-thick pieces.

- Beat the eggs with a dash of salt and pepper and 1 teaspoon oil. Put the flour on a sheet of wax paper and put the bread crumbs on another sheet of wax paper.

- Wash the whiting fillets, and dry them with paper toweling. Flour them, then using a pastry brush (see advice) brush some of the egg over one side of the fillets. Invert the coated side onto the bread crumbs, then coat the second side of the fish with egg and invert again on the crumbs. Place on a cake rack to dry a bit before cooking.

- Heat the mixture of oil and butter preferably in a large electric frying pan. When the butter starts turning golden, add the fillets and brown on one side, then turn over and brown on the second side. Reduce the heat to cook fillets to the center. Remove to a crumpled paper towel to absorb the oil, then arrange on a platter.

- While the fish is cooking, heat the tomato sauce in a small pan, seasoning it with herbs of your choice. Serve sauce separately.

STUFFED CLAMS
(Praires Farcies)

Choosing wine: A nice and fresh Muscadet is ideal with this dish.

■ Easy
6 servings
**From cheap to expensive, depending on
  your location**
40 minutes
Best season: September to April

3 garlic cloves
1 bunch of parsley
US ½ cup, UK 4 oz., butter (120 g)
salt (little)
pepper
**US ⅔ cup, UK ½ cup, dry bread crumbs (4
  TB)**
**6 dozen small hardshell clams of any
  edible species**

- Preheat the broiler.
- Peel the garlic and chop almost into a purée. Chop the parsley.
- Cream the butter in a small bowl, add garlic, chopped parsley, salt (little), pepper to taste and dry bread crumbs.
- Open the clams with a knife and gather all the meat into the bottom half shell. Separate the small shell-opening muscle from the bottom shell. Spread a small amount of the prepared stuffing on each clam.
- Sprinkle coarse salt into 1 or 2 jelly-roll pans and set the clams into the salt (to prevent them tipping over and losing their stuffing). Broil for 3 to 4 minutes, or until golden brown. Serve hot.

CHOOSE YOUR CLAMS WITH CARE
*They should be shut extremely tightly. Use
them the same day as purchased.*

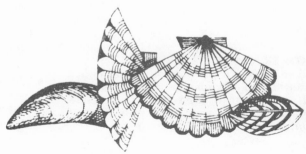

CRABS FORT DE FRANCE
(Crabes Fort de France)

No live crab? Use canned or frozen crab meat of your choice. Alaskan or Russian king crabs would be excellent.

- Medium difficult
  6 servings
  Expensive
  1½ hours
  Best season: summer, when crab is least expensive

suitable amount of live crabs (see note below)
salt
5 oz. slab bacon (150 g)
2 garlic cloves
3 shallots
several parsley sprigs
3 slices of bread (white or French), crusts removed
enough milk to moisten bread, but not soak it through
pepper
US 2 TB, UK 1 TB, butter (30 g)
US ½ cup, UK ⅓ cup, dry bread crumbs (4 to 5 TB)
dark rum, approximately US ½ cup, UK ⅓ cup (1 generous dl)

CHOOSING THE CRABS
Blue crabs: 1 per person
Rock crabs, small: 1 per person
Dungeness crabs: 1 crab per 2 persons

- Bring a large pot of water to a boil. Add salt and the crabs. Bring back to a boil and barely simmer for 10 to 20 minutes depending on size of crabs.
- Meanwhile, cut the bacon into fine dice, put in a cold frying pan, and let it turn golden.
- Chop garlic and shallots; chop the parsley.
- Remove the bacon from the heat and add the garlic, shallots and parsley mixture to the still hot pan.
- Soak the bread in the milk; squeeze dry. Crumble well and add to the bacon pan.
- Shell the crabs and chop all their meat including the legs and the soft, light brown material in the center, which is the liver and extremely tasty.
- Mix the crab meat with the bacon-aromatics-bread mixture. Correct the seasoning and stuff either into the crab shells or into ramekins. Dot with small pieces of butter. Cover with dry bread crumbs.
- Bake in a 425°F., 220°C. or 7 Regulo oven until the top turns brown.
- Heat the rum in a small pan. Remove the crab shells or ramekins from the oven. Ignite the rum. Pour an equal amount of it flaming over each crab.

LOBSTER WITH RIESLING SAUCE
(Homards au Riesling)

To complete the meal, serve a dish of braised rice (p. 209) and a chilled bottle of excellent Riesling. Alsatian Riesling would be the best for this preparation since German and Californian wines may have a tendency to be too sweet for this purpose.

■ Difficult
6 servings
Expensive
30 minutes
Best season: summer when lobster is less expensive

3 shallots
2 small garlic cloves
US 3 TB, UK 1½ TB, butter (1½ TB)
3 live 1½-lb. lobsters (750 g each)
1½ oz. Cognac, whisky or brandy
salt, little
pepper
US 1½ cups, UK 1⅓ cups, Riesling, preferably Alsatian (3.5 dl)
½ lb. fresh mushrooms, sliced (250 g)
2 egg yolks
US ½ cup, UK ⅓ cup, heavy cream (1 generous dl)
chopped parsley

- Peel the shallots and garlic. Chop them finely.
- Heat the butter in a large sauteuse.
- Cut the lobster into pieces as described in the note. Add the pieces of lobster to the hot butter as soon as you have cut them. Toss well in the hot butter until shells turn bright red.
- Heat and ignite the Cognac and pour flaming over the lobster. Shake the pan well to distribute the liqueur.
- Add salt (little), pepper to taste, the shallots and garlic, the Riesling and the sliced mushrooms. Mix well. Cover and let cook for a maximum of 10 minutes.

- Meanwhile, heat the serving dish, which should be a country-style deep dish. Remove the cooked lobster to the deep dish.
- Break egg yolks into a bowl and mix well with the cream. Mix one third of the cooking juices of the lobster into the egg-cream mixture to make a *liaison*. Reduce the remainder of the juices a bit to concentrate them. Remove the pan from the heat and quickly whisk the *liaison* into the reduced juices and mushrooms. The sauce should thicken somewhat; reheat well without boiling.
- Correct the seasoning and pour sauce over the lobsters. Sprinkle with chopped parsley.

TO KILL A LIVE LOBSTER WITHOUT FEAR
1. Wet your thumb, rub the top of the lobster head until the lobster stands still.
2. Cut the claws off at the big joint, crack them with the back of your blade. Cut the head lengthwise into halves, remove the gravel bag behind the eyes. Finally, cut the tail into three "rings" following the natural hinges of the shell. Important: Make sure that the claws are pegged before you start.

MUSSELS MEDITERRANEAN STYLE
(Moules Méditerranée)

This may be served hot or cold since it tastes as good cold as hot. Also, any leftover mussels can always be used in a mixed salad or a fish gratin.

■ Easy
6 servings
Thrift recipe
25 minutes
Best season: September to April

3 shallots
1 large onion
2 garlic cloves
several parsley sprigs
4 quarts mussels
US 2 TB, UK 1 TB, olive oil (1 TB)
US 2 TB, UK 1 TB, tomato paste (1 TB)
½ tsp. paprika
salt only if needed
pepper
chopped parsley

BE CAREFUL
Mussels are liable to be full of sand. Soak them in heavily salted water for a while. Test the freshness by squeezing the shell sideways; if the mussel is dead it will slide open; if it is fresh and alive it will let out a cute little sigh!

- Peel and chop the shallots, onion, garlic and parsley very finely. Set aside.
- The soaked mussels should be first scrubbed carefully and rinsed in more salted water, then put to steam in a large kettle.
- As the mussels steam, shake the kettle every second minute to bring to the surface the mussels at the bottom of the pot that are opened. As soon as the mussels are opened, they are cooked.
- Pour off the cooking juices and filter them through several layers of cheesecloth or a paper filter.
- Heat the olive oil in a saucepan. Sauté the aromatics for a few minutes, or until light golden. Add the cooking juices of the mussels, the tomato paste, paprika, salt (only if needed) and pepper to taste. Simmer for 10 minutes.
- Discard the empty half shell of each mussel and arrange the shells containing a mussel in a country-style deep dish. Keep warm.
- Just before serving pour the sauce over the mussels. Sprinkle with chopped parsley.

SKEWERED SEA SCALLOPS
(Brochettes de Coquilles Saint-Jacques)

A few nice variations: On each skewer you can also use presautéed whole large mushrooms, presteamed mussels or large cubes of fish such as scrod, cod, halibut, bluefish, haddock or swordfish.

- A bit difficult
  6 servings
  Medium expensive
  30 minutes
  Best season: September to April

  30 deep-sea scallops
  3 slices of slab bacon, ⅓ inch thick
  3 garlic cloves
  salt and pepper
  1 recipe Béarnaise Sauce (p. 63), or
  Noisette Butter (p. 95) (optional)
  chopped parsley

  You will need 6 skewers.

SCALLOPS
If well refrigerated, scallops last very well. Use them as fresh as possible. Frozen and defrosted scallops are also excellent, but should be used as soon as defrosted.

- Wash the scallops and dry with paper towels.
- Cut the bacon into 1-inch pieces, making 24 pieces altogether. Put them in a cold frying pan. Let the bacon pieces render their fat, then slowly bring the pan to a higher heat, to brown them lightly.
- Preheat the broiler.
- Peel the garlic cloves and push each skewer through one of the cloves, over its whole length, to coat skewer with garlic juice and flavor it well.
- Thread 5 scallops on each skewer, alternated with 4 pieces of bacon. Brush the scallops with some of the bacon fat in the pan.
- Broil 4 inches from the source of heat for 3 minutes on each side.
- Present the skewers on a platter and serve them with either Noisette Butter or Béarnaise Sauce. Sprinkle with chopped parsley.

BEEF
(Le Bœuf)

COOKING METHODS FOR BEEF

Broiled (in electric or gas broiler or barbecue)
1- to 1¼-inch thickness: Sear on each side for 2 to 3 minutes, 4 inches from the source of heat.
2-inch thickness: Sear on each side for 2 to 3 minutes, 4 inches from the source of heat. Move 2 inches farther from the source of heat and continue cooking for another 4 minutes on each side.
3½-inch thickness: Sear on each side for 5 to 6 minutes, 4 inches from the source of heat. Move 2 inches farther from the source of heat and continue cooking for another 5 to 6 minutes on each side.

Oven-Roasted
Rare: 12 minutes for the first pound plus 10 minutes for each additional pound.
Medium-rare: 15 minutes per pound. Oven temperature: 400°F., 200°C. or 6 Regulo.

Panfried
1-inch thickness: Sear on first side for 2 minutes, turn over, season seared side. Sear on second side for 2 minutes, and cook until droplets of blood appear at surface of steak.
1¼- to 1½-inch thickness: Sear on first side for 3 minutes, turn over, season seared side. Sear on second side for 3 minutes; turn heat down until droplets of blood appear at surface of steak.

Pan-Roasted
3-inch thickness: Sear on first side for 3 minutes, turn over, season seared side. Sear on second side for 3 minutes, and turn heat down. Keep turning every 2 minutes for 8 minutes. Cover for 2 minutes more. Let rest for 3 minutes before cutting into slices across the grain.
The times here are for rare to medium-rare steak. Cook longer on each side if medium-well-done or well-done steaks are desired.

Braised Beef
All stews braised in a regular oven must cook for a minimum of 2½ hours at these temperatures: 325°F., 165°C. or 3 Regulo. *In a pressure cooker* 1 hour will be sufficient.

Boiled Beef
Bring to a boil the liquid in which the beef is to be cooked; add the beef and bring the liquid back to a second boil. Turn heat down and simmer for a minimum of 3½ hours in a regular stockpot. *In a pressure cooker* 1 hour will be sufficient.

POT-AU-FEU
(The French Version of Boiled Beef)

Add pepper during the last half hour of cooking only.

Potatoes should not be cooked in the main pot with the other vegetables because their starch clouds the bouillon.

Keep by storing or freezing (allow space for expansion) any leftover bouillon, to use it for your sauces, soups and other dishes.

- Relatively easy
  6 servings
  Thrift recipe
  4 hours, 1½ hours in pressure cooker
  Best season: fall and winter months

  3 lbs. boiling beef (1.5 kg)
  3½ quarts water (3 L)
  1 veal shank
  1 large marrowbone
  8 carrots
  3 white turnips, or ½ large rutabaga
  4 leeks (white and green parts), tied into a bundle
  2 onions, each stuck with 3 cloves
  1 sprig of celery leaves
  1 large garlic clove
  bouquet garni (p. 293)
  1 tsp. salt
  freshly grated nutmeg
  1 cabbage
  6 peppercorns

THE BASIC RULE OF POT-AU-FEU:
It is an important one: if you want the meat to have the best eating qualities and the bouillon to be light, immerse the meat into boiling water. If, on the contrary, you plan to have a strong bouillon, immerse the meat into cold water; the meat will then not be as tasty.

- Pour 3½ quarts water (3 L), either cold or brought to a boil according to the rule explained above, into a large stockpot. Add the meat and bones and bring, or bring back, to a boil. Skim well of all the scum rising to the top. Let cook uncovered for 15 minutes, skimming every 5 minutes.

- Meanwhile peel and trim all the vegetables with the exception of the cabbage. Cut the carrots lengthwise into halves.

- Add to the pot the onions stuck with the cloves, the sprig of celery, the garlic, a large bouquet garni, salt (not much) and a bit of grated nutmeg. Add then the carrots, turnips and leeks. Cover and cook for about 3 hours, in a pressure cooker approximately 1 hour.

- Clean the cabbage. Bring a pot of water to a boil, add salt, and put in the cabbage to blanch it for 5 to 10 minutes. Drain it and squeeze it dry. Transfer the cabbage to the pot-au-feu and cook for another 20 minutes, 10 in pressure cooker. Pepper the bouillon only after you add the cabbage.

- Serve on a huge platter with a jar of Dijon mustard.

- If you wish to have also some potatoes, peel and cut 6 medium-size ones, wash them well, and cook them in enough of the bouillon just to cover them, until tender.

CHOOSE
rump, shin, short rib or plate beef, or brisket of beef.

The veal shank is not an absolute necessity but it gives both excellent taste and texture. You can replace it by a good pound of moderately salted pork brisket if you prefer.

BEEF BOURGUIGNON
(Bœuf Bourguignon)

To separate fat from gravy, let the gravy stand until all fat has risen to the top, then pump the fat-free gravy out with a bulb baster.

This dish reheats very successfully. So why not double the recipe and refrigerate or freeze one half for another day? You will gain time.

■ Relatively easy
  6 servings
  Thrift recipe
  3 hours and 50 minutes, 1 hour in pressure cooker
  Best season: fall and winter months

4 large onions
1 large carrot
1 bottle of dry red wine (Burgundy or Côtes du Rhône)
1 tsp. dried thyme
1 small bay leaf
1 bundle of parsley stems
5 to 6 oz. slab bacon (150 to 180 g)
cold water
US 4 TB, UK 2 TB, butter (60 g)
½ lb. tiny silverskin onions, fresh or frozen (250 g)
pinch of sugar
2½ lbs. beef chuck (1.25 kg)
salt and pepper
US 3 TB, UK 1½ TB, flour (25 g)
beef bouillon as needed
US 1 TB, UK ½ TB, tomato paste (1 TB)
chopped parsley

- Peel the large onions and the carrot; cut them into thin slices.
- Empty the bottle of wine into a saucepan. Add onion and carrot slices and thyme, bay leaf and parsley stems tied into a bundle. Bring to a boil and simmer for 20 to 25 minutes.
- Cut the bacon slab into pieces ⅓ inch wide. Put pieces in cold water, bring to a boil, and simmer for 3 to 4 minutes. Discard the water.
- Put blanched bacon pieces in a cold braising pot over medium heat. Let them render their fat and become light

golden all around but not crisp and dry. Remove to a plate.

- Add the butter to the bacon fat and brown the silverskin onions in the mixture. Add the pinch of sugar for better coloring. Remove to a plate. Do not discard the fat in the pot.
- Cut the beef into 1½-inch cubes. Brown them on all sides in the same fat, doing it in two batches if necessary so the meat is well browned all around. Remove to a plate. Salt and pepper lightly.
- Remove the onion and carrot from the wine and pat them dry. Add those vegetables to the braising pot and brown them in the same fat. Their moisture will loosen up all the beef juices caramelized in the pot.
- When the vegetables have lost all their moisture, add the flour and cook until the onion starts browning.
- Off the heat, add the wine and all the aromatics, stirring well with a wooden spoon, and bring to a boil. Add the meat; then add enough bouillon to cover the meat by ¼ inch. Add the tomato paste and mix well. Cover meat with a sheet of aluminum foil placed upside down flush on the meat and large enough to be used as an inverted lid to catch the condensation if any builds.
- Cover the pot and bake for 1¾ hours.
- After that time, remove the meat to a plate. Strain the sauce into a measuring cup and defatten it well with a

spoon or a bulb baster (see advice). Return the meat to the pot, mix it with the onions and bacon, add the sauce, and re-cover both with foil and lid.

- Continue cooking for another 25 to 30 minutes. The meat is done when a skewer inserted in it comes out clean and without effort. If the skewer lifts the meat out of the pot, it is not ready.
- Serve in a country-style deep dish sprinkled with chopped parsley. As a

vegetable, use noodles or steamed potatoes.

YOUR MEAT
Please use exclusively beef chuck (shoulder). The cuts in the round (leg) are much too lean and become stringy. This recipe is the simple way to make Bourguignon. You could, to make it fancier and even better tasting, marinate the meat in the wine and add mushrooms.

BEEF MIROTON
(Bœuf Miroton)

The same recipe can be applied to leftover pork roast, leg or shoulder of lamb, shoulder of veal or even roast beef. Should you use rare roast beef, remember to cook it slowly for a scant hour.

- Easy
  6 servings
  Thrift recipe
  25 minutes
  Best season: year around, but better adapted to cold months

  1½ lbs. boiled beef (760 g)
  2 onions
  6 oz. slab bacon (180 g) or brisket of pork
  US 4 TB, UK 2 TB, butter (60 g)
  US 3 TB, UK 1½ TB, flour (25 g)
  US 2½ cups, UK 2 cups, bouillon (.5 L)
  US 2 TB, UK 1 TB, tomato paste (1 TB)
  salt and pepper
  3 small sour pickles

A BIT OF FRENCH LORE
Every woman in France knows this dish as "Monday's meat" and almost every household has it either for dinner or lunch, using leftovers of Sunday's boiled beef dinner or Pot-au-Feu (see p. 109).

- Remove all gristle and fat from the meat. Slice it.
- Peel the onions and slice them. Cut the bacon or brisket of pork into ⅓-inch-wide strips.
- Cook the bacon strips in a braising pot over medium heat until they render their fat.
- Add the butter; heat it well and add the sliced onions. Cook both bacon and onions until golden. Add the flour and let cook until flour turns light brown.
- Add the bouillon, tomato paste, and salt and pepper to taste. Stir until the mixture boils. Reduce to a simmer.
- Chop the pickles coarsely and add them to the sauce. Finally add the meat. Simmer for 10 to 15 minutes.
- As a vegetable, consider steamed potatoes, mashed potatoes, boiled carrots cooked during the last minutes of cooking in the gravy of this dish.

BEEF À LA MODE
(Bœuf à la Mode)

No veal foot or shank? Add any gelatinous bone such as veal breast cut into small pieces, or if you have absolutely no bones add ¼ ounce (7 g) unflavored gelatin and ½ pound silverskin onions (250 g) 30 minutes before the end of the cooking. In this case discard the larger onions before serving.

■ A bit difficult
6 servings
Medium expensive
3½ hours, 1½ hours in pressure cooker
Best season: year around, but better adapted to cold months

US 2 TB, UK 1 TB, oil (1 TB)
US 4 TB, UK 2 TB, butter (60 g)
2½ lbs. beef chuck (shoulder), in one piece (1.25 kg)
2 large onions
2 garlic cloves
2 lbs. carrots (1 kg)
½ bay leaf, sprig of thyme, bundle of parsley stems, tied into a bouquet garni
1 veal foot or shank
½ quart dry white wine (.5 L)
US 3 cups, UK 2¾ cups, bouillon (.75 L)
freshly grated nutmeg
salt and pepper

- Mix oil and butter in a braising pot and heat both together well. Add the meat and brown well all around.
- While the meat browns, peel the onions, garlic and carrots. Cut all into ¼-inch-thick slices. Prepare the *bouquet garni*.
- Blanch the veal foot or shank in boiling water for 10 minutes.
- Remove the browned meat to a plate. Put all the aromatics in the braising pot and sauté them until they lose their moisture and dissolve the meat juices in the pot.
- Return the meat to the pot. Add also the veal shank or foot, the white wine and enough bouillon to cover the top of the meat by ¼ inch. Bring to a boil.

Add the nutmeg, salt and pepper to taste. Cover with a large piece of foil placed flush on the surface of the meat and shaped as an inverted lid. Cover with the pot lid and let simmer for 2½ hours, or until a skewer inserted into the meat comes out free.

- To serve, put the piece of beef and all the vegetables into a country-style deep dish. Bone the veal foot or shank and chop it finely. Add it to the dish; keep warm.
- Pour the sauce through a strainer into a measuring cup and defatten it completely. Reheat the sauce if necessary and pour it into the dish.

WITH THE SAME METHOD
Jellied Beef: Follow the recipe exactly. At the end of the operation, slice the meat, arrange it in a deep dish or a mold lightly oiled and dabbed dry with paper towels. Surround the meat with the vegetables and the veal foot cut into small pieces. Defatten the sauce completely and pour over the mixture. Refrigerate overnight and unmold to serve.

ANOTHER BIT OF FRENCH LORE
This dish is the glory of bourgeois kitchens and is often prepared with great expense of energy on the vegetable decoration. But feel free to keep it humble and informal for it came through centuries of history as people's food par excellence, often more satisfying to the soul and the palate than the greatest haute cuisine dish.

ROAST BEEF
(Rôti de Bœuf)

No meat thermometer? Use a skewer, insert it at one end of the roast beef almost all the way to the other end. Test the heat of the needle at its center on the top of your hand or the inside of your wrist: cold needle: uncooked meat; lukewarm needle: rare meat; warm needle: medium rare meat.

- Relatively easy
  6 servings
  Expensive
  45 minutes
  Best season: year around

  3 lbs. roast beef (cut of your choice) (1.5 kg)
  no more than US 1 TB, UK ½ TB, oil (½ TB)
  salt and pepper

WITH THE SAME METHOD
Roast Beef with Port Sauce: When the roast beef is done, deglaze (see p. 117) the roasting pan with approximately US ½ cup, UK ⅓ cup, bouillon (1 generous dl) and US ¼ cup, UK 2 tablespoons, dry white Port. Reduce well and add ½ pound mushrooms (250 g), sautéed, with their juices. You may thicken the gravy with a little slurry of cornstarch.

- In our modern day please do without the fat coverings of pork or beef around the meat. Trim the meat to the bare muscle for less calories and rub it with an extremely thin layer of oil before roasting.
- Preheat oven to 400°F., 220°C. or 7 Regulo.
- Set the beef on a roasting pan fitted with a rack. Do not salt and pepper before roasting. Put in the oven and roast for approximately 12 minutes per pound. Ribs, sirloin strip, rump and eye of the round cook more slowly than the tenderloin.
- Salt and pepper the meat on all sides when three quarters done and remove from the oven 3 to 4 minutes before desired degree of doneness is reached. The meat thermometer should register 130°F. if the final degree is to be 140°F., for the meat continues cooking from its own acquired heat while resting.
- Let meat rest at room temperature for 5 minutes before carving. Season more if desired at this point.

BEEF BROCHETTES
(Brochettes de Bœuf)

Marinating can be skipped if you are in a hurry. All you do then is toss the cubes in the olive oil, skewer, and broil. Or marinating can, for even better flavoring, be extended overnight. Choose whichever fits your timetable best.

- Easy
  6 servings
  Expensive
  1½ hours, plus 1 hour for marinating
  Best season: summer when you can cook on the barbecue and tomatoes are sun-ripened

  1½ lbs. best-cut beef, in 1 piece (750 g)
  1 lb. calf's liver, in 1 piece (500 g)
  1 lb. fresh pork brisket, in 2 pieces each ½ inch thick (500 g)
  US 1 TB, UK ½ TB, dried Provençal herbs, well crumbled (½ TB)
  salt and pepper
  US ½ cup, UK ⅓ cup, olive oil (1 generous dl)
  6 medium-size ripe tomatoes

A BROCHETTE

is nothing else than a skewer: the name is so charming in French, why change it?

Use the best cuts: tenderloin, sirloin strip, sirloin, etc.

Would you like a sauce? Choose mustard, ketchup, Béarnaise (p. 63), tartar or Worcestershire.

- Cut the meat into 18 cubes. Discard all fat and gristle as you cut. Cut the liver also into 18 cubes. Cut the brisket into 18 strips 1 inch wide and the thickness of the piece of brisket.
- Put the brisket in a cold frying pan with a bit of water. Heat gradually to medium and let cook until some of the fat has run out and the pork is barely starting to brown. Cool.
- On a plate, mix the Provençal herbs, salt and pepper to taste, and the oil; mix very well with a fork. Toss the meats into the oil and let them stand (see advice).
- Cut each tomato into 4 quarters. Set them aside on a plate as long as you can.
- Preheat the broiler or barbecue.
- Skewer the ingredients on brochettes in this order: 1 tomato quarter, 1 piece of beef, 1 piece of brisket, 1 piece of liver, repeating until the meats are used and all 6 brochettes are filled.
- Broil 4 inches from the source of heat for a total of 10 minutes, 5 minutes on each side.

BROILED RIB OF BEEF WITH COGNAC SAUCE
(Côte de Bœuf Grillée, Sauce au Cognac)

Would you prefer another sauce? Try Béarnaise (p. 63) or any of the prepared "steak" sauces.

If you prefer no sauce at all, serve a dish of vegetables with the meat, instead of a plain salad.

- Difficult
  6 servings
  Expensive
  35 minutes, plus time for overnight marinating
  Best season: summer when you can cook on the barbecue

BEEF
thyme, bay leaf (½), fennel seeds, chives, basil, tarragon, mint, parsley, savory, sage
6 juniper berries
1 rib of beef, approximately 3 lbs. (1.5 kg)
oil (preferably olive)
salt
pepper, preferably coarsely ground from the mill

SAUCE
US ⅔ cup, UK ½ cup, bouillon (2 scant dl)
US ⅓ cup, UK ¼ cup, dry white wine (1 scant dl)
US 3 TB, UK 1½ TB, Cognac (1½ TB)
US 2 TB, UK 1 TB, prepared Dijon mustard
US ½ cup, UK 4 oz., butter (120 g)

- *The day before,* chop the herbs or crumble finely depending on whether they are fresh or dried; crush the juniper berries to a powder. Rub the beef rib with oil and coat it with the herbs on both sides, using the flat side of a large knife blade. Marinate overnight between 2 soup plates placed in the refrigerator.

- *The day you will serve the meat,* preheat the broiler or fire the barbecue pit. Broil beef 4 inches from the source of heat for approximately 8 minutes on each side. Salt and pepper the seared side before turning over. Salt and pepper the second side as soon as the broiling is completed. The meat will be rare.

- For medium rare, move the meat so it is 6 to 7 inches from the source of heat and let it cook for 5 more minutes.

- Transfer the rib to a heated platter and keep it warm while you prepare the sauce.

- *To make the sauce,* dissolve the drippings in your broiler pan with the bouillon and white wine mixed together. Scrape well over heat so all the browned juices melt into the mixture.

- Add the Cognac and cook for 1 more minute. Strain into a heated small pot. Off the heat add the mustard, and bit by bit the butter.

- Reheat over low heat, stirring with a whisk. Do not boil.

- If you barbecue the meat, reduce bouillon, white wine and Cognac by one third. Add mustard and butter.

- Serve the rib on its heated platter and slice it against the grain in paper-thin slices. Serve the sauce in a boat. Garnish with fresh watercress.

DO YOU KNOW THAT
pepper exposed to broiler heat turns very acrid and very bitter? Add it only when the broiling is completed.

You can prepare yourself a mixture of dried Provençal herbs and keep it in a jar (p. 302).

RIB STEAK MARCHAND DE VIN
(Entrecôte Marchand de Vin)

How to judge the doneness of a thick steak:
It is very rare when your finger pushes a ⅓-inch depression into it.
It is rare when your finger pushes a ¼-inch depression into it.
It is medium rare when your finger pushes a ⅛-inch depression into it.
It is well done when it resists the pressure of your finger.

■ Easy
6 servings
Affordable
25 minutes
Best season: year around

1 rib of beef, approximately 2½ lbs. (1 heavy kg)
1 onion
1 shallot
US ¼ cup, UK 2 TB, butter (60 g)
salt and pepper
US 1½ cups, UK 1⅓ cups, dry red wine (3.5 dl)
1 tsp. flour
salted water or bouillon
chopped parsley

- Remove the bone and gristle of the meat.
- Peel the onion and chop it extremely finely. Do the same with the shallot.
- Heat 2 tablespoons butter in a large skillet until it foams well. Add the onion, toss well in the butter, then add the shallot and let cook gently for 2 to 3 minutes.
- Raise the pan at a 45-degree angle. With a slotted spoon remove the aromatics to a plate. Do not remove the butter, but press it out of the onion and shallot pieces with the back of the spoon.
- Reheat that butter very well and add another ½ tablespoon. When it is hot, sear the meat well. Turn the meat over, season the seared side with salt and pepper, and let cook over medium-high heat, turning the meat over every 3 minutes, until the meat has reached the doneness you like (see advice). Cover during the last 3 to 4 minutes of cooking. A rib 1½ inches thick should cook in 15 minutes for rare and 18 minutes for medium rare.
- Remove to a plate placed over hot water, and cover to keep warm.
- Return the onion/shallot mixture to the pan. Add the wine. Over medium heat, and scraping the bottom of the pan well, reduce it by half to evaporate the alcohol well. Turn the heat down.
- Meanwhile, mix the remaining butter on a plate with the teaspoon of flour and whisk it into the simmering liquid. It will thicken instantly. Should it get too thick, add enough salted hot water or bouillon to dilute to the desired texture.
- Should any juices run out of the meat while it waits, add them to the sauce while it is still simmering until you obtain the texture you like again. Correct the seasoning. Pour the sauce over the steak and sprinkle with chopped parsley.
- To serve, cut into slivers against the grain.

FRENCH FOOD LORE
A "Marchand de Vin" is a wine seller. France has thousands of them. Since a wine seller would obviously cook with some of the wines he sells the name becomes obvious. Every "bistro" in France offers a personalized version of this favorite dish.

SIRLOIN STEAK AU POIVRE
(Entrecôte au Poivre)

Deglazing is what you do when you add liquid to a skillet to dissolve the meat juices that have cooked and browned to the point of hardness. Deglazing is a must since it gives taste to your sauce and forms a "bouillon" of sorts. The bouillon is single if you deglaze with water and double if you deglaze with bouillon. When using canned bouillon or cubes, beware of salt. Homemade bouillon is best (see p. 109).

- Easy
6 servings
Medium expensive
15 minutes
Best season: year around

2 lbs. boneless sirloin strip, in 1 piece (1 kg)
US 2 TB, UK 1 TB, white peppercorns (1 TB)
US 2 TB, UK 1 TB, oil (1 TB)
salt
US ¼ cup, UK 2 TB, Cognac (2 TB) or whisky or brandy

FOR OPTIONAL SAUCE:
US 3 TB, UK 1½ TB, water or bouillon (1½ TB)
US ⅓ cup, UK ¼ cup, heavy cream (80 g)

- Make sure that you remove all traces of fat and gristle from the meat and that it is cleaned to the bare muscle. Flatten the piece of meat so the slice is not more than 1½ to 1¾ inches thick.
- Crush the white peppercorns with a pastry rolling pin. This is best done by enclosing the corns between 2 layers of wax paper.
- Using the flat of a knife blade and pressing well, embed the crushed peppercorns into each side of the meat.
- Heat the oil in a large skillet and sear the meat over high heat on both sides. Salt it, turn it over, and salt the second side. Turn the heat down to medium high and continue cooking, turning

the piece every 4 minutes until done to your taste. Cover for the last few minutes of cooking.
- When the steak is done to your taste, heat the Cognac in a small pot. Turn the heat off under the steak. Ignite the Cognac and pour it flaming over the steak. Cut across the grain to serve (see note below).

OPTIONAL SAUCE
- Remove the steak and keep warm on a plate. Do not flambé.
- Blot the oil off the frying pan with paper towels.
- Pour the Cognac into the pan, on the turned-off burner, scraping well to deglaze the pan (see advice). Add the water or bouillon and cream and reduce over high heat until the sauce starts coating the spatula. No flour is necessary. Correct the seasoning.

IN FRANCE
an entrecôte is cut either out of the rib or the sirloin strip. When cut into thick steaks to serve 6 persons, the rib must be sliced against the grain lengthwise and the strip across the grain crosswise. A 2-pound piece of sirloin is about 5 inches long and once flattened is about 1¾ inches thick.

TENDERLOIN OF BEEF WITH MADEIRA
(Filet de Bœuf au Madère)

With a tenderloin of beef all green vegetables such as braised lettuce, spinach, green beans, braised Belgian endives are very fitting garnishes.

■ Difficult
6 servings
Very expensive
40 minutes
Best season: year around

2 lbs. fillet of beef (tenderloin) (1 kg)
¼ lb. fresh pork brisket (125 g) (uncured "bacon")
2 small onions
US 3 TB, UK 1½ TB, butter (45 g)
US 3 TB, UK 1½ TB, oil (1½ TB)
salt and pepper
US 1 cup, UK 1 scant cup, bouillon (2.5 dl) (see note below)
US ⅓ cup, UK ¼ cup, dry Madeira (1 scant dl) (Sercial or Rainwater, see p. 306)
US ¼ cup, UK 2 TB, tomato paste (2 TB)

- Trim the beef of all fat and gristle. Cut the pork brisket into small pieces. Peel the onions and cut into thin slices.
- Heat the butter in an oblong braising pot. Add the brisket and the onions and let cook gently without browning. Drain and transfer to a plate, using a slotted spoon.
- Add the oil to the butter already in the pot and heat well. Brown the piece of beef on all sides over rather high heat. Season the meat after it is seared. Remove the meat to a plate.
- Discard all the fat in the braising pot. Add the bouillon and deglaze (see p. 117) well. Add the Madeira and the tomato paste. Bring to a boil and mix well. Add the pork brisket and onion and finally the beef.
- Cook uncovered over low heat, turning the meat over every 5 minutes, for a total of 20 minutes. *Do not overcook.*
- Serve the meat sliced with the sauce around.

YOU MUST KNOW THAT
the tenderloin is the most tender cut of beef but not the tastiest; the sirloin strip and the rib are the tastiest. Bouillon for such an expensive piece of meat should be homemade if at all possible. If you use canned bouillon or cubes, please beware of the salt.

TENDERLOIN STEAK IN TARRAGON SAUCE
(Tournedos Sauce Estragon)

To cook large artichokes: Cut the stems off. Immerse in boiling water and cook for 40 to 45 minutes. To clean the bottoms, remove the leaves of each artichoke, one by one (a quick process), remove the choke, and trim each bottom or heart with a paring knife. The leaves make a superb lunch with Vinaigrette (p. 65), or, if you have time to remove the pulp from the leaves, use for a small soup.

■ Difficult
6 servings
Very expensive
25 minutes
Best season: year around

6 artichoke bottoms, cooked (see advice)

SAUCE
2 shallots, chopped fine
US 1 TB, UK ½ TB, fresh tarragon, or 1 tsp. dried tarragon
US ⅓ cup, UK 3 TB, vinegar (3 TB)
hot water
salt and pepper
2 egg yolks
US ¾ cup, UK 6 oz., butter (175 g)
US 2 TB, UK 1 TB, tomato paste (1 TB)

STEAKS
6 tournedos, 4 to 6 oz. each (120 to 180 g)
US 3 TB, UK 1½ TB, butter (1½ TB)
salt and pepper

- Reheat the artichoke bottoms slowly in a small pat of butter.

SAUCE
- Peel the shallots; chop them and the tarragon. If the tarragon is dry, crumble it very fine.
- Put shallots and tarragon in a small pan, preferably of enameled cast iron. Add the vinegar and cook down slowly until the vinegar has almost completely evaporated.
- Add 2 tablespoons of hot water (UK 1 tablespoon), a dash of salt, pepper to taste and the egg yolks. Whisk the yolks over very low heat until very foamy. (See Hollandaise.) As soon as a heavy foam is reached, add the lukewarm melted butter very gradually, whisking well all the time. Finally add the tomato paste, still whisking well. Correct the salt and pepper seasoning.

STEAKS
- Heat the butter in a large skillet for 2 minutes. Sear the meat on one side, turn over, salt the seared side, and reduce heat to medium. The steak will be done when the blood beads in droplets at the surface of the steak.
- To serve, put the steaks on a heated platter. Spoon a bit of sauce over each steak. Put 1 artichoke bottom upside down over each steak and spoon a bit more sauce over them. Serve the remainder of the sauce in a sauceboat.

THE BEEF CUT
A tournedos is a steak cut from the center of the tenderloin. It is called "turn your back" because being very tender it is said to cook in the time needed to do just that. It can be replaced by sirloin strip. In that case, cut the artichoke bottoms into slivers.

BEEF TONGUE IN TOMATO SAUCE
(Langue de Bœuf, Sauce Tomate)

Two important points: Keep the cooking broth, it is excellent as the base of a soup or as bouillon to cook and deglaze with.

Transform the recipe into a summer dish. Serve the tongue lukewarm with a very "herby" vinaigrette (see p. 65).

■ Easy
6 to 8 servings
Very affordable
3¼ hours, 1¾ hours in pressure cooker
Best season: fall and winter

TONGUE
1 beef tongue
water
8 carrots
4 white turnips
4 leeks
2 onions, stuck with 3 cloves
thyme, parsley, bay leaf
1 lb. slab bacon (500 g)
salt and pepper

SAUCE
US 3 TB, UK 1½ TB, butter (45 g)
1 onion, chopped fine
3 garlic cloves
US 3TB, UK 1½ TB, flour (25 g)
US 1½ cups, UK 1¼ cups, tongue cooking broth (3.5 dl)
US ½ cup, UK ⅓ cup, dry white wine (1 generous dl)
US 6 TB, UK 3 TB, tomato paste (3 TB)
fresh or dried tarragon (1 TB or 1 tsp.)
US 2 to 3 TB, UK 1 to 1½ TB, dry Madeira (1 to 1½ TB)
chopped parsley

- Put the tongue in a large pot and cover with cold water. Bring to a boil and simmer for 10 minutes.
- Bring another pot of water to a boil while the tongue is "blanching."
- Peel and trim all vegetables. Cut carrots and turnips into chunks. Tie the leeks, thyme, bay leaf and parsley stems into a big *bouquet garni.*
- Discard the tongue blanching water. Replace it by the boiling water in the second pot and bring immediately back to a boil. Add all the vegetables and the slab of bacon.
- Bring back to a boil and add salt (not too much because of the bacon) and a bit of pepper. Simmer for as long as needed. The tongue is done when a skewer inserted at its center comes out without resistance.
- Turn the heat off and let the tongue and vegetables sit in the broth. Remove approximately US 2 cups, UK 2 scant cups, of broth (.5 L) and defatten it well.
- *For the sauce,* sauté the onion and garlic in the butter until golden. Add the flour; cook until golden also. Add the hot broth, white wine and tomato paste, whisking all the while. Add the fresh or dried tarragon. Bring to a boil and simmer for 15 to 20 minutes.
- Add the Madeira and correct the seasoning.
- Drain the tongue; remove the elastic skin (watch your hands, it stays awfully hot), using scissors to cut it open.

• Slice the tongue and the bacon and present them, alternated and surrounded with the vegetables, on a heated platter. Spoon some sauce over the meat; sprinkle with parsley. Present the remainder of the sauce in a boat.

FROZEN OR FRESH TONGUES?
It depends; for best taste and a bit of loss in gristle and connective tissues on the undersides of the tongue, choose a fresh tongue. For lesser taste, but less loss, since frozen tongues are mostly pared of all inedible parts, choose a frozen tongue.

Most children will like it.

BEEF HEART IN RED-WINE SAUCE
(Cœur de Bœuf au Vin Rouge)

Would you like additional flavor? Then cook the potatoes separately in boiling salted water and add ½ pound quartered mushrooms (250 g) to the stew 10 minutes before the stew is finished.

■ Relatively easy
6 servings
Thrift recipe
1¾ hours, 45 minutes in pressure cooker
Best season: fall and winter

4 onions or 18 small white onions
bouquet garni (see p. 293)
US 6 TB, UK 3 TB, oil (3 TB)
US 3 TB, UK 1½ TB, butter (45 g)
2½ lbs. beef heart (1.25 kg)
US 2 TB, UK 1 TB, flour (15 g)
US 2 cups, UK 2 scant cups, red wine (.5 L)
US 2 cups, UK 2 scant cups, bouillon (.5 L)
salt and pepper
12 small potatoes
3 slices of white bread
chopped parsley

• Peel and slice the onions. Prepare the *bouquet garni.*

• Heat half of the oil and butter in a braising pot, add the onions, and sauté until translucent. Remove them to a plate, pressing the fat out with a slotted spoon.

• Place the heart in the braising pot and brown it well over high heat. Sprinkle the heart with the flour and brown it lightly. Return the onions to the pot.

• Add the red wine, bouillon, salt and pepper to taste, and the *bouquet garni.* Cover and reduce the heat; let cook gently for 1½ hours, *30 to 35 minutes in pressure cooker.*

• While the meat cooks, peel the potatoes, cut each into 4 pieces, and add them to the stew 20 minutes before the stew is done.

• Remove the crusts of the 3 slices of white bread and fry them in the remainder of the oil. Cut each slice into halves to obtain 6 triangles.

• To serve, remove the *bouquet garni* and check the final seasoning of the stew. Pour the stew into a country-style deep dish. Sprinkle with chopped parsley and decorate with the fried croutons.

BEEF HEART
It is ideal for stewing or stuffing and is nutritious for children who mistake it for beef stew. Have the butcher give you as thick a slice as possible and cut it across into ½-inch strips.

BEEF CROQUETTES
(Croquettes de Bœuf)

If you have the time and are in the mood for a sauce, prepare a well-spiced Tomato Sauce (p. 61), or doctor up a can of tomato sauce.

- Relatively easy
  6 servings
  Thrift recipe
  30 minutes
  Best season: winter and fall months, early spring months

1¼ lbs. "boiled beef" (625 g)
US ⅓ cup, UK ¼ cup, milk (1 scant dl)
3 slices of white bread, crusts removed
1 onion
1 garlic clove
several sprigs of parsley
salt and pepper
oil bath for frying
flour to dust the meat

A SUGGESTION
When you buy beef for boiling, buy twice as much as needed; use the leftover in a dish such as these croquettes.

A mixture of chopped meats and aromatics, either cooked or raw, has the technical name of "forcemeat."

- Trim the cooked meat of fat and gristle. Grind finely with a grinder or in a food processor.
- Put milk and soft centers of bread in a small pot; heat to lukewarm. Squeeze the milk out of the bread and mash the bread with a fork.
- Peel the onion and garlic. Chop them together with the parsley very finely.
- Mix this mixture with the meat, bread, and salt and pepper to taste. Mix well to obtain a smooth forcemeat.
- Heat the oil bath. Put the flour on a plate. Shape meatballs with about 4 tablespoons of forcemeat for each one. Roll them in the flour.
- When the meatballs are all ready, immerse them in the hot oil, making sure that you proceed in about 3 batches, so as not to cool the oil bath too much. The meatballs should not touch one another in the bath.
- When each croquette is nice and golden, transfer it to crumpled paper to drain well. Serve very hot.

WITH THE SAME FORCEMEAT
Beef Patties: Flatten the meatballs to become 3 inches wide and ⅓ inch thick. Flour them and brown them on both sides in butter or oil.

Shepherd's Pie: Add a couple of pinches of sweet spices to the forcemeat. Enclose the forcemeat between 2 layers of mashed potatoes. Top the dish with any grated melting cheese and bake until golden.

LAMB
(L'Agneau ou le Mouton)

COOKING METHODS FOR LAMB

Broiled
Rib or loin chops, ⅔ inch thick, broil for 4 to 5 minutes on each side, depending on personal taste.

Panfried
Rib and loin chops, ⅔ inch thick, panfry for 4 to 5 minutes on each side, depending on personal taste. Slices of leg ⅓ inch thick, cut against the grain of the meat, panfry for 3 minutes on each side.

Oven-Roasted
Leg: roast for 10 minutes for the first pound, plus 6 minutes for each additional pound for rare lamb: 10 to 12 minutes for each additional pound for medium-rare lamb; 14 minutes for each additional pound for medium-well-done lamb. Oven temperatures: 400°F., 200°C., 6 Regulo.

Shoulder: English and American square-cut shoulder on the bone, roast for 1 hour at 400°F., 200°C., 6 Regulo.

Shoulder: French-style, rolled and boned, with or without light stuffing, roast for 1½ hours at 400°F., 200°C., 6 Regulo.

Casserole-Roasted
Shoulder: Square-cut unboned English and American style, sear in any chosen fat, season, cover, and bake for 1½ hours at 325°F., 165°C., 3 Regulo.

In a pressure cooker, using the same method, the same cut of meat will be done in 1 hour.

Shoulder: French-style, rolled and boned, sear in any chosen fat, season, cover, and bake for 1 hour and 50 minutes at 325°F., 165°C., 3 Regulo.

In a pressure cooker, using the same method, the same cut of meat prepared identically will be done in 1 hour and 10 minutes.

Stews and Sautés
On top of the stove in a regular sauté pan, cook for 1 hour and 20 minutes. In a pressure cooker, cook for 15 to 20 minutes only.

Variety Meats
These look a bit discouraging, will you say? and strange? Yes, maybe, but they are loaded with a lot of good vitamins and most of them are inexpensive and delicious. So give them a try. Children may balk at some of them; a note will tell you which recipes are less attractive for the young fry. On the contrary, they will eat those that are marked: "good for kids" because the taste is similar to that of muscle meats of beef, lamb or veal.

ROAST LEG OF LAMB IN THE FRENCH MANNER
(Gigot de Mouton Rôti)

Fell versus no fell: The fell or membrane which surrounds the leg of lamb and its layer of fat is usually not removed in Classic French Cuisine. However, in modern 20th-century France, quite a few chefs and home cooks trim all legs of lamb and mutton down to the bare muscle. This makes the lamb lighter and does away with the so called "lamby" taste to which many people object. Suit your own taste. Should you want to keep fell and fat on and minimize the lamby taste, then marinate the leg in red wine and vinegar for a day or so. Wipe dry the next day and roast as usual.

- Easy
  6 to 8 servings
  Very expensive
  Cooking time: 8 to 10 minutes per pound
  Best season: spring to early fall

  1 leg of lamb, 2 to 4 lbs. (1.5 to 2 kg)
  1 large garlic clove
  US 2 TB, UK 1 TB, butter (30 g)
  salt and pepper
  **approximately US 1 cup, UK 1 scant cup,
  bouillon (3 dl), if needed**

THIS IS THE FRENCH COOKING METHOD
The lamb is cooked medium rare and mutton rare. In French cuisine only the shoulder can be well done. Try lamb medium rare; it is a treat. Mutton cooked rare is very special to the French taste; nothing prevents your cooking mutton medium rare also.

- Preheat oven to 425°F., 220°C. or 6 Regulo.
- Trim the leg of lamb of all fat if you desire (see advice). Peel the garlic clove and insert it along the bone between the two muscles. Spread the butter over the whole leg. Put the leg on a rack fitted over any roasting pan and put to roast in the preheated oven.
- Cooking time is about 8 minutes per pound for rare and 10 minutes per pound for medium rare. While the meat cooks, baste it at regular intervals with any juices accumulating at the bottom of the roasting pan. If none happens to materialize, baste with a bit of bouillon added to the roasting pan.
- Remove the leg of lamb from the oven as soon as done and let it sit for a few minutes before carving. Should you have to delay serving, keep the meat in the oven with the door open. Salt and pepper the meat well before serving.

LAMB BOULANGÈRE
(Agneau Boulangère)

À la boulangère, or "baker's wife style," is an old French expression going back to the days when lower- and middle-class people had only chimneys and no ovens to bake breads or meats. They used to prepare their dish, write their name on it, and carry it to a baker who, for a small fee, would bake it for them. This custom is still observed; when a French housewife needs her oven for several dishes at a time she will easily take a leg or shoulder of lamb or a large roast beef to the baker.

■ Relatively easy
6 to 8 servings
Very expensive to medium expensive (see note below)
1 hour 30 minutes to 1 hour 40 minutes
Best season: spring to early fall

1 cut of lamb of your choice (see note below)
US 1 TB, UK ½ TB, oil (½ TB)
2½ lbs. baking potatoes (1.25 kg)
salt and pepper
2 large garlic cloves
US 5 TB, UK 2½ TB, butter (75 g)
US 2 cups, UK 2 scant cups, bouillon (4.5 dl)
chopped parsley

• For this recipe, whatever the cut, in all cases the fell remains on the meat. Score it in a criss-cross pattern applied every ½ inch in both directions. Rub the cut with the oil.

• Peel the potatoes and slice into a bowl. Salt and pepper them. Chop the garlic cloves finely and mix them into the potatoes. Toss well together.

• Preheat oven to 400°F., 200°C. or 6 Regulo.

• Put the potatoes in a large baking dish buttered with one fifth of the butter. Add the bouillon and bake for 30 minutes to swell the potato starch and moisten the slices.

• Rub lamb with the rest of the butter. Put it in the dish with the potatoes and bake until done. To check the doneness of the saddle and of the leg plunge a skewer into the back bone or the leg bone marrow. The cut is done when this skewer feels lukewarm when touched to the top of your hand.

• Carve the meat and serve the slices over their bed of potatoes. Sprinkle with chopped parsley.

SPECIAL INSTRUCTIONS FOR CARVING THE SADDLE
Cut along the backbone and snug against it, curving your blade downward to lift the meat off the bone. Continue cutting until you reach the tip end of the short lumbar bones. You will see a long strip of lean rare meat; cut it off from the main piece. This is the sirloin strip; you can either cut it across in *noisettes* or lengthwise into what the French call *aiguillettes*. The 2 sirloin strips represent 4 servings. Then turn the cut over and you will see the tenderloins; lift them with your blade. Each tenderloin, whole, represents a portion.

YOUR CHOICE OF LAMB CUTS
The saddle or whole loin, known as "Pic" to butchers, is very expensive; it may be left on the bone and will bake in 35 to 40 minutes, or it may be boned and rolled and will bake in 1 hour.

The leg will bake in 1¼ hours and is expensive.

The square-cut shoulder will bake in 1 hour and is medium expensive.

STUFFED SHOULDER OF LAMB
(Épaule de Mouton Farcie)

Too much forcemeat left? Butter a piece of aluminum foil. Roll it around the forcemeat, enclosing it in the shape of a sausage, and put the package to cook beside the shoulder. Remove the package 15 minutes before serving. Unwrap the forcemeat and immerse it in the sauce for better taste and a few last minutes of cooking. Serve around the shoulder, cut into slices, or keep refrigerated for a lunch sandwich or high protein salad.

- A bit difficult
  6 to 8 servings
  Medium expensive
  2 hours, 1½ hours in pressure cooker
  Best season: fall, winter to early spring when served hot; late spring to early fall when served cold.

5 oz. liver of your choice (150 g)
2 slices of white bread, crusts removed
milk for soaking
½ lb. sausage (250 g)
1 egg
1 large onion, finely chopped
2 small garlic cloves, finely chopped
salt and pepper
chopped parsley
1 shoulder of lamb, boned
US 2 TB, UK 1 TB, oil (1 TB)
US 2 TB, UK 1 TB, butter (30 g)
US 2 cups, UK 2 scant cups, bouillon (4.5 dl)

- Chop or grind the liver, using a knife, an electric grinder or a food processor. Soak the bread in milk, squeeze dry, and mash the bread with a fork.
- Squeeze the sausage meat out of its casing and put in a mixing bowl with the liver, bread, egg, chopped onion and garlic, and salt, pepper and chopped parsley to taste. Mix very well into a homogenous forcemeat.
- Fill the pocket of the shoulder with the forcemeat. With a large needle threaded with strong white thread (see note, p. 128) sew the pocket closed.
- Heat the mixture of oil and butter in a braising pot and brown the shoulder on all sides. Use 2 spatulas to turn the meat for even browning.
- When the shoulder is nice and golden, add the bouillon, and salt and pepper to taste. Cover and let cook gently for at least 1½ hours, 1 hour in pressure cooker. The meat is done when a skewer inserted at its center comes out easily. The meat is not cooked as long as the piece of meat can be lifted with the skewer.
- Strain the gravy into a measuring cup and separate the lean gravy from the fat, using a bulb baster. If the gravy is too thin, boil it hard for 5 minutes to concentrate it.
- Serve on very hot plates.

BONING THE SHOULDER, HANDLING THE FORCEMEAT
Any butcher will bone the shoulder for you.

The best way to mix a forcemeat is with your well-scrubbed hands, dipped into cold water so the forcemeat does not stick to your fingers.

RICE-STUFFED SHOULDER OF LAMB
(Épaule de Mouton au Riz)

In this type of pot-roasting it may happen that evaporation is strong and that all gravy disappears. Check at regular intervals and add a bit of bouillon or water to the pot as needed.

■ A bit difficult
6 to 8 servings
Medium expensive
2 hours, 1½ hours in pressure cooker
Best season: fall to early spring

4 medium-size onions
US 4 TB, UK 2 TB, butter (60 g)
water
salt and pepper
US ½ cup, UK ⅓ cup, rice of your choice (100 g)
1 shoulder of lamb, boned
dried thyme
tiny piece of bay leaf
chopped parsley
US 2 TB, UK 1 TB, oil (1 TB)
3½ oz. fresh salt pork (not too old) or slab bacon (110 g)
1 large garlic clove
bouquet garni
US ⅓ cup, UK ¼ cup, white Port (1 scant dl)

- Peel the onions and cut into thin slices. Heat a tablespoon or so of butter in a frying pan and brown the onion slices lightly.

- Meanwhile, bring 2 quarts water to a boil, add salt and pepper to taste and the rice. Cook it for 14 minutes. Drain rice, do not rinse it, and add it to the onions. Empty the mixture onto a plate and let it cool thoroughly.

- Open the shoulder flat on a cutting board. Spread the rice mixture over three quarters of the meat. Add salt, pepper, crumbled thyme, small piece of bay leaf, well crumbled, chopped parsley. Roll the shoulder, starting with the edge entirely covered with rice, and sew tightly closed.

- Heat the oil and remaining butter in a braising pot and brown the rolled shoulder on all sides.

- Meanwhile, cut the salt pork into strips ⅓ x 1 inch. Blanch them in boiling water for 5 minutes.

- Add the salt pork around the meat, as well as the garlic clove and the *bouquet garni*. Cover, reduce the heat, and let cook gently for about 1 hour, *30 minutes in pressure cooker.*

- Ten minutes before the end of the cooking, add two thirds of the Port.

- When ready to serve, remove the shoulder to a serving plate. Add the remainder of the Port to the sauce and do not reboil. Strain the sauce, defatten it with a bulb baster if need be, and pour it into a sauceboat.

PAY ATTENTION TO THE FACTS
You need solid white thread to sew the shoulder (black or colored threads leach their color into the meat!).

If you use Converted rice the dish will be lighter and less tasty and also the rice will not stick to the meat but will roll out of it when cut; if you use round starchy rice the dish will be heavier and tastier and the slicing easier.

LAMB CHOPS WITH CANADIAN BACON
(Côtes d'Agneau au Bacon)

As a vegetable try mashed potatoes and either green beans or zucchini.

■ Easy
6 servings
Expensive
20 minutes
Best season: spring to early fall

6 large lamb chops, rib or loin
3 slices of Canadian bacon
US 2 TB, UK 1 TB, butter (1 TB)
US 3 TB, UK 1½ TB, oil (1½ TB)
salt
water
coarse pepper from the mill
chopped parsley

- Remove the fat around the meat and on top of the bone if you are using rib chops.
- Sauté the Canadian bacon slices in butter. Remove to crumpled paper and keep the butter. Let bacon cool. Halfway through the *noisette* (see note below) thickness of the chop, cut a pocket that will reach all the way to the bone but do not separate the meat from the bone.
- Slide ½ slice of cooled bacon into each pocket and press closed.
- Heat the oil in 1 or 2 skillets. When the oil almost starts smoking, sear the chops for 2 minutes and turn over. Salt the seared side, let the meat cook for 4 minutes, then turn over again. Salt the second side and let cook for another 2 minutes.
- Discard the oil in the pan, dissolve the caramelized lamb juices with US ¼ cup, UK 2 tablespoons, water (2 TB). Empty this little gravy into the frying pan where the bacon was sautéed and add some coarsely cracked pepper from the mill. Add more water if needed and reheat well.
- Put the lamb chops on a heated platter and spoon a bit of gravy over each chop. Sprinkle with chopped parsley.

WITH THE SAME METHOD
Breaded Lamb Chops: When the chops are stuffed with the bacon, flour them, brush them with beaten egg, and coat them with a mixture of bread crumbs and grated Gruyère cheese. Sauté in butter over medium high heat.

USE
either rib or loin chops. Noisettes are obtained as follows: when the eye of the rib or the sirloin strip attached to the rib and backbone of a lamb or any other animal are entirely boned, a long strip of lean meat results, which can be cut across the grain into ½-inch slices. A slice is called a noisette.

If you like the stronger flavor of mutton, by all means use mutton in this recipe.

LAMB CHOPS EN PAPILLOTES
(Côtes d'Agneau en Papillotes)

Any one late for dinner? Turn the oven off but keep the packages in it; the worst that can happen is that the chops will be well done and extremely tender the longer they wait; the aluminum foil keeps the meat very hot for a long time.

A bit of French food lore: The mixture of garlic and parsley is called persillade; *it is a favorite of Southern French cooks. East of the Rhône Delta, in Provence, it is usually browned lightly in butter; try it that way for a change, the dish takes on another dimension. West of the Delta, in the Languedoc, it is used exactly as described here.*

■ Relatively easy
6 servings
Expensive
45 minutes
Best season: spring to early fall

6 to 8 boiling potatoes (Red Bliss)
salt
6 loin or rib lamb chops
US 7 TB, UK 3½ TB, butter (100 g)
pepper
3 garlic cloves
large bunch of parsley

● Wash the potatoes. Immerse them in cold water in a saucepan, bring to a boil, and add salt to taste. Simmer for 20 minutes.

● Preheat oven to 350°F., 200°C. or 5 to 6 Regulo.

● While potatoes cook, trim the chops of all fat and sear them in 1 tablespoon butter on both sides without attempting to cook them. The center should remain almost uncooked. Salt and pepper on both sides.

● Cut 6 large squares of aluminum foil. Butter each lightly.

● As soon as potatoes are cooked, peel them and slice them.

● Put an equal amount of potato slices on each piece of foil, leaving 2 inches free all around the potatoes. Put 1 chop per package on the potatoes. Top the chops with a piece of butter.

● Chop the garlic and parsley into a fine mixture (see advice). Sprinkle over the chops and close all 6 packages "drugstore" fashion.

● Bake the *papillotes* on the middle rack of the preheated oven for 8 to 10 minutes.

● Serve the *papillotes* closed. It is fun and a real olfactory pleasure for each guest to open the foil package.

CHOOSE WELL
The chops should be either rib or loin.

The potatoes should be waxy and not too starchy.

If you like mutton, by all means use mutton chops instead of lamb chops.

BROCHETTES OR SKEWERS OF LAMB
(Brochettes d'Agneau)

Would you like a small sauce? There will be quite a bit of caramelized lamb juices at the bottom of the broiler pan. Dissolve them with ½ cup or so of warm water; add a bit of tomato paste and salt and pepper. Sauté a very finely chopped small onion in 1 tablespoon or so of butter. Pour the deglazing mixture over the onion and simmer together for 5 minutes.

■ Easy
  6 servings
  Expensive
  40 minutes
  Best season: spring to early winter

  US ¾ cup, UK 6 TB, oil (6 TB)
  salt and pepper
  finely crumbled dried thyme
  18 silverskin onions
  6 bay leaves
  6 medium-size tomatoes, or 18 cherry
     tomatoes
  2 lbs. lamb, free of fat and gristle, cut into
     1¼-inch cubes (1 kg)

WISE BUYING
Buy a whole shoulder of lamb, bone it, and cut it into 1¼-inch cubes. You can use the bone in a soup such as Velouté of Dried Legumes (p. 29); it will give the soup an excellent flavor. If you have no time to bone and cube the shoulder yourself, ask the butcher.

- In a bowl, mix the oil with salt, pepper and thyme to taste, and let stand.
- Peel the silverskin onions; cut the bay leaves into 2 or 3 pieces; if the tomatoes are large, cut them into quarters.
- Add the meat cubes and the onions to the oil and toss them very well together.
- Skewer the meat, tomatoes, pieces of bay leaf and small onions in that order on 6 skewers. Brush any oil left of the marinade over the tomatoes.
- Preheat the oven broiler. Put the brochettes on a rack placed over a broiler pan and broil 4 inches from the source of heat, for about 10 minutes, turning the brochettes several times during the cooking.
- Serve the brochettes on a dish of rice (p. 209) or accompany with green beans (p. 215).

WITH THE SAME METHOD
Brochettes of Liver: Skewer pieces of lamb, pieces of liver of your choice, mushroom caps and lightly presautéed bacon pieces, ¼ inch wide. Broil as above.

Mixed Grill: Skewer pieces of lamb, cleaned half lamb kidneys, pieces of bell peppers, cherry tomatoes, half links of breakfast sausage and 1¼-inch pieces of lightly presautéed bacon.

OLD-FASHIONED FRENCH LAMB STEW
(Navarin de Mouton)

This dish reheats very well. Prepare 2 recipes except for the potatoes, which must be cooked just before serving. Freezes very well.

To eliminate defattening with the bulb baster, cook the first part of the stew the day before serving it and refrigerate the sauce in a separate container. You will be able to lift off the layer of fat in one piece.

■ Relatively easy
  6 servings
  Thrift recipe
  2½ hours, 1 hour in pressure cooker
  Best season: in spring with baby carrots

  2½ to 3 lbs. lamb stew or shank (1.25 to 1.5 kg)
  US 2 TB, UK 1 TB, oil (1 TB)
  US 3 TB, UK 1½ TB, flour (25 g)
  US 2¼ cups, UK 2 cups, water or bouillon (.5 L)
  1 large onion
  1 large garlic clove
  salt and pepper
  bouquet garni
  4 carrots
  6 medium-size potatoes
  chopped parsley

- Trim as much fat as possible from the pieces of lamb.

- Heat 1 to 2 tablespoons oil in a braising pot and in it brown the lamb on all sides.

- Remove the lamb from the pot and discard all traces of the fat. Return the meat to the pot, dust meat with the flour, and toss well over medium heat so it browns nicely.

- Add the water or bouillon, the onion, garlic, salt and pepper to taste and *bouquet garni*. Cover and bring to a boil. Reduce to a simmer and cook for 45 minutes.

- Meanwhile, peel the carrots and cut into thick slices. Add them to the pot and let cook for another 40 minutes.

- Peel the potatoes. Wash them, cube them.

- Remove the stew from the heat. Put the meat and vegetables in a bowl. Strain the sauce into a large glass measuring cup. Let all the fat come to the surface and pump out all the fat-free sauce, using a bulb baster. Return the sauce to the braising pot, add the vegetables and the meat, and bring back to a boil. Add the potatoes. Cook for another 20 minutes.

- To serve, heat a country-style deep dish as well as the dinner plates. Spoon off the additional fat at the surface of the stew and empty the stew into the dish. Sprinkle with chopped parsley.

SPECIAL INSTRUCTIONS FOR THE PRESSURE COOKER
Put carrots and potatoes at once in the pot and cook for at least 15 minutes after the correct pressure is reached.

CHOOSE WELL
Shank is excellent and lean after you remove the fatty flap, and it is inexpensive.

Neck pieces are cheap but a bit fat; trim them well.

Choose either new potatoes or Red Bliss boiling potatoes.

BAKED LAMB BRAINS
(Cervelles de Mouton au Four)

Would you like a sauce? Use a nice bowl of mayonnaise flavored with herbs.

- Easy
  6 servings
  Well affordable
  35 minutes
  Best season: year around

  6 lamb brains
  vinegar
  2 eggs
  US 4 TB, UK 2 TB, heavy cream (75 g)
  salt and pepper
  bread crumbs, dry or fresh
  flour
  US 4 TB, UK 2 TB, butter (60 g)
  parsley
  1 lemon, cut into 6 wedges

ABOUT BRAINS
While children do not like the idea of brains, they will generally eat them happily when they are prepared this way.

Also, on portioning brains: 1 lamb brain is 1 portion; 1 veal brain is 2 portions; 1 beef brain is 3 portions.

- Wash the brains in running cold water, then immerse them in slightly vinegared water. Bring slowly to a boil and reduce to a bare simmer. Poach for about 4 minutes. Remove to a bowl of cold water to cool them rapidly.
- Add 1 egg to the saucepan of water and hard-boil it for 10 minutes.
- Beat the second egg with the cream and salt and pepper to taste. Put the bread crumbs on a piece of wax paper. Put the flour on another piece of wax paper.
- Preheat the broiler.
- Cut the brains crosswise into thick slices; flour the slices, coat each slice with egg and cream, and roll in the bread crumbs.
- Butter a baking dish. Put the slices of brains in it and broil 4 inches from the source of heat until nice and golden. Add a bit more butter if necessary.
- Peel and chop the hard-boiled egg and the parsley. Mix well.
- Serve the brains in the baking dish, sprinkled with the mixture of egg and parsley and surrounded by the 6 lemon wedges.

LAMB KIDNEYS AND MUSHROOMS
(Rognons aux Champignons)

- A bit difficult
  6 servings
  Medium expensive
  20 minutes
  Best season: cold months

2 lbs. lamb kidneys (1 kg)
¾ lb. fresh mushrooms (375 g)
US 4 TB, UK 2 TB, butter (60 g)
salt and pepper
US 2 TB, UK 1 TB, flour (15 g)
US 1 cup, UK 1 scant cup, bouillon (2.5 dl)
**US ½ cup, UK ⅓ cup, dry white wine (1
    generous dl)**
small bouquet garni
1 tsp. tomato paste
US 2 TB, UK 1 TB, oil (1 TB)
US 2 TB, UK 1 TB, dry sherry (1 TB)
US 2 TB, UK 1 TB, heavy cream (optional)
chopped parsley

- Cut kidneys lengthwise into halves. With sharp scissors cut out all white membrane. Cut kidneys into ½-inch cubes.
- Prepare the mushrooms (see p. 300). Slice them.
- Heat half of the butter in a pan. Add the mushrooms and sauté them for 1 minute. Salt and pepper them, then cover them and let them render their juices, about 7 minutes.
- Prepare a roux with the remainder of the butter and the flour. Add the bouil-

lon and white wine, whisking very well, and bring back to a boil. Add the *bouquet garni* and the tomato paste. Simmer for 15 minutes. Skim any scum coming to the surface of the sauce.

- Add mushrooms and their juices to the sauce. Simmer for 2 or 3 minutes more.
- Heat the oil in a large skillet and in it stir-fry the kidneys very quickly over very high heat until they turn gray. Add the sherry. *This will take only 1 minute or so.*
- Empty the kidneys into a colander and let them drip all the blood they possibly can drip. When they stop dripping, add them to the sauce.
- Reheat the sauce and kidneys well but do not even approach boiling. Just before serving add a dollop of cream if you like.
- Spoon into a heated serving dish and sprinkle with chopped parsley. Serve very hot on hot plates with buttered rice.

NOT A CHILDREN'S CHARMER

FRESH KIDNEYS
are shiny bright and have no smell.

PORK
(Le Porc)

COOKING METHODS FOR PORK

Overcooking or overroasting pork is a common mistake which must be avoided or the meat will be extremely dry and unpalatable. Use a meat thermometer and cook to 170°F., for best flavor and best texture.

Contrary to beef or lamb, pork cannot be trimmed to the bare muscle for most of the flavor of pork is in its fat, not in its meat. Always leave ¼ inch of fat on a roast or chop.

Cold pork makes excellent eating for the summer months with a salad, so cook larger pieces to have some leftovers. It keeps well for several days when refrigerated properly.

Broiled
Large loin and rib chops ¾ to 1 inch thick: broil for 8 to 10 minutes on each side, depending on thickness.

Panfried
Follow the timing for broiled chops.

Oven-Roasted
Roast at 30 minutes per pound. Oven temperature: 350°F., 180°C., 5 Regulo.

Casserole-Roasted
Sear, season, and cover; then cook for 30 minutes per pound.

Boiled
Bring water to a boil, add salted pork cuts, bring back to a boil, and reduce to a simmer for the following lengths of time: salted brisket: cook for 1½ hours; salted picnic ham shoulder: cook for 2 to 2½ hours.

PORK ROAST IN HAZELNUT COAT
(Rôti de Porc aux Noisettes)

A luscious vegetable with this roast would be a well-buttered chestnut purée. There are some good canned chestnut purées, but do not reheat any of them in an aluminum pan.

- A bit difficult
  6 servings
  Medium expensive
  2½ hours
  Best season: winter

  10 whole hazelnuts
  1 boneless pork loin roast, 3 lbs. (1.5 kg)
  US 3 TB, UK 1½ TB, oil (1½ TB)
  salt and pepper
  US 1 cup, UK 1 scant cup, dry white wine (2.5 dl)
  2.5 oz. finely ground hazelnuts (75 g) (see note below)
  US 2 TB, UK 1 TB, sugar (1 TB)
  US 2 TB, UK 1 TB, butter (30 g)

- Preheat oven to 400°F., 220°C. or 6 Regulo.

- Cut the whole hazelnuts into halves. Punch small holes with a knife ½ inch below the surface of the roast and insert the hazelnut halves in the holes.

- Heat the oil in a large pot and brown the roast on all sides. Salt and pepper the roast. Discard the fat mixture in the pan and add the dry white wine. Cook for 2 minutes, scraping the bottom of the pan well to dissolve the caramelized pan juices.

- Place the roast at the center of a large sheet of aluminum foil. Bunch the sheet around the meat to form a container. Empty the white wine into that container, then close the sheet at the top of the roast, making several "drugstore" style folds to seal the wine in.

- Roast the "meat package" for about 1½ hours. Prepare a mixture with the ground hazelnuts, the sugar and the melted butter.

- Fifteen minutes before the end of the cooking time pull the rack out of the oven. Open the foil. Spread the hazelnut mixture over the whole roast. Do not reclose the foil. Push the rack back into the oven, close the door, and let the topping brown.

- To serve, present the whole roast in its foil, or remove the foil and slice the meat.

THE BEST CUT
for this roast is a boned loin, which can be trimmed of all its fat, for cooking in tightly sealed foil will prevent the roast from drying out.

To grind hazelnuts: chop them coarsely, put the sugar in the blender, add the nuts, and process until a fine powder is obtained.

PORK RIB ROAST ISLAND STYLE
(Carré de Porc des Isles)

To prevent the tips of the ribs from burning, wrap them in aluminum foil as soon as they are golden brown.

■ A bit difficult
6 servings
Medium expensive
2 hours
Best season: fall and winter

4 to 5 lbs. pork rib roast (about 2 kg)
1 tsp. crystallized sugar
salt and pepper
oil of your choice
US ¼ cup, UK 2 TB, dark rum (2 TB)
6 green apples
US 6 TB, UK 3 TB, butter (90 g)
1 fresh pineapple, ready to eat

• Preheat oven to 325°F., 180°C. or 5 Regulo.

• Sprinkle the cut of pork with the sugar and salt and pepper to taste. Brush with some oil.

• Set the pork on a roasting pan fitted with a rack and roast for approximately 1 hour. When the top is nice and golden, baste with half of the rum. During the last half hour of cooking, baste several times with the cooking juices in the pan.

• Peel and core the apples while the pork roasts. Cut the apples into quarters and sauté them in butter until they are tender but do not let them fall apart.

• Cut the pineapple lengthwise into halves. Scoop out the fruit without breaking the shell; remove and discard the center core and dice the fruit. Heat some butter in a frying pan and heat the dice without browning them.

• When the roast is done, remove it from the oven and to a platter.

• Add any pineapple juice oozing out of the dice to the roasting pan and mix very well, scraping to dissolve caramelized pork juices. Empty into a small saucepan and spoon off surface fat. Pour the remainder of the rum into a small pan, ignite it, and pour it flaming into the gravy.

• To serve, return the hot pineapple cubes to their shells. Put one shell at each end of the dish. Slice the pork and set the slices at the center of the dish with the hot apples on each side. Serve the gravy in a gravy boat.

ABOUT THE RECIPE
It can be applied to several cuts of pork beside the rib: the loin on the bone, or boneless and rolled; the Boston butt or shoulder (very moist and tender).

BRAISED PORK IN BEER
(Carbonnades de Porc)

This is a regional recipe. It is from Flanders which straddles the border of France and Belgium. The beer used there is slightly sour and is called Lambic. Try any light beer, or if you like a good solid beer with a tinge of bitterness try dark beer or even Guinness.

■ Easy
  6 servings
  Thrift recipe
  2 hours, 45 minutes in pressure cooker
  Best season: fall and winter

  4 or 5 onions
  US 4 TB, UK 2 TB, oil (2 TB)
  2½ to 3 lbs. pork stewing meat, cut into cubes (1.5 kg)
  US 2 TB, UK 1 TB, flour (15 g)
  bouquet garni
  US 1¼ cups, UK 1 cup, beer (.25 L)
  US 1¼ cups, UK 1 cup, water (.25 L)
  salt and pepper
  1 slice of French or Italian bread
  Dijon mustard

● Peel the onions and cut them into ¼-inch-thick slices.

● Heat the oil in a braising pot over high heat. Add the pieces of pork and brown them well on all sides. Add the onions and toss the mixture of meat and onions well together. The onions should not brown beyond light golden.

● Add the flour and toss well again. Add the *bouquet garni*, beer, water, salt and pepper.

● Spread a slice of bread with mustard and set it on top of the mixture. (It will disintegrate into the sauce as the stew cooks.)

● Bring the liquid to a boil, reduce the heat, and let cook very slowly for 2 hours, *30 minutes in pressure cooker.*

WITH THE SAME METHOD
Braised Beef in Beer: Use 2½ to 3 pounds beef chuck (1.5 kg), cut into thick slices (chicken or blade steaks are perfect; use 1 per person). Cook exactly the same way, for 2½ to 3 hours, *1 hour in pressure cooker.*

THE VERY BEST CUT
is the shoulder (Boston butt), cubed, but short ribs are also very good as well as cut-up neck.

The best vegetable is steamed potatoes prepared by setting potatoes enclosed in a steaming basket on the surface of the cooking meat.

PORK BRAISED IN MILK
(Porc Braisé au Lait)

If you enjoy a more potent taste to a sauce, add a large spoonful of mustard to it while it is boiling hot, and do not reboil.

■ Relatively easy
6 servings
Medium expensive
2¾ hours, 1 hour and 25 minutes in pressure cooker
Best season: the depth of winter

6 small white onions
US ¼ cup, UK 2 TB, butter (60 g)
1 boneless pork roast, about 3 lbs. (1.5 kg)
US 2¼ cups, UK 2 cups, scalding milk (.5 L)
salt and pepper
1 bay leaf
1½ tsp. cornstarch
US 3 TB, UK 1½ TB, scallion tops, cut into small rings (1½ TB)
US 2 TB, UK 1 TB, prepared Dijon mustard (1 TB) (optional, see advice)

WHICH CUT TO USE?
What meat stores call "boneless" pork roast, which is a rolled and tied roast, is made of half rib roast boned and part of the shoulder, boned. The roast usually shows a flap at its larger end; it is the pocket left by the removal of the shoulder blade.

- Peel the onions and cut them into slices.

- Heat the butter in the braising pot and add the onions. Brown them well and remove them to a plate, pressing the butter out.

- In the same pot, brown the pork roast on all sides. Return the onions to the pot. Add the hot milk. Add salt, pepper and bay leaf, and bring to a boil. Turn down to a simmer and cover.

- Let pork cook very slowly for 2 hours, 1 hour in pressure cooker.

- When the meat is cooked, remove it to a serving platter and keep it hot.

- The sauce will have a "curdled" and separated look, which is normal and due to the onions acting on the milk. Remove the bay leaf. Pour the sauce, onions and all, into a blender container and whirl until smooth.

- Return sauce to pot. Dilute the cornstarch with a drop or so of cold milk or water. Bring the sauce back to a simmer and stir in the starch until sauce is smooth and boiling. Let simmer for another 2 to 3 minutes.

- Remove the sauce from the heat; add the scallions. Slice the roast and spoon the sauce over it.

PORK AND LEMON
(Porc au Citron)

Salt and acid balance each other. If a sauce like this one is too acid, add salt or a small piece of bouillon cube. Conversely, if a sauce is too salty, add an acid. Most of the time that acid will be lemon juice, sour cream or yogurt.

■ Easy
  6 servings
  Medium expensive
  1¼ hours
  Best season: year around

  US 2¼ cups, UK 2 cups, water (.5 L)
  1 boneless pork roast, about 3 lbs. (1.5 kg)
  salt and pepper
  4 lemons

THE CHOICE OF CUT
The same as in the recipe for Pork Braised in Milk. This recipe is excellent cold and makes a pleasant meat for a summer evening with a plain green salad.

- Pour the water into a braising pot. Add the pork; bring the water to a boil. Keep turning the pork roast in the boiling water until the water evaporates completely. The fat will by then have melted.

- Brown the roast well in its own fat until golden on all sides. Season with salt and pepper.

- Add to the pot the juice of 3 lemons and the last lemon, *unpeeled* and cut into thick slices.

- Cover and let cook very gently for 1¼ hours. The meat is done when a skewer inserted at the center comes out clear and without lifting up the piece of meat.

- As the meat cooks, taste the gravy at regular intervals. It should take on a slight edge of bitterness. This is from the lemon rind; as soon as this taste has been acquired, remove the slices of lemon and discard them.

- Before serving, defatten the gravy, using a bulb baster, and correct the salt and pepper (see advice).

ROAST PORK BOULANGÈRE
(Rôti de Porc Boulangère)

For a delicious treat, arrange potatoes in alternating rows or layers with rows or layers of onions.

- Relatively easy
  6 servings
  Medium expensive
  1½ to 2 hours
  Best season: fall and winter

  2½ lbs. baking potatoes (1 heavy kg)
  salt and pepper
  US 6 TB, UK 3 TB, butter (90 g)
  1 boneless pork roast, about 3 lbs. (1.5 kg)
  thyme to suit your taste, well crumbled
  ¼ bay leaf, well crumbled
  US 1 to 2 cups, UK 1 scant cup to 2 scant
     cups, water or bouillon (3 dl to .5 L)

CUTS TO USE
The best cut for this dish is the same as that used for Pork Braised in Milk (p. 140). You can also use a whole Boston butt or shoulder.

- Preheat oven to 325°F., 200°C. or 5 Regulo.
- Peel the potatoes, wash them, and cut them into thin slices. Toss them with salt and pepper to taste.
- With half of the butter, coat a baking dish. Set the pork roast at the center. Surround the roast with the potatoes; sprinkle with thyme and bay leaf. Dot the potatoes with the remainder of the butter.
- Bake for about 1 hour, then add the water or bouillon to the potatoes and continue baking until a skewer inserted into the roast comes out without difficulty. The amount of liquid needed depends on the absorbency of the potatoes.
- For the last half hour or so of cooking, cover the roast with a loose sheet of aluminum foil; the meat will be more moist and tender.
- Serve in the baking dish.

PORK CHOPS WITH SWEET SPICES
(Côtes de Porc aux Quatre Épices)

Flambéing: If you have a table hot plate, you can flambé the dish at the table; it is a joy for children and fun for adults. A dish of Creole Rice (p. 206) would be pleasant with the chops as well as some heated pineapple and orange slices.

- Easy
  6 servings
  Medium expensive
  30 minutes
  Best season: the depth of winter

  juice of 1 large juice orange
  finely grated rind of ⅔ lemon
  3 cloves
  ½ tsp. ground cinnamon
  ⅓ tsp. freshly grated nutmeg
  **US ⅔ cup, UK ½ generous cup, dark rum
      (1.5 dl)**
  salt and pepper
  6 loin pork chops
  flour
  US 3 TB, UK 1½ TB, butter (45 g)

IT IS ESSENTIAL
that you leave only ¼-inch of fat on the edge of the chop; if there is more, trim it; that you score the fat band 3 times along the broad side of each chop so chops can remain flat in the skillet and not buckle while cooking. This will prevent uneven cooking.

- Prepare a small marinade with the orange juice, lemon rind, the crushed heads of the cloves, the cinnamon and nutmeg, half of the rum, and salt and pepper to taste. Mix well.
- Put the pork chops into a 2-quart glass baking dish and pour the marinade over them. Let them marinate for about 15 minutes, turning the chops once or twice so they take on the taste of the spices and aromatics.
- Drain the chops. Pat them dry and flour them.
- Heat the butter in a large skillet or electric frying pan. Cook the chops over medium heat so they can cook to the center without hardening too much. Turn them over and cook on the second side. Season both sides well with salt and pepper.
- Remove the chops to a heated platter. Empty the marinade into the skillet. Boil hard for 1 to 2 minutes. Pour the sauce over the chops. Heat the other half of the rum in a small pan, ignite it, and pour it flaming over the chops.

SAUTÉED PORK AND EGGPLANTS
(Sauté de Porc aux Aubergines)

Sauce textures: If you dust your eggplant with flour the sauce will have an added degree of thickness. If you do not, it may still be too liquid after the pork has finished cooking. Remove the meat to a plate and cook sauce down until it loses moisture. See Reduce (p. 302).

- Relatively easy
  6 servings
  Medium expensive
  1 hour
  Best season: late summer and fall with baby eggplants and fresh tomatoes

3 onions
3 garlic cloves
US ½ cup, UK 4 TB, olive oil (4 TB)
2½ to 3 lbs. pork meat, cut into 1½-inch cubes (1.5 kg)
US 1 cup, UK 1 scant cup, dry white wine (3 dl)
salt and pepper
6 baby eggplants or 2 medium-size eggplants
flour (optional, see advice)
6 medium-size tomatoes
chopped parsley

- Peel the onions and cut into thin slices. Peel the garlic cloves and mash them.
- Heat half of the oil in a braising pot and brown the onions until golden. Press the oil out of them with the back of a spoon and remove them to a plate.
- In the same oil, brown the cubes of pork very well on all sides. Return the onions to the pot, add also the mashed garlic, the wine, and salt and pepper to taste. Cover and let simmer gently for 30 minutes.

- Peel the eggplants; cut them into ½-inch cubes. Set aside on a plate. Sprinkle with salt and let stand for 10 minutes (see note).
- Peel the tomatoes if you have the time. Cut them into quarters; squeeze the seeds out. Set them aside on a plate.
- Rinse the eggplant cubes; pat them dry. Heat the remainder of the oil and sauté the cubed eggplant over high heat so the pieces brown. Dusting the eggplant with flour could be helpful.
- When the eggplant is ready, add the tomatoes, stir well, and add the mixture to the braising pot. Cook for 20 to 30 minutes longer. Correct the final seasoning.
- To serve, empty the stew into a deep dish and sprinkle with chopped parsley.

THE BEST CHOICES HERE ARE
cubed Boston butt (shoulder).
Olive oil.
Italian baby eggplants. If you use larger eggplants, salt the cubes, rinse them, pat them dry, and flour them before sautéing in oil.

HAM SLICES THE CREOLE WAY
(Jambon à la Créole)

Would you like more rum flavor? Heat another tablespoon or so of rum in a small pot and pour it flaming over the dish before serving.

■ Easy
6 servings
Thrift recipe
25 minutes (see note below)
Best season: year around

US 4 TB, UK 2 TB, butter (60 g)
US 2½ TB, UK 1¼ TB, flour (22 g)
US 1½ cups, UK 1¼ cups, hot bouillon
   (3.5 dl)
1 tsp. vinegar
salt and pepper
US 3 TB, UK 1½ TB, dark rum (1½ TB)
2 boxes (10 oz. each) frozen spinach
   leaves (285 g each)
nutmeg
12 slices of boiled ham

IF YOU USE FRESH SPINACH
You will need 30 more minutes for complete preparation: cleaning, sorting, blanching and sautéing.

● Sauce: Melt half of the butter in a saucepan. Add the flour, stir well, and cook until the flour has browned ever so slightly. Whisk in the bouillon and the vinegar, season with salt and pepper to taste, and bring to a boil. Simmer for a few minutes. Add the rum and simmer for another 2 to 3 minutes.

● Meanwhile, bring some water to a boil. Add the spinach, and break apart to thaw it completely. Drain well.

● Heat a tablespoon or so of butter in a small pan and add the spinach. Season with salt and pepper and a dash of nutmeg.

● Preheat oven to 325°F., 165°C. or 4 Regulo.

● Butter a baking dish with the last of the butter. Spread the spinach on the bottom of the dish. Add the rolled slices of ham and cover with the hot sauce. Reheat, well covered, in the oven for just a few minutes. *Do not let the ham boil.*

JELLIED TERRINE OF HAM
(Terrine de Jambon en Gelée)

For a picnic bring the terrine along in a cooler. Do not unmold.

■ Easy
6 to 8 servings
Medium expensive
15 minutes, plus an overnight stay in the refrigerator to set the dish
Best season: summer to early fall

US 1¼ cups, UK 1 cup, bouillon (.25 L)
US 1¼ cups, UK 1 cup, dry white wine (.25 L)
4 tsp. unflavored gelatin
salt
coarsely ground pepper
1 lb. boiled ham, preferably with some fat (500 g)
1 large bouquet of parsley leaves
fresh tarragon leaves

DO YOU PLAN A LARGE PARTY?
This keeps so well in the refrigerator, do not hesitate to double or even triple these proportions.

- Prepare the jelly as follows: Heat the bouillon. Soften the gelatin in the white wine and add to the hot bouillon; stir until well dissolved. Let cool. Add salt and pepper to taste; be generous with the pepper.
- Pour about one third of this mixture into a 1-quart terrine, and let it set in the refrigerator.
- Chop the ham in irregular pieces; if it has some fat, leave it on also. Chop the parsley and mix with the ham.
- Take the terrine out of the refrigerator and dip some of the leaves of tarragon into the remaining jelly. Arrange them attractively on the already set jelly. Then add the ham and parsley. Gently pour the cool unset jelly over the ham. Pack well with your hand, cover with a sheet of plastic wrap, and refrigerate overnight.
- To serve, pass a hot knife blade around the dish and unmold onto a chilled platter.

HAM SLICES IN PORT SAUCE
(Jambon au Porto)

Vegetable suggestions: braised lettuce, braised zucchini, braised endives would be very complementary to this dish.

- Easy
  6 servings
  Thrift recipe
  20 minutes
  Best season: year around

  12 slices of boiled ham
  US 3 TB, UK 1½ TB, butter (45 g)
  US 2½ TB, UK 1¼ TB, flour (22 g)
  US 1½ cups, UK 1⅓ cups, hot bouillon
     (3.5 dl)
  salt and pepper
  US ½ cup, UK ⅓ cup, white Port (1
     generous dl)
  US ½ cup, UK ⅓ cup, heavy cream (110 g)

YOU CAN USE ANY
ham or pork shoulder left over and thinly sliced.

Also, if you use cubes for bouillon, use only part of one for ham is very salty.

- To *heat the ham:* roll the slices into "cigars," and put them on a plate. Cover the plate with another plate inverted, and set over a saucepan full of water kept simmering.

- *Make the sauce:* Melt the butter in a saucepan. Add the flour and mix the roux well. Cook the flour until light golden, then add the hot bouillon with a whisk and stir until the mixture comes back to a boil. Add salt and pepper to taste and gradually add two thirds of the Port and let cook for a few minutes. Then off the heat add the cream and the remainder of the Port. Reheat very well but do not reboil. Correct the seasoning.

- Pour one quarter of the sauce into a baking dish buttered with 1 tablespoon of butter. Add the ham rolls and top with the remainder of the sauce. Serve immediately.

SAUSAGE SKEWERS AGEN STYLE
(Brochettes d'Agen)

Would you rather, instead of brushing the oil on the ingredients of the brochettes, put the oil in a bowl and toss everything in it before skewering? You will use less oil.

Also, Agen, in the valley of the river Garonne, is the major area of prune-plum production in France.

- Easy
  6 servings
  Thrift recipe
  30 minutes
  Best season: late summer and fall with tomatoes and peppers

  2 dozen soft pitted prunes
  water
  12 links of Italian sausage
  3 tomatoes or 12 cherry tomatoes
  3 red or green sweet bell peppers
  3 white boiling onions
  2 bay leaves, cracked in small pieces
  salt and pepper
  olive oil

THE BEST CHOICES HERE ARE
Italian fennel-flavored sausage links ¾ inch in diameter and 3½ inches long, but any other sausage of your choice will do.

If you can find them, try cherry tomatoes instead of large tomatoes, they need not be cut and they broil so well.

- Put the prunes to soak in just enough water to cover them for 1 hour.
- Preheat the broiler.
- Cut the Italian sausages into 1-inch pieces, about 3 pieces per sausage.
- Wash the tomatoes and cut them into quarters, or if you use cherry tomatoes, keep them whole.
- Cut the peppers into 1-inch strips, removing all seeds and ribs in the process.
- Peel the onions; cut them into quarters.
- On each of 6 skewers, thread a piece of sausage, a prune, an onion quarter, another piece of sausage, a piece of tomato, a piece of pepper and end with a piece of sausage. Here and there, squeeze a bit of bay leaf between the other ingredients.
- Sprinkle with salt and pepper, brush with oil, and set the skewers on the rack of your broiler pan.
- Broil 4 inches from the source of heat for a total of 10 minutes, turning the skewers over halfway through the cooking.

SAUSAGES IN WHITE-WINE SAUCE
(Saucisses au Vin Blanc)

This recipe comes from the Savoie. It is one of its great regional recipes. It is served there with a pot of noodles.

■ Easy
6 servings
Thrift recipe
25 minutes
Best season: year around

12 links of Italian sausage
water
US 2 TB, UK 1 TB, butter (30 g)
1 onion, finely chopped
US 2 TB, UK 1 TB, flour (15 g)
US 1¼ cups, UK 1 generous cup, dry
**   white wine (3.5 dl)**
salt and pepper

INSTEAD OF SAUSAGE LINKS
Instead of links, you can use patties made with sausage meat, lightly floured. In this case you will need no flour for the thickening of your gravy.

- Prick the sausage skins with the tines of a fork so they do not burst open during the cooking.
- Put US 1 cup, UK 1 scant cup, cold water (3 dl) in a skillet. Add the sausages and bring slowly to a boil. The fat will slowly ooze out of the sausages. Let them cook gently in that fat until they are nice and golden. The sausages will be done in 10 to 15 minutes.
- Remove the sausages to a plate. Discard the fat and replace it by the butter. Add the onion and sauté it until soft.
- Add the flour and cook for a few minutes. Finally add the white wine, off the heat, Whisk until the mixture is homogenous and bring to a boil. Simmer for a few minutes. Add pepper and salt if necessary. Return the sausages to the pan to reheat in the sauce.

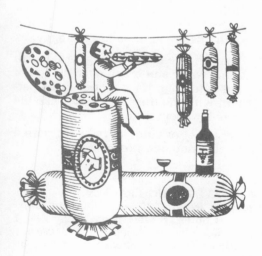

EASTER PÂTÉ FROM THE BERRY
(Pâté de Pâques du Berry)

Should the top of the pâté color too fast toward the end of the cooking, cover it with a loose-fitting sheet of foil, shiny side up.

■ Difficult
6 to 8 servings
Medium expensive
2½ hours
Best season: a specialty for Easter

4 whole eggs
1 extra egg yolk
5 oz. sausage meat (150 g)
3½ oz. boiled ham in one piece (100 g)
5 oz. boneless raw veal (150 g)
1 onion
several sprigs of parsley
3 slices of white bread, without crusts
milk
salt and pepper
quatre-épices
Pastry: enough for two 10-inch pies (see note below)

- Hard-boil 3 eggs in boiling salted water for 10 minutes.
- Cut the meats into small pieces and grind them. Also grind the onion and parsley. Add the bread soaked in milk, squeezed dry, and crumbled well.
- Mix all those ingredients very well; add salt, pepper and quatre-épices to taste and 1 raw egg. Mix to obtain a smooth forcemeat. Test a bit of the forcemeat to check the seasoning.
- Preheat oven to 375°F., 200°C. or 5 to 6 Regulo.
- Also butter a baking sheet.
- Roll out the pastry to a thickness of ⅛ inch. Cut it into 2 rectangles, one of which should be 1 inch wider than the other one. Cut a hole at the center of the smaller rectangle.
- With the rolling pin transfer each rectangle to a floured sheet of paper and refrigerate both for 30 minutes.

- Meanwhile peel the hard-boiled eggs and cut ½ inch of white off each of their ends, so they will fit into each other when you put them in the forcemeat.
- When the pastry has cooled properly, set the larger rectangle on the buttered baking sheet. Put half of the forcemeat on the sheet, leaving 2 inches free of the forcemeat around the edge of the pastry. Arrange the eggs end on end on the forcemeat. Cover with the remainder of the forcemeat.
- Brush the edge of the pastry with water and put the second rectangle of pastry over the forcemeat. Lift the edge of the bottom layer of pastry and fold it over the top one. Apply a pattern of fork tines, pressing down to seal the layers of pastry together.
- Roll a small piece of foil into a small tube and fit it into the hole previously cut in the top rectangle of pastry. This little "chimney" will keep the meat juices from running down over the top of the pastry and making it soggy.
- Beat the remaining egg yolk with some water and brush over the top of the pâté, then trace a criss-cross pattern with the tines of a fork. Bake the pâté for about 1 hour.
- Serve hot or cold, and always with a lively crisp and green salad.

TO HAVE ENOUGH PASTRY
prepare it with 2½ cups flour, 12 tablespoons butter, 6 tablespoons water and 1 teaspoon salt (see method, p. 48). Or use any prepackaged pastry or frozen pastry that you like.

VEAL
(Le Veau)

COOKING METHODS FOR VEAL

The cuts of veal in France are very different from the cuts of veal in England and America. Here is a list of the common cuts to be found in English-speaking countries and recommended methods of cooking them.

CUT	COOKING METHOD
Veal Shoulder	Pot-Roasting
	Braising
	Fricassee or Blanquette (cubes)
Veal Rib	Roasting
	Panfrying (chops or steaks)
Veal Loin	Panfrying (sirloin or tenderloin steaks)
Veal Leg:	
Top Round	Panfrying (steaks, escalopes)
Bottom Round	Panfrying (steaks, escalopes)
Shank	Braising

Broiled
Large European-size chops, broil for 5 to 6 minutes per side. Small American-size chops are better prepared in a frying pan.

Panfried
Large European-size chops, ½ to ¾ inch thick, panfry for 5 minutes on each side.
Small American-size chops, ½ inch thick, panfry for 4 minutes on each side.
Scallops or *escalopes*, European, ⅓ inch thick, panfry for 3 minutes on each side.
Scaloppine Italian and American, ¼ inch thick, panfry for 2 minutes on each side.

Poached
This method applies to veal shoulder cut into cubes for *blanquette*. Cook in barely simmering stock or water for 50 minutes to 1 hour and 10 minutes, depending on the quality of the veal. *In a pressure cooker*, 20 minutes will be sufficient.

Sautés and Stews
From 50 minutes to 1 hour, depending on the age and quality of the meat. *In the pressure cooker*, 20 minutes will be sufficient.

ROAST SADDLE OF VEAL CREOLE STYLE
(Selle de Veau à la Créole)

About the gravy: A fine piece of meat of this high a quality, roasted at a high temperature, releases very little moisture and as a result the quantity of gravy is very small. To prepare more gravy have a small pot of very lightly salted bouillon and add it to the roasting pan after the roast has been seared for 20 minutes. If you add to it a sautéed chopped onion, the taste will be even better.

- Relatively easy
  6 servings
  Very expensive
  1 hour
  Best season: year around

  US 2 TB, UK 1 TB, dark raisins (50 g)
  US 2 TB, UK 1 TB, light raisins (50 g)
  2 oz. dark rum (.75 dl)
  1 saddle (pic) of veal, boned
  4 thin rashers of bacon, rindless
  pepper from the mill
  US 4 TB, UK 2 TB, butter (60 g)
  salt
  1 tsp. paprika
  bouillon as needed (see advice)
  1 onion, chopped (see advice)

THIS CUT OF VEAL
is made up of the sirloin strip and the belly flap or flanken. As you roll the piece of meat around the sirloin strip, the belly flap will be on the outside and keep the strip nice and tender while roasting. Have the butcher remove the backbone for you. Ask him for a good piece of string to tie the roast.

- Soak the raisins in 1 ounce of the rum while the roast bakes.
- Preheat oven to 400°F., 220°C. or 6 Regulo.
- Spread the saddle of veal on the table top upside-down. Lay the rashers of bacon on the inside, add a few turns of pepper from the mill, and roll the roast starting with the thick meaty sirloin strip. Tie well crosswise.
- Spread the roast with butter, salt and pepper it. Put it to roast for about 20 minutes, then add 1 ounce of rum to the roasting pan. Baste with the juices in the roasting pan and continue roasting for another 25 minutes.
- Check the doneness of the roast by inserting a skewer at the center of the meat; the juices are clear when the meat is done.
- Remove the roast to a platter. Pour the cooking juices of the roast into a small saucepan, straining them through a conical strainer. Add the raisins and the paprika. Add also the rum in which the raisins soaked. Boil hard for a minute to evaporate the alcohol, and season with salt and pepper to your taste.
- Pour the sauce into a heated sauceboat. Remove the strings from the meat and slice it.

BASQUE COUNTRY VEAL ROAST
(Veau Basquaise)

The recipe is from the Basque country which straddles the border of Spain and France across the Western Pyrénées. The sauce being highly seasoned, serve with it a plain blanched vegetable such as cauliflower, or plain rice or potatoes.

■ Easy
6 servings
Expensive
2 hours and 10 minutes, 45 minutes in pressure cooker
Best season: year around

1 can (8 oz.) tuna (250 g)
1 large onion
US 2 TB, UK 1 TB, butter (30 g)
US ¼ cup, UK 2 TB, olive oil (2 TB)
1 rolled veal roast, 2 lbs. (1 kg)
5 anchovies, preserved in oil
US 1¼ cups, UK 1 cup, dry white wine (3 dl)
salt and pepper
1 large lemon
3 oz. sour dill pickles, chopped fine (100 g)

TO BE THRIFTY
A rolled veal loin is expensive; you can replace it by a piece of bottom round or a rolled shoulder. You can also limit expenses by using light tuna.

Do not hesitate to increase the ingredients to have more servings since the dish is excellent when served cold.

- Empty the can of tuna onto a plate; mash finely using a fork. Peel and mince the onion.
- Heat the butter and 2 tablespoons of olive oil well in a braising pot; brown the roast well in this mixture of hot fats.
- Arrange the tuna, anchovies and minced onion around the veal roast; add the white wine and salt and pepper to taste. Bring to a boil, cover the pot, reduce to a simmer, and let cook gently for about 2 hours, *30 minutes in the pressure cooker.*
- Remove the meat from the pot; keep it warm.
- Pour the gravy into a blender container and process until smooth. Return the gravy to the pot, add the juice of the lemon, the remaining olive oil and the chopped pickles. Whisk the sauce over heat until hot. Correct the seasoning.
- Slice the veal; arrange the slices on a serving platter and coat them with the sauce.

STUFFED SHOULDER OF VEAL
(Épaule de Veau Farcie)

This is as good cold as it is hot and perfect for a summer luncheon or buffet dinner or even a nice picnic. For the dish in its cold version, you may want to use olives stuffed with anchovies, in which case you will not blanch them. Cold dishes always need more seasoning than hot dishes.

- A bit difficult
  6 servings
  Medium expensive
  2 hours, 1¼ hours in pressure cooker
  Best season: fall and winter

  US ½ cup, UK ⅓ cup, centers of white
      French bread (50 g)
  a little milk for soaking
  3 dozen green olives
  1 garlic clove
  a few parsley sprigs
  5 oz. liver of your choice (150 g)
  5 to 6 oz. sausage meat (150 to 180 g)
  1 egg
  salt and pepper
  1 shoulder of veal, boned
  US 4 TB, UK 2 TB, butter (60 g)
  US 2 TB, UK 1 TB, oil (1 TB)
  US ½ cup, UK ⅓ cup, hot water (1
      generous dl)

- Soak the bread in the milk. Pit the olives and blanch them in boiling water for 2 minutes.

- Peel and chop the garlic. Chop the parsley. Cut the liver into ¼-inch cubes (you will need a chopping board and a good sharp knife for this operation).

- In a bowl put the bread after squeezing most of the milk out of it, the sausage meat, liver, egg, garlic and parsley, salt and pepper to taste, and a dozen or so of the olives cut into slices. Mix well.

- Spread the boned shoulder on the table, forming a sheet of meat as even as possible. Salt and pepper it. Put the forcemeat at the center of the meat shaped like a huge cigar tapered at both ends.

- Roll the shoulder around the filling and sew the piece of meat closed, leaving 6 inches of thread free at each end.

- Heat the mixture of oil and butter very well and brown the shoulder well on all sides. Season with salt and pepper. Add the remainder of the olives and the hot water. Cover. Reduce the heat as soon as the boiling point is reached and let cook gently for 1¼ hours. Toward the end of the cooking time, insert a skewer at the center of the meat; the meat is done if the skewer is hot and the juices run clear and without a trace of blood. *In the pressure cooker, count 45 minutes.*

- To serve, cut the meat into rather thick slices. Defatten the gravy well and serve it and the olives in a sauceboat.

TO BONE THE SHOULDER
Do not hesitate to ask the butcher to remove the bone for you; he will do in a minute what would take you a good half hour.

As a choice of liver, you can think of calf's, pork or chicken livers.

STUFFED VEAL BREAST
(Poitrine de Veau Farcie)

For a delicious vegetable, peel small potatoes and bake them in the gravy of the roast. They will be delicious.

■ A bit difficult
6 to 8 servings
Medium expensive
2 hours
Best season: fall and winter

1 veal breast, about 3 lbs (1.5 kg)
salt and pepper
US ½ cup, UK ⅓ cup, centers of white or French bread (6 TB)
milk for soaking
3½ oz. sausage meat (100 g)
3½ oz. liver of your choice (veal, pork, chicken) (100 g)
3½ oz. chopped veal meat (100 g)
1 egg
1 onion
1 large garlic clove
chopped parsley
butter
hot salted water or bouillon

- Have the butcher cut a pocket between the bone and the meat of the breast. Salt and pepper the inside of the pocket.
- Soak the bread in just enough milk to saturate it.
- Crumble the sausage into a bowl. Chop the liver into ¼-inch cubes, and add it with the chopped veal to the same bowl. Add the soaked bread and 1 egg.
- Chop the onion, garlic and parsley very finely. Stir into the forcemeat and mix very well (see p. 298). Season well with salt and pepper.
- Fill the pocket of the veal with the forcemeat. Tie the breast like a package all around in both directions. Then slide a sheet of parchment paper over the forcemeat where it peeks out of the pocket. Spread butter over the top of the meat.
- Preheat oven to 400°F., 220°C. or 6 Regulo. Place the breast on the bottom of a roasting pan; sear for 20 minutes.
- Reduce heat to 350°F., 180°C. or 5 Regulo, and continue baking for another 1 to 1½ hours.
- Baste at regular intervals, using the juices accumulating in the roasting pan. Remove parchment paper for the last half hour of roasting.
- To serve, untie the roast and cut into thick slices between the ribs of the veal.
- Prepare a small gravy by adding some hot, salted water or bouillon to the roasting pan and deglazing well. Strain this gravy into a boat, correct the seasoning, and pass separately.

WITH THE SAME METHOD
Veal Breast Stuffed with Spinach: Prepare a forcemeat with 3½ ounces boiled ham (100 g), ½ pound chopped spinach, fresh or frozen (250 g), 3½ ounces sausage meat (100 g), 3½ ounces chopped veal (100 g), 1 egg, 1 onion, chopped, and salt and pepper to taste. Use this forcemeat to stuff the veal breast. Proceed as above.

IF YOU PREFER A LESS BULKY
roast, have the butcher bone the breast completely. To stuff it, lay it flat on the table and roll the stuffing in it. You will then be able to use the pressure cooker; the meat will cook in just about 1 hour.

BROILED VEAL CHOPS MAÎTRE d'HÔTEL
(Côtes de Veau Grillées Maître d'Hôtel)

As a vegetable, any sautéed mushroom, whether cultivated or wild, would be the best garnish for these chops. Pasta is also very good in winter.

- Easy
  6 servings
  Expensive
  20 minutes
  Best season: year around

  US 10 TB, UK 5 TB, butter (150 g)
  salt and pepper
  6 veal chops
  US ½ cup, UK 4 TB, dry bread crumbs (4 TB)
  US 2 TB, UK 1 TB, water (1 TB)
  US 1 to 2 TB, UK ½ to 1 TB, lemon juice (½ to 1 TB)
  watercress bunches

A THRIFTY COOK
keeps all the heels of bread, dries them lightly in the oven, and processes them in the blender or with a rolling pin to obtain dry bread crumbs (see p. 294).

- Preheat the broiler.
- Melt half of the butter over low heat. Turn the heat off as soon as it is liquid.
- Salt and pepper the chops, roll them in the melted butter, then immediately after in the dry bread crumbs.
- Broil the chops 6 inches from the source of heat for 7 to 8 minutes on each side. The veal may remain light pink but should not be rare or bloody.
- Make the sauce: Put the water and the lemon juice in a small pot. Add salt and pepper to taste. Bring to a boil, then add remaining butter, whisking the sauce and keeping it at a high boil until the butter has been completely added.
- Put the chops on a watercress-garnished platter and serve the sauce in a small boat.

VEAL CHOPS AU GRATIN
(Côtes de Veau Gratinées)

As a vegetable serve sliced eggplants, floured and browned in olive oil, and season them with a browned persillade (see p. 302).

- Easy
  6 servings
  Expensive
  40 minutes
  Best season: late summer and fall with
     fresh sun-ripened tomatoes

  5 medium-size onions
  US 6 TB, UK 3 TB, butter (90 g)
  5 medium-size tomatoes
  6 veal chops
  flour
  salt and pepper
  US ½ cup, UK ⅓ cup, dry white wine (1
     generous dl)
  US 1 oz., UK 1 TB, dark rum, whisky, or
     Cognac (1 TB)
  US ½ cup, UK ⅓ cup, dry bread crumbs (4
     TB)
  US ½ cup, UK ⅓ cup, grated Gruyère
     cheese (4 TB)

- Preheat oven to 400°F., 220°C. or 6 Regulo.

- Peel the onions and chop coarsely. Heat a tablespoon or so of butter in a small frying pan and sauté the onions until translucent; do not let the onions take on any color. Let simmer gently until soft.

- While the onions cook, cut the tomatoes into ⅓-inch-thick slices and lightly dust the chops with a bit of flour.

- Heat 2 tablespoons butter in a large skillet and brown the chops over very high heat, so they are seared outside and remain raw at the center. Season with salt and pepper.

- Butter lightly a large baking dish. Put the chops in the dish, sprinkle the onions over, and top with the sliced tomatoes. Pour the wine mixed with the chosen spirit all around the sides of the dish. Sprinkle the tomatoes with a dash of salt and pepper and a mixture of bread crumbs and grated Gruyère.

- Bake for 25 to 30 minutes, or until the top of the dish is golden and crusty.

BE CAREFUL
You need thick large chops for this recipe; smaller chops or steaks would overcook badly.

BLANQUETTE OF VEAL
(Blanquette de Veau)

The word blanquette: it is untranslatable in English and would have to be transliterated as "white stew." The word blanc (white) is readily visible in blanquette and refers to the fact that the sauce is off-white in color.

■ Relatively easy
6 servings
Medium expensive
1½ hours, 40 minutes in pressure cooker
Best season: year around

2½ to 3 lbs. veal shoulder, cut into 1-inch
    cubes (1.25 to 1.5 kg)
water
salt
1 lemon
pepper
2 large onions
2 cloves
bouquet garni (see p. 293)
½ lb. fresh mushrooms (250 g)
US 3 TB, UK 1½ TB, cornstarch (1½ TB)
1 egg yolk
US 4 TB, UK 2 TB, heavy cream (2 TB)
freshly grated nutmeg
chopped parsley

• Immerse the veal cubes in enough water just to cover them. Add a good pinch of salt, the juice of ½ lemon, and only a bit of pepper. Bring to a boil. Skim well. Simmer for 10 minutes and skim again. Add the onions stuck with the cloves and the *bouquet garni.*

• Cover and let simmer for just about 1 hour, *20 minutes in the pressure cooker.*

• While the meat cooks, clean the mushrooms (see p. 300). Slice them and put them in a small saucepan with a bit of the meat cooking broth. Add a pinch of salt and pepper and a drop of lemon juice and let cook for 7 to 8 minutes.

• Remove the cooked meat to a bowl and strain the cooking broth into another saucepan large enough to contain the stew.

• Place the saucepan over heat and bring the broth to a simmer. Dissolve the cornstarch with a little cold water and pour this mixture into the sauce, stirring all the while. Stir until the sauce thickens.

• Add all the mushrooms and their cooking juices to the sauce. Bring back to a simmer.

• In a small bowl, mix the egg yolk and the heavy cream. Add a few tablespoons of the hot sauce, whisking very quickly to heat the yolk gradually. Then, stir this *liaison* into the bulk of the sauce, continuing to reheat gradually until one or two boils can be seen at the surface of the sauce.

• Add the meat to the sauce. Reheat until very hot, but avoid reboiling. Correct the salt and pepper and add nutmeg to your taste. If you would like, add a dash of lemon juice.

• Serve in a country-style deep dish and sprinkle with chopped parsley.

THE BEST CHOICES FOR THIS DISH
Use shoulder of veal for the meat. If you cannot find fresh mushrooms, use a can of sliced mushrooms in their canning juices (7½ oz. or 225 g).

VEAL SCALLOPS IN PORT SAUCE
(Escalopes au Porto)

In a hurry? Use a can of mushrooms.

Green beans or artichoke bottoms are two vegetable garnishes especially well suited to this dish.

■ Easy
  6 servings
  Very expensive
  15 minutes
  Best season: year around

  ½ lb. fresh mushrooms (250 g) (see advice)
  US 4 TB, UK 2 TB, butter (60 g)
  salt and pepper
  US 6 TB, UK 3 TB, white Port (1 scant dl)
  US ⅓ cup, UK 3 TB, heavy cream (75 g)
  flour seasoned with salt and pepper
  1 veal top of the round, cut into escalopes (see note below)

USE A VEAL "TOP"
Veal top or top of the round, 8 inches long and 5 to 6 inches wide, and cut into slices or scallops approximately ⅓ inch thick against the grain of the meat. A veal steak cut out of either the top or bottom round is called an escalope in French.

- Clean the mushrooms (see p. 300). Slice them.

- Heat one third of the butter in a skillet, add the mushrooms, sprinkle with salt and pepper, and cook until mushrooms lose their moisture. Add half of the Port and all the cream and let reduce until you have a saucelike consistency. Remove to a bowl. Wash the skillet.

- Flour the veal scallops lightly with the seasoned flour.

- Heat the remainder of the butter in the skillet. Brown the scallops until golden on each side. Remove to a plate.

- Pour the remainder of the Port wine into the frying pan and deglaze the pan with it, boiling hard for a minute or so. Now add the mushroom sauce and the meat and reheat well together without boiling. The meat will harden if it boils. Serve immediately.

VEAL STEAKS MIMOLETTE
(Escalopes Mimolette)

The veal will finish cooking properly from the heat of the mushroom ragout and that of the oven. Do not let the cheese heat beyond the melting point or it will turn hard and bitter.

■ A bit difficult
6 servings
Expensive
30 minutes
Best season: fall and winter

½ lb. fresh mushrooms (250 g)
3 onions
US 4 TB, UK 2 TB, butter (60 g)
salt and pepper
5 oz. fresh chicken livers (150 g)
flour
12 veal steaks, ⅓ inch thick by 5 to 6
  inches long
US ½ cup, UK ⅓ cup, water (1 generous
  dl)
1 tsp. cornstarch
US 1 oz., UK 1 TB, Cognac or other spirit
  (1 TB)
12 slices ⅙ inch thick, of Mimolette or
  Gouda cheese

• Prepare the mushrooms (see p. 300). Slice them. Peel the onions and cut into thin slices.

• Heat half of the butter in a frying pan. Sauté the onions in it. Salt and pepper them. Turn the heat down and let the onions cook until translucent. Add the mushrooms; cook them gently so that they lose all their moisture.

• Cut the chicken livers into ¼-inch cubes. Set them aside on a plate.

• Flour the veal steaks, patting them carefully to discard excess flour. Heat the remainder of the butter in another large skillet or electric frying pan. Sear the steaks and let them cook for 2 minutes on each side. They should not be quite done at their center so they can continue cooking while they are in the oven.

• Remove steaks to a baking dish; replace them with the cubed livers; toss very quickly. Spread livers over the slices of meat. Salt and pepper both meats.

• Pour the water into the same frying pan to deglaze all the meat juices, then add the mushroom and onion mixture. Simmer together for a few minutes.

• In a small bowl, mix a teaspoon or so of cornstarch with the Cognac and add it to the simmering mushrooms. Correct the salt and pepper and cook for 1 more minute. Spoon sauce evenly over the steaks.

• Set the slices of Mimolette over the mushrooms and slide the baking dish under the broiler until the cheese starts melting.

YOU NEED
thick steaks cut against the grain of the veal top. You can cut these yourself if your knife is very sharp.

Mimolette is a French cousin to Gouda. If you cannot find one, replace it by the other.

Chicken livers must be cleaned of all green traces of bile and gall bladder.

SIRLOIN OR TENDERLOIN OF VEAL STEAKS WITH BABY PEAS
(Grenadins de Veau aux Petits Pois)

Just as there are two ways of cooking beef steaks, there are two ways of cooking veal steaks. Contemporary French cuisine prefers the steaks medium rare, still pink and juicy at the center. The still classic cuisine of 30 to 50 years ago preferred veal done to the center. Choose what answers best to your personal taste.

- Easy
  6 servings
  Extremely expensive
  45 minutes
  Best season: year around

  1 package (10 oz.) frozen baby peas (300 g), or 1½ lbs. fresh peas in pods (750 g)
  2 packages (10 oz. each) frozen artichoke hearts (300 g each), or 2 dozen fresh baby artichokes
  US 6 TB, UK 3 TB, butter (90 g)
  bouillon or water
  ½ lemon
  salt and pepper
  fresh chopped tarragon or revived dried tarragon
  6 slices of veal, ⅓ inch thick, trimmed
  US ½ cup, UK ⅓ cup, heavy cream (125 g)

THE WORD GRENADIN
designates in French a small steak cut out of the tenderloin. By extension it is also applied to steaks cut out of the sirloin strip and out of the top of the round.

If you use fresh peas and fresh baby artichokes, add 30 minutes to your preparation time to shell, pare, and blanch both vegetables.

- Defrost both baby peas and artichokes under running cold water.
- Melt and heat half of the butter in a large saucepan. Add both peas and artichokes, a few tablespoons bouillon or water, a squeeze of lemon juice, salt and pepper to taste and half of the chopped tarragon. Cover and simmer together until very hot and until the artichoke hearts are tender.
- In a large skillet, melt the remainder of the butter and add the veal slices; sear them well on both sides, salt and pepper them, and reduce the heat for 1 to 2 minutes (see advice).
- Remove the steaks to a heated platter. Add the cream to the frying pan and scrape well to deglaze the meat juices (see p. 296). Add the remainder of the tarragon. Correct the seasoning.
- Serve the veal steaks surrounded by the peas and the artichoke hearts. Serve the sauce in a boat.

VEAL LOAF
(Pain de Veau)

If you bake in the pressure cooker, cover the top of the loaf with a sheet of foil, dull side up, and tie it securely all around the edges of the mold. Fill the pressure cooker with water to reach halfway to the top edge of the mold.

■ Easy
6 servings
Relatively expensive
1 hour and 20 minutes, 55 minutes in pressure cooker
Best season: year around

4 slices of white bread
milk
2 onions
1 garlic clove
¼ lb. mushrooms (125 g)
several sprigs of parsley
1 lb. boneless veal, ground (500 g)
3½ oz. sausage meat (100 g)
2 eggs
salt and pepper
quatre-épices
US 1 TB, UK ½ TB, butter (15 g)

- Preheat oven to 400°F., 220°C. or 6 Regulo.
- Remove crusts from bread and soak the crumbs in just enough milk to cover them. Squeeze them dry. Crumble well.
- Chop the onions and the garlic as well as the mushrooms and the parsley.
- In a bowl, mix very well the meats, chopped vegetables, bread crumbs, eggs, salt and pepper to taste and a good dash of *quatre-épices*.
- Butter heavily a glass or porcelain loaf pan and pack the mixture in it.
- Bake in the oven for about 1 hour. Should the loaf cook too fast, cover it with a sheet of foil, shiny side up.
- To serve, unmold the loaf and slice it.

THIS VEAL LOAF
is good hot as well as cold and does well with a good tomato sauce (see p. 61) when served hot, or an herb mayonnaise when served cold. Should you have to extend the recipe to feed more people, add another 3 ounces of sausage meat (90 g) and 1 more egg.

VEAL KIDNEYS FLANDERS STYLE
(Rognons de Veau des Flandres)

This recipe is a favorite in Flanders, which spreads over the upper Northern part of France and Southern Belgium. The gin used to prepare this dish can be either regular English style or Dutch gin, which is more often used there.

■ Difficult
6 servings
Expensive
20 minutes
Best season: year around

6 large veal kidneys
5 oz. pork brisket or bacon (150 g)
2 dozen juniper berries
US 4 TB, UK 2 TB, butter (60 g)
flour for dusting the kidneys
salt and pepper
1 oz. gin of your choice (1 TB) (see advice)
chopped parsley

- Cut kidneys lengthwise into halves. With sharp scissors remove all the white tissues. Set aside on a plate after snipping all around with the scissors to make sure that the kidneys will lie flat.

- Cut the pork brisket or bacon into strips ⅓ x 1 inch, and slowly render until golden. Remove to a plate.

- Crush the juniper berries.

- Discard the bacon fat; replace it by the butter. Flour the kidneys and put them to cook over medium heat for no more than 2½ minutes on each side. Sprinkle with salt and pepper.

- Return the bacon to the pan; add the juniper berries.

- Last pour the gin into the pan, tilt the pan, and ignite the gin. Shake the pan back and forth until the flames die.

- Serve sprinkled with chopped parsley. Accompany with braised endives (p. 222), braised lettuce or creamed mushrooms.

NOT A CHILDREN'S CHARMER

THE DIFFICULTY LIES
in not overcooking the kidneys. Be careful and very gentle.

BRAINS IN BROWN BUTTER
(Cervelles à la Meunière)

Would you like to make things easier? Then poach the brains ahead of time and cool them so they are cold and very firm when you are ready to flour and sauté them.

■ Easy
6 servings
Very affordable
1 hour
Best season: year around

3 veal brains
vinegar
1 onion
1 clove
1 carrot
thyme
bay leaf
1 lemon
½ generous quart water (.5 L)
salt and pepper
flour
US ½ cup, UK ⅓ cup, butter (120 g)
parsley bouquets

• Soak the brains in lightly vinegared water for at least 30 minutes.

• Peel the onion, stick the clove in it, and cut into quarters. Peel the carrot and cut it into thick slices.

• Put the carrot, onion quarters, thyme, bay leaf, 1 thick slice of lemon and a generous ½ quart of water (.5 L) in a large saucepan. Add salt and pepper to taste. Bring to a boil and simmer for 15 minutes. This will constitute a court-bouillon (see p. 295).

• Remove the skin on top of each brain by sliding your index finger under the skin after you cut an opening approximately ½ inch wide in it on the underside of each brain along the medulla. Move the tip of your finger back and forth and you will see the skin lifting easily.

• Immerse the brains in the *court-bouillon*. Bring the bouillon to a bare simmer, but do not boil. Let brains poach for 20 to 25 minutes.

• Drain the brains, cut them into thick slices, and flour them.

• Heat two thirds of the butter in a large skillet. Put the slices of brains in the hot butter and let them turn golden on each side.

• Serve on a hot platter decorated with parsley bouquets. Add the remainder of the butter and a good squeeze of lemon juice to the frying pan and heat until the butter turns to hazelnut butter. Add salt and pepper and pour over the meat.

• Serve with steamed buttered potatoes, heavily parsleyed.

NOT A CHILDREN'S FAVORITE
You can use the same method for veal, lamb or beef brains. Make sure that they are fresh, with a clean smell and as few traces of blood under the membrane as possible. If your choice is frozen brains, put them to soak while they are solidly frozen; they will defrost as they soak. Change the water twice during soakings.

CALF'S LIVER PROVENÇALE
(Foie de Veau à la Provençale)

In winter prepare the same dish using a large can of the Italian or Mediterranean pear-shaped tomatoes known as pelati. You may use all kinds of dried herbs to perk up the sauce, in moderate amounts to obtain a pleasant blend. Try alone or in combination: fennel seeds, mint, orégano, basil, rosemary, marjoram and any of the sweet herbs such as tarragon.

■ Relatively easy
6 servings
Medium expensive
40 minutes
Best season: late summer to early fall with
sun-ripened tomatoes

8 large tomatoes
2 onions
3 garlic cloves
US 6 TB, UK 3 TB, olive oil (3 TB)
salt and pepper
bouquet garni
18 black olives
flour
6 pretty slices of calf's liver
chopped parsley

• Wash the tomatoes, remove the stem ends, and cut them into quarters. Squeeze water and seeds out. Peel and chop onions and garlic.

• Heat one third of the olive oil in an enameled cast-iron pot. Add the onions and garlic and brown lightly. Add the tomatoes, toss well. Add salt, pepper and *bouquet garni*. Cover and reduce the heat as soon as the boiling point has been reached. Cook for 30 minutes.

• Meanwhile, pit the black olives, flour the slices of liver, and have them ready to use.

• When the tomatoes are cooked, purée them through a food mill or a strainer to obtain a smooth purée. Correct the seasoning; if too liquid do not hesitate to reduce the purée a little to concentrate the flavor and thicken the texture.

• Add the olives to the sauce just long enough to reheat them without boiling them.

• Heat the remainder of the oil in a large skillet, and very quickly sauté the slices of liver. They should remain pink throughout; watch over- or under-cooking. Season only after you have seared the meat.

• Pour the tomato sauce into a shallow serving platter or dish. Add the liver slices and sprinkle with chopped parsley.

CALF'S LIVER
is the best looking, the best tasting. Make sure that you buy large slices 7 inches long and 2 to 3 inches wide and that you remove the surrounding membrane.

Although it is so good for them, children may give you some difficulty.

BRAISED VEAL TONGUE
(Langue de Veau Braisée aux Carottes)

In American markets tongues are very often sold already soaked and cleaned. You will be able to see for yourself whether this has been done: the underside of the tongue will show no trace of blood. In European shops, the tongues are more often sold without presoaking. Soaking serves to dissolve and flush away any blood on the connective tissue.

- A bit difficult
  6 servings
  Affordable
  2½ hours, 1 hour in pressure cooker, plus 2 hours for soaking tongues
  Best season: fall and winter

  as many veal tongues as needed depending on size (see note below)
  water
  vinegar
  1 gelatinous veal bone
  5 oz. fresh pork brisket or bacon (150 g)
  6 white onions
  12 carrots
  US 2 TB, UK 1 TB, butter (30 g)
  salt and pepper
  US ⅔ cup, UK ½ cup, dry white wine (2 scant dl)
  bouillon or water
  bouquet garni

CHOOSE AS WELL AS YOU CAN
The size of the tongue varies with the size of the carcass of the animal. Use 2 or 3 larger tongues or 1 small one per person.

Tongues make excellent eating when cold with salad dressing and salad greens.

Most children like it.

- Soak the tongues in water for 2 hours, adding a few drops of vinegar (see advice).

- Put the tongues and the veal bone in a pot, cover with cold water, bring to a boil, and blanch for 10 minutes. Rinse under cold water and remove the skin as well as all the connective tissues on the underside of the tongue.

- Cut the brisket or bacon into pieces ⅓ x 1 inch (lardoons). Peel the onions and carrots and cut both of them into thick slices.

- Render the bacon or pork lardoons slowly, adding a bit of butter if necessary. Sauté them until golden. Add the onions and carrots and sauté until golden. Add the tongues and salt and pepper to taste.

- Add the white wine, bouillon or water, the veal bone and *bouquet garni*. Bring to a boil, add a bit of salt and pepper, cover, and cook slowly until the tongues are tender when tested with a skewer. Check once in a while to make sure that no more liquid is needed.

- To serve, cut the tongues into slices and arrange on a platter surrounded with the carrots and onions. Serve the cooking juices in a sauceboat with a separator lip.

- Potatoes or rice make a good second vegetable.

VEAL SWEETBREADS WITH MUSHROOMS
(Ris de Veau aux Champignons)

The French favorite vegetable with sweetbreads is fine baby peas, but fine green beans or plain sautéed spinach leaves would also be extremely good.

■ A bit difficult
6 servings
Very expensive
45 minutes, plus a few hours for soaking
Best season: year around

2 lbs. finest sweetbreads (1 kg)
cold water
¾ lb. fresh mushrooms (375 g)
US 6 TB, UK 3 TB, butter (90 g)
1 lemon
salt and pepper
flour to dust the sweetbreads
US ¾ cup, UK ⅔ cup, heavy cream (180 g)
1 oz. Cognac, Armagnac, whisky or
**   brandy**
chopped parsley

- Soak the sweetbreads in cold water for 2 to 3 hours, changing the water several times (see note below).

- Transfer the sweetbreads to a large pot. Cover them with cold water, bring slowly to a boil, and blanch in simmering water for 3 to 4 minutes. Drain the water, refresh under running cold water, and remove all tough membranes and traces of blood. Do not remove the thin outside membrane or the sweetbreads would fall apart.

- Squeeze the sweetbreads between 2 dinner plates and put a weight on top of the plate. You will see the sweetbreads lose their bloody juices, which will run very pink indeed.

- While the sweetbreads are resting, prepare the mushrooms (see p. 300).

Quarter them. Cook them in butter in a small pot with a good dash of lemon juice and salt and pepper to taste. Cover and let cook for 7 to 8 minutes, until the mushrooms are floating in their own juices. Reserve.

- Cut the sweetbreads into ⅓- to ½-inch-thick slices. Flour the slices and brown them until golden on both sides. Remove to a platter; keep warm.

- Using the same frying pan, pour in the cream, the chosen spirit and the mushrooms, and let simmer until saucelike. The sauce will coat a spoon lightly.

- Correct the salt and pepper. Add lemon juice as needed and pour the sauce over the sweetbreads. Sprinkle with chopped parsley.

NOT A CHILDREN'S CHARMER
SWEETBREADS ARE THE THYMUS GLAND
of young animals. As the animal grows the gland atrophies and shrinks. Each sweetbread is made of two parts: the heart or large sweetbread is the best and finest. The throat sweetbread, the smallest. The largest sweetbreads are the best.

Sweetbreads are sometimes sold soaked and cleaned, sometimes not. Uncleaned they are reddish and bloody. A 1-hour soaking period is recommended even if the sweetbreads appear rather clean.

POULTRY AND GAME
(La Volaille et le Gibier)

CHOOSE THE RIGHT BIRD OR GAME
FOR YOUR COOKING METHOD

CHICKEN

Chickens are very different in Europe, which still has some corn- and wheat-fed animals; American does not have them anymore. For *roasting* choose a bird of 4 to 4½ pounds maximum, a small roaster. For sautéing or fricasseeing choose broilers and fryers, whole or in pieces, 2½ to 3½ pounds maximum.

DUCK

Ducks are different in Great Britain and America from what they are in France. The French like their duck rare and, as a result, raise it so it can be cooked this way; it is slaughtered while very young and with still very little fat. The birds are then roasted very fast at 400°F., 200°C. or 6 Regulo for barely 1 hour. British and American taste runs to crisp and very well-cooked duck, which honestly can be more delicious than the French style.

The recipes here have been adapted to the second type of roasting, which is done at the medium-low temperature of 325°F., 165°C. or 4 to 5 Regulo, and which produces a lot of good gravy to make the sauces better.

TURKEY

America raises better turkeys than Europe. The best turkey for taste, flavor and texture weighs from 10 to 12 pounds.

PIGEON OR SQUAB

Fresh pigeon or squab is to be found all over Europe. In America it is usually frozen. Pigeons come in two sizes, 12 ounces and 1 pound. A 12-ounce pigeon is an adequate portion. Pigeon, like duck, is considered "red" meat in France where it is casserole roasted for no more than 15 minutes and comes to the table succulent with juices. Longer cooking is more acceptable to the British and American taste.

RABBIT

In Europe, whole rabbits are available almost everywhere. In America they are a bit more difficult to find, but Italian neighborhoods make a great specialty of it. Buy small young rabbit. Older animals do not become tender. One rabbit may be just about enough for 6 persons. Prepare plenty of vegetables to round out the meal. America produces excellent young rabbit, cut up and frozen. This rabbit must be defrosted in the refrigerator for over 24 hours. Use frozen rabbit for sautéing.

COQ AU VIN

According to many French food authorities, the original recipe for this French specialty was created at the dead center of France, in the mountainous province of Auvergne, and from there extended to all the vineyard areas of France. So that Burgundy now has Coq au Chambertin, Touraine has Coq au Chinon, etc.

■ Relatively easy
  6 servings
  Medium expensive
  1 hour and 20 minutes
  Best season: fall to June

  5 oz. slab bacon (150 g)
  2 chickens, each 3½ lbs. (about 1.5 kg each)
  24 silverskin onions
  1½ bottles of dry red wine of excellent quality
  salt and pepper
  2 garlic cloves, chopped
  thyme
  parsley
  basil
  ¾ lb. fresh mushrooms (375 g)
  1 oz. Cognac or Armagnac (1 TB)
  US 1½ TB, UK ¾ TB, butter (22 g)
  US 1½ TB, UK ¾ TB, flour (1½ TB)
  chopped parsley

CHOOSE VERY WELL
The chickens should be nice.

The wine should be of excellent quality, from either Burgundy or the Rhône valley. Offer the same wine to drink as you used to cook the chicken.

- Cut the bacon into pieces ½ x ⅓ inch. Place in a cold braising pot and render gently. Let pieces turn light golden, but not crisp. Remove to a plate.

- Meanwhile, cut the chickens into 6 pieces each and brown them well on both sides in the bacon fat. Remove to the same plate as the bacon.

- Peel the silverskin onions and sauté them until nice and golden. Remove the onions to the same plate as the bacon and chicken pieces.

- Discard the fat in the braising pot. Add the wine and salt and pepper to taste and scrape well all the meat juices at the bottom of the pot. Bring to a boil. Add the chopped garlic and salt, pepper, thyme, parsley and basil to your taste. Return the chicken pieces, bacon and onions to the pot, cover, leaving the lid slightly askew to allow for evaporation, and let cook for 20 minutes.

- Clean the mushrooms, quarter them, and add them to the pot. Let cook for another 30 minutes.

- When the chicken is nearly done add the Cognac or Armagnac and correct the seasoning.

- Remove the pieces of chicken to a country-style dish. On a plate mash the butter with the flour and add to the sauce, stirring all the while. Turn the heat off as soon as the sauce is thickened and pour it over the chicken.

- Sprinkle with chopped parsley.

CHICKEN IN COCOTTE
(Poulet Cocotte)

Only 4 guests? You can, if you want, leave out the stuffing if there are only 4 guests at the table.

To complete dinner, prepare a soup or a substantial first course and end the meal with a salad and a lovely dessert. Even if portions seem small to you, you will see that the dish really is "rich" enough to serve 6 persons.

- Easy to medium difficult
  6 servings
  Affordable
  1¼ hours
  Best season: year around

  STUFFING
  1 chicken liver
  1 chicken gizzard
  5 oz. sausage meat (150 g)
  2 slices of white bread soaked in milk
  1 onion, chopped fine
  1 garlic clove, chopped fine
  tarragon, fresh chopped or dried
  salt and pepper

  CHICKEN
  1 roaster, 4½ lbs. (2 kg)
  salt and pepper
  5 oz. slab bacon (150 g)
  3 dozen silverskin onions
  US 6 TB, UK 3 TB, butter (90 g)
  6 medium-size potatoes, preferably waxy type
  1 lb. fresh mushrooms (500 g)
  chopped parsley

- Have an 8-quart braising pot at hand, preferably oval.
- *Prepare the stuffing:* chop the liver and the gizzard very fine, mix both with the sausage, bread soaked in milk and squeezed dry, the chopped onion and garlic and the tarragon. Season well with salt and pepper. Mix until homogenous.
- Salt and pepper the cavity of the roaster and stuff with the forcemeat. Truss the chicken or sew the opening closed if it is easier for you.

- Cut the bacon into strips ⅓ x ½ inch. Let them render slowly in the braising pot until they are golden but not crisp. Remove them to a plate.
- Put the silverskin onions in the pot. When those have been well browned, remove them to the same plate as the bacon, using a slotted spoon.
- Remove the bacon fat to a large skillet and reserve it.
- Replace the bacon fat in the pot by two thirds of the butter. Heat it well and in it brown the chicken on all sides until golden brown.
- Salt and pepper the chicken. Cover the pot and let it cook over low heat for 20 minutes.
- Meanwhile, peel the potatoes and cut them into ½-inch cubes. Wash them three times in cold water to discard all the starch and pat them completely dry.
- Heat the bacon fat in the skillet, add the last tablespoon of butter, and fry the potatoes. Keep them on high heat until a crust forms all around them, then turn the heat down to cook them to their centers. Keep warm.
- Prepare the mushrooms, quarter them.
- After chicken has cooked for 20 minutes, arrange bacon pieces, onions and mushrooms around the chicken. Let the chicken finish cooking until a skewer inserted at the thickest part of the thigh lets out a clear liquid free of any traces of blood.

- Remove the chicken to a deep country-style dish. Tilt the pot and spoon two thirds of the gravy into a small boat.
- Add the potatoes to the pot and reheat well all the garnishes. Pour into the chicken dish, arranging the vegetables all around the bird. Sprinkle with chopped parsley.

WHAT IS A COCOTTE?
Besides two other meanings, one childish, the other a bit risqué, the word "cocotte" in French is. the name of a round braising pot made of cast iron. The old-style black pots are the best. The new-style, which is enameled in orange, blue, yellow or brown, is pretty enough to bring to the table.

CHICKEN IN PORT SAUCE
(Poulet au Porto)

The method used here is called "sautéing". It can be done with many, many vegetables and using a natural wine, broth, bouillon or even water, since the chicken, while cooking, builds its own gravy.

■ Easy
  6 servings
  Very affordable
  1 hour, 35 minutes in pressure cooker
  Best season: year around

  1 lb. mushrooms (500 g)
  2 chickens, each 3½ lbs. (1.5 kg each)
  US 2 TB, UK 1 TB, oil (1 TB)
  US 3 TB, UK 1½ TB, butter (45 g)
  salt and pepper
  US ¼ cup, UK 2 TB, water (.75 dl)
  US ½ cup, UK ⅓ cup, dry white Port (1 generous dl)
  1 tsp. cornstarch
  US ½ cup, UK ⅓ cup, heavy cream (75 to 80 g)
  chopped parsley

- Prepare the mushrooms (see p. 300). Quarter them.
- Cut each chicken into 6 pieces, or have the store or butcher do that for you if you prefer.
- Heat oil and butter and brown the chicken in the mixture, browning only as many pieces as will fit comfortably in the pot so the pieces do not overlap. Salt and pepper the chicken.

- Discard the fat in the pot. Add the water and half of the Port and scrape well to dissolve the juices. Add the mushrooms in a single layer and set the pieces of chicken over them. Cover and cook over gentle heat for 35 to 40 minutes.
- When the chicken is cooked, remove it to a deep country-style dish. Dilute the cornstarch with the remainder of the Port and stir into the mushroom sauce until the mixture thickens. Add the cream, correct the salt and pepper, and pour over the chicken. Sprinkle with chopped parsley.

WITH THE SAME METHOD
Follow the same method using any fortified wine such as Madeira, Marsala or Sherry, all in their dry versions.
  Or use whisky or any other spirit. Use half Port and half whisky or Cognac, Armagnac, Calvados or applejack. Bourbon is especially good. Mix cornstarch with water, then heat the spirit and pour it flaming into the pot.

ROAST CHICKEN THE FRENCH WAY
(Poulet Rôti à la Française)

To carve a chicken easily: First, remove both legs and cut through the joint of the thigh and drumstick to obtain 2 small portions on each side. Then, cutting down along the breast bone and through the wing joint, lift each breast fillet and cut each into 2 small portions. In France 1 small piece per person is customary because meals always have a first course and cheese. In English-speaking countries, we prefer a small piece each of dark and white meat.

■ Easy
6 servings
Very affordable
20 minutes per pound
Best season: year around

2 chickens, 4 lbs. each (2 kg each)
salt and pepper
water to deglaze the pan
butter
watercress

SOME CHICKENS ARE BETTER THAN OTHERS
Always choose a bird that looks "rounded" and squat, rather than long and angular.

● Preheat oven to 400°F., 220°C. or 6 to 7 Regulo.

● Season the chickens in their cavities with salt and pepper. Do not season the skin at all.

● Set the chickens on the rack of a roasting pan. Put some water in the roasting pan so the juices drip into it, forming a good gravy.

● Roast the chickens for 20 minutes per pound, which will be about 1 hour and a few minutes for our chickens. Heavier chickens cook relatively faster and you will find that a 4-pound chicken will cook just as fast as a 3½-pound chicken.

● Roast in the following positions: one third of the time resting on one side, another half of the time on the other side, and the remainder of the time breast up. When you finish the roasting, brush each chicken with a small pat of butter.

● When the birds are done, salt and pepper the skins. Remove them from the oven and cover them loosely with a sheet of foil, to allow the salt to melt. Keep the cooked chickens on a heated platter. Carve (see advice) and surround with watercress.

● Remove all the fat from the cooking juices. Add water to deglaze the roasting pan and scrape well to dissolve all the meat juices. Strain these juices into a sauceboat.

DUCK WITH CHERRIES
(Canard aux Cerises)

Sour cherries are difficult to come by. When they are in season, remove the stems, stuff them into ½-quart jars, and sterilize them in a pressure cooker for 1 minute.

■ A bit difficult
6 servings
Medium expensive
2½ hours
Best season: September to May; a bit heavy for the summer months

2 ducks, 4 lbs. each (2 kg each)
salt and pepper
water
1½ lbs. fresh sour cherries (750 g)
US 1½ cups, UK 1¼ cups, red wine (generous .25 L)
US 2 TB, UK 1 TB, sugar (1 TB)
1½ tsp. cornstarch

• Preheat oven to 325°F., 165°C. or 4 Regulo. Salt and pepper the ducks in the cavities.

• Set the ducks in the rack of a roasting pan. Add US 2 cups, UK 2 scant cups, water (.5 L) to the roasting pan. Salt and pepper the ducks.

• Roast the ducks for about 45 minutes, then prick the sides of the ducks below the breast with a skewer to release the fat. Continue roasting until the juice from the cavity runs clear. Tilt the ducks forward every half hour to release those juices into the roasting pan.

• Meanwhile, pit the cherries. Add them to a saucepan containing the red wine and the sugar. Bring slowly to a boil. When the cherries come floating to the top of the pot they will be done. Using a slotted spoon, remove the cherries to a bowl, and let the sauce reduce by about one third.

• Return the cherries to the juices and bring back to a simmer. Mix the cornstarch with a tablespoon or so of cold water and add the mixture to the simmering cherry compote. Stir until thickened. Keep warm. (See note on Slurry, p. 304.)

• Put the duck on a hot platter for serving. Keep warm.

• Empty the gravy into a measuring cup and let fat and gravy separate. With a bulb baster remove the lean gravy to the pot containing the cherry compote. Simmer together for 6 to 8 minutes.

• Spoon a bit of the cherry sauce over the duck and serve the remainder in a sauceboat.

QUANTITY TO BUY
Duck being very rich and high in calories, 1 leg of duck or 1 breast is an ample enough portion for 1 person. Two ducks will give 8 portions, the 2 additional portions can be shared by more hungry members of the family.

DUCK WITH APPLES AND CALVADOS
(Canard à la Normande)

To carve a roasted duck, first remove the legs, then, sliding the blade along the breast bone on each side of the bird, cut downward until the knife reaches the wing joint. Cut through it. This will give you one whole side of breast in one piece. In France when the duck is carved, the breast, being still rare and bright red, is cut lengthwise into paper-thin slivers called aiguillettes.

■ A bit difficult
  6 servings
  Medium expensive
  2½ hours
  Best season: September to May, a bit heavy for the summer months

  12 tart green apples
  lemon juice
  2 ducks, 4 lbs. each, with giblets (2 kg each)
  US ½ cup, UK 4 TB, butter (120 g)
  2 oz. Calvados or applejack (.75 dl)
  salt and pepper
  fresh or frozen baby peas (optional)

- Preheat oven to 325°F., 165°C. or 4 to 5 Regulo.

- Peel the apples. Cut 2 apples into 8 slices each. Sprinkle them with a drop of lemon juice.

- Cut off the strong ligaments from the gizzards and slice them into paper-thin slivers. Cut the livers also into thin slivers.

- Heat a bit of the butter in a large skillet and first brown half of the apple slices well over high heat. Remove the pan from the heat and toss in liver and gizzard slivers. Heat the Calvados in a small pot and ignite it. Pour it flaming into the apple mixture, shaking the pan very well. Cool. Correct the seasoning.

- Salt and pepper the cavities of the ducks and fill each with half of the Calvados filling.

- Roast the ducks for 2 to 2½ hours. Test the doneness by inserting a skewer at the thickest part of the legs. The duck is done when no juices ooze out of the joint.

- When the ducks are nearly cooked, heat the remainder of the butter and brown the remaining apples, cut into quarters. Reduce the heat and cook gently until the apples are tender.

- Empty the cooking juices of the duck into a measuring cup. Using a bulb baster, remove the lean juices to a small pan. Add a drop or so of Calvados and turn the heat off. Spoon a few tablespoons of the gravy over the meat and present the remainder in a sauceboat.

- As a second vegetable offer a dish of braised small peas or, if you are in a hurry, some frozen baby peas.

YOUR APPLES AND BRANDY
The apples should be of a tart breed: try Granny Smith, Greenings, Pippins, etc., or an apple from your local orchards that is not too sweet.

Calvados is a double brandy, distilled from apple cider in French Normandy; it can always be replaced by applejack.

DUCK WITH ORANGES
(Canard à l'Orange)

White "Peking" ducks are the best for slow roasting; "Muscovy" or farmyard ducks are leaner and would be better casserole-roasted like the chicken on page 172.

- A bit difficult
  6 servings
  Medium expensive
  2½ hours
  Best season: fall to early spring

  2 tart oranges
  2 ducks, 4 lbs. each, with giblets (2 kg each)
  salt and pepper
  US ¼ cup, UK 2 TB, butter (60 g)
  1 onion
  1 small carrot
  parsley stems
  thyme
  bay leaf
  US 2 TB, UK 1 TB, flour (15 g)
  US 2 cups, UK 2 scant cups, water (.5 L)
  US ½ cup, UK ⅓ cup, dry white wine (1 generous dl)
  US 1 TB, UK ½ TB, tomato paste (½ TB)
  juice of 1 lemon
  1 oz. orange liqueur of your choice (1 TB)

- Preheat oven to 325°F., 165°C. or 4 to 5 Regulo.

- Peel the rind of 2 oranges with a potato peeler, taking care not to lift any of the white pith. Put 2 large strips of rind into the cavity of each duck as well as salt and pepper.

- Chop the rind of 1 whole orange extremely fine. Put rind in a small pot, add cold water, and bring to a boil. Simmer for 2 minutes and drain. Reserve the rind.

- Remove the wingtips and the neck of the ducks. Chop them and the gizzards into small pieces. Heat three quarters of the butter in a saucepan and brown those meats well.

- Put the ducks to roast on a roasting pan fitted with a rack.

- Meanwhile, chop the onion and carrot; tie parsley, thyme and bay leaf into a *bouquet garni*. Remove the meats to a plate. Place the onion and carrot in the pot and brown them well. Add the flour and cook until light golden. Add the water, white wine, tomato paste, *bouquet garni* and the browned giblet and wing pieces, and bring to a boil. Simmer, skimming a bit, until a nice tasty sauce is obtained, about 1 hour. During the last 15 minutes of cooking, add a piece of orange rind about 1 inch long (see Brown Sauce, p. 58).

- As soon as the sauce is done, strain it into a clean pot and add the blanched chopped orange rind.

- Slice the oranges and remove all their pith and pits.

- When the ducks are cooked, empty their gravy into a measuring cup. With a bulb baster, separate gravy from fat. Add the fat-free gravy to the prepared sauce and simmer together for 10 minutes. Add a squeeze of lemon juice.

- Pour a few tablespoons of the final sauce into a skillet, and in it heat the orange slices very well. The orange slices will lose quite a bit of juice. Add the juices to the sauce as well as the ounce of orange liqueur, preheated in a small pot and ignited.

- Present the ducks on a platter decorated with the orange slices, and serve the gravy in a boat.

TURKEY WITH SAUSAGE AND CHESTNUT STUFFING
(Dinde Farcie aux Marrons)

Canned chestnuts, whole and delicious, all peeled and ready to use, can be bought in specialty grocery stores. They are sold in glass jars. To make a chestnut purée, heat the chestnuts in milk and purée them in a blender or food processor. Chestnut purée is also available in cans. Choose whichever you prefer depending on the time you have.

■ Demands attention
10 to 12 servings
Affordable to medium expensive
20 to 22 minutes per pound
Best season: fall and winter

STUFFING AND TURKEY
5 oz. sausage meat
¼ tsp. thyme
½ bay leaf, crumbled
salt and pepper
6 oz. chestnut purée (180 g)
3½ oz. boiled ham (100 g)
1 turkey, 10 lbs. (4.5 kg)
butter
salted water
¾ lb. peeled shelled chestnuts, cooked (340 g)

SAUCE
giblets and wingtips of turkey, chopped
US 1 TB, UK ½ TB, butter (½ TB)
1 onion, chopped
US ½ cup, UK ⅓ cup, dry white wine (1 generous dl)
US ½ cup, UK ⅓ cup, bouillon (1 generous dl)
bouquet garni
1½ tsp. cornstarch
US 2 TB, UK 1 TB, Cognac (1 TB)
hot water

• Put the sausage meat in a bowl, add thyme and bay leaf crumbled fine, salt and pepper to taste, and the chestnut purée; mix well. Cut the ham into ¼-inch cubes and add to the forcemeat.

• Preheat oven to 325°F., 165°C. or 4 to 5 Regulo.

• Stuff the forcemeat into the cavity. Sew the opening closed. Truss the bird and set it on its back, breast side up, on a rack fitted over the roasting pan. Spread butter all over the skin.

• Roast for an average of 20 minutes per pound. If during the last stage of roasting the skin becomes too crisp, cover it loosely with a tent of foil, dull side up. Make sure to baste the turkey at regular intervals with the pan juices. To keep making pan juices, add a small amount of salted water to the roasting pan now and then to keep the gravy liquid. The turkey will be done when a skewer inserted at the thickest part of the thigh releases only clear juices.

• While the turkey cooks, prepare a small sauce. Brown all of the giblets (wings, necks, gizzards) in butter; add the chopped onion, white wine and bouillon; add the *bouquet garni* and let simmer for an hour or two.

• When this sauce is tasty, strain it into a small pot. Dilute the cornstarch with a drop or so of water and stir into the simmering sauce to thicken it. Heat the Cognac and add it flaming to the sauce.

• Add the chestnuts to two thirds of this sauce and heat them well.

• Remove the turkey to a platter, defatten the cooking juices, and add juices to the remainder of the sauce with as much hot water as needed to obtain a good gravy. Correct the seasoning and strain into a sauceboat.

• Surround the turkey with the chestnuts; slice the breast, carve the legs, and serve the stuffing in slices or large spoonfuls. Pass the sauce separately.

STUFFED TURKEY ROAST
(Rôti de Dinde Farci)

A few additional garnishes: During the last half hour of cooking, you can add a dozen or so blanched green olives and ½ pound of sliced young carrots.

■ A bit difficult
6 servings
Medium expensive
2 hours
Best season: fall and winter

STUFFING
3½ oz. boiled ham (100 g)
2 slices of white bread
US 2 TB, UK 1 TB, milk (1 TB)
1 onion
5 oz. sausage meat (150 g)
1 egg
salt and pepper

TURKEY
1 boned turkey roll, about 1½ lbs. (700 g)
US 4 TB, UK 2 TB, oil (2 TB)
US ⅔ cup, UK ½ cup, dry white wine (2 scant dl)
1 garlic clove
US ⅔ cup, UK ½ cup, bouillon or water (2 scant dl)
bouquet garni
salt and pepper
watercress

ABOUT THIS DISH
It tastes as good cold as warm, so do not hesitate to use it for luncheon with a salad.

ALL STUFFINGS
They may be prepared ahead of time and kept refrigerated, but should be stuffed into the cavity of any bird only minutes before roasting to prevent unhealthy fermentations.

STUFFING
- Chop the ham finely. Remove the crusts of the bread, soak the centers in milk, and squeeze dry. Peel and chop the onion very finely. Mix the ham, bread, onion, sausage, egg, and salt and pepper to taste very well to obtain a homogenous stuffing.

TURKEY
- Untie the turkey roll. Spread the roll open and cover the center with the forcemeat. Close the meat over the stuffing, and sew it or tie it closed, whichever is easiest for you.

- Heat the oil in a braising pot. Brown the meat on all sides until golden.

- Discard the oil, replace it by the white wine. Add also the garlic clove, crushed and peeled, the bouillon or water, the *bouquet garni*, and salt and pepper to taste. Bring to a boil, cover, and let cook gently for 1½ hours. The meat is done when a skewer inserted at the thickest part comes out without difficulty, and the juices run clear and transparent.

- Remove the roast from the cooking pot. Slice it and present it on a platter surrounded with watercress.

- Strain the sauce into a heated sauceboat. Correct the seasoning and serve.

QUAILS WITH GRAPES
(Cailles aux Raisins)

Do you have one more minute at your disposal? Remove the crusts of as many slices of white bread as you have birds. Fry slices in butter on both sides to make large golden croutons. Put them on the serving plate. As soon as you have removed the ties of a bird, tilt it forward and let the juices escape onto a crouton; set the quail on it. Delicious!

- Relatively easy
  6 servings
  Expensive
  30 minutes
  Best season: at shooting season for wild quail, year aound for hatchery quails

  6 to 12 quails (see note below)
  salt and pepper
  US 4 TB, UK 2 TB, butter (60 g)
  1 oz. Cognac or other spirit (1 TB)
  60 to 70 seedless white grapes
  US 1 cup, UK 1 scant cup, dry white wine (2.5 dl)
  US ½ cup, UK ⅓ cup, Ruby Port (1 generous dl)
  juice of ½ lemon
  white bread (see advice)

PORTIONS
Quails are tiny and weigh no more than 3½ ounces. If you entertain, 2 quails per person are necessary. For your family count 2 per adult and 1 per child.

Wild quails keep no longer than 2 days after having been shot, but hatchery quails will last at least 4 days if well refrigerated.

- Preheat oven to 400°F., 200°C. or 6 Regulo.
- Salt and pepper the quail cavities and tie their legs together, so they remain tightly closed.
- Rub each quail with butter. Set the quails in a roasting pan and roast with the lid open for 10 minutes.
- Remove from the oven and sprinkle with salt and pepper. Add the Cognac and ignite it. Cover the pan and finish cooking on top of the stove for another 7 to 8 minutes. Quails will be and must be rare and succulent with juice.
- While the quails cook, wash the grapes. Mix the white wine and Port. Bring to a boil and reduce by half. Add the grapes and lemon juice and simmer until the grapes come floating to the surface of the sauce.
- When the quails are done, remove the strings and place them on a warm platter. Strain the cooking juices into the sauce, mix well, and reheat well. Correct the seasoning. Spoon a few tablespoons of sauce and a few grapes over the birds and serve the remainder of the sauce in a gravy boat.
- As a vegetable, serve the Gratin Dauphinois on page 231.

SQUAB AND BABY PEAS
(Pigeons aux Petits Pois)

Are you adventurous? Then try a taste experience! Roast the pigeons alone for 15 minutes after you brown them. They will be medium rare and succulent.

■ Relatively easy
6 servings
Expensive
1½ hours
**Best season: spring with young squabs
  and tiny spring vegetables**

3½ oz. bacon (100 g)
2 dozen silverskin onions
2 dozen baby carrots
**2½ lbs. baby peas in pods (1 kg), or 1 lb.
  snow peas (500 g)**
US 1 TB, UK ½ TB, flour (10 g)
US 1 cup, UK 1 scant cup, bouillon (2.5 dl)
bouquet garni
US 3 TB, UK 1½ TB, butter (45 g)
3 lovely pigeons
salt and pepper
chopped parsley

- Cut the bacon into ⅓-inch cubes. In a braising pot render it slowly and let it turn golden in its own fat.

- Meanwhile, peel the onions and carrots. Shell the peas or string the snow peas.

- Add a bit of flour to the bacon fat and brown it lightly. Add the bouillon and stir until thickened. Add the *bouquet garni*, the carrots, onions and baby peas. Cover and let cook for 10 minutes.

- Heat the butter in a skillet and brown the pigeons well in it on all sides. Transfer the pigeons to the braising pot and set them on the vegetables. Season with salt and pepper, cover, and cook for about 45 minutes.

- To serve, remove the pigeons to a wooden board and cut them into halves. Empty the vegetables into a deep country-style dish and set the half pigeons in a row over them. Sprinkle with chopped parsley.

BEFORE YOU START THIS DISH
You must have very young pigeons, weighing 12 ounces to 1 pound (375 to 500 g).

You must also have very young peas in pods. If you have none, use Chinese pea pods. These are known in France as mange-tout.

CASEROLE-ROASTED PHEASANT
(Faisan à la Cocotte)

To make the dish prettier and better, remove crusts from slices of white bread. Toast slices lightly, then rub them with a peeled garlic clove. Butter them on both sides, then fry them to golden. Surround the birds with these croutons.

- Difficult
  6 servings
  Expensive
  1 hour and 40 minutes
  Best season: hunting season with wild birds; hatchery birds are not worth their price

2 pheasants
2 oz. Cognac or other spirit of your choice
1 lb. slab brisket of pork or fatback (500 g) (see p. 297)
US 3 TB, UK 1½ TB, oil (1½ TB)
salt and pepper
1 large onion, sliced
1 lb. fresh mushrooms (500 g)
US ½ cup, UK ⅓ cup, heavy cream (125 g)
lemon juice
chopped parsley

- Pluck the pheasants and clean the insides as close as possible to the time you are going to cook them. Heat 1 ounce of Cognac in a pan and ignite it. Place the pheasants over the flames on all sides to burn off the pin feathers.

- Cut the brisket or fatback into thin sheets. Lay them over the birds and tie them securely all around.

- In a large oval braising pot, heat the oil. Brown the pheasants on all sides. Salt and pepper them. Add the sliced onion, cover, and let cook for 40 minutes.

- Cut the stem end of the mushrooms, clean as on page 000, and slice them thinly. Add them to the braising pot and let cook for another 15 minutes.

- Open the pot, remove the pheasants to a plate, and remove the fatback or brisket. Tilt the pan forward. Above the mushrooms, oil and melted pork fat will come floating to the top. Spoon most of it off or even all of it if you can.

- Return the pheasants to the pot. Heat another ounce of Cognac and pour it flaming over the birds. Cover and let stand for 5 minutes.

- Remove the pheasants to a board and carve them into serving pieces. Meanwhile, add the cream and lemon juice to taste to the pan and simmer gently. Correct the seasoning of the sauce.

- Pour half of this sauce into a heated deep country-style dish and arrange the pieces of pheasant on top. Coat them well with the remainder of the sauce. Sprinkle with chopped parsley.

THE BEST PHEASANTS
are 12 to 15 months old, with a semisoft, pliable beak and large enough to serve 4. A pheasant hen is smaller and serves only 3 persons. Only wild pheasants are considered here. They must be hung and drawn at home. They are ready to eat when a feather pulled from the breast comes off easily. When plucking a pheasant, wrap a wet cloth around your nose and pull the feathers away from you, with a backward motion of the hand.

JELLIED RABBIT TERRINE
(Terrine de Lapin en Gelée)

You can use the pressure cooker for this terrine. Add a cup or so of water to the pot. Build up the pressure very slowly, and then cook for 45 minutes.

- Medium difficult
  6 servings
  3 hours
  Medium expensive
  Best season: summer

  1 lb. fresh pork brisket (500 g)
  1 rabbit
  1 lb. fresh pork meat, semilean, semifat, from throat or shoulder (500 g)
  4 carrots, sliced
  2 onions, chopped
  1 garlic clove, chopped
  thyme
  bay leaf
  US ¼ cup, UK 2 TB, chopped parsley (2 TB)
  salt and pepper
  1 veal foot or knuckle, blanched
  1 bottle of dry white wine
  a bit of flour
  water

OTHER CHOICES
Instead of a whole rabbit, use a box of frozen rabbit and defrost it. Bone the rabbit.

No veal foot or knuckle? Use 2 pig's feet.

Make sure that your wine is good and has body: a Mâcon Blanc would be perfect.

- Cut brisket into ⅛-inch slices. Cut rabbit into pieces and bone the pieces.
- Line a 3-quart braising pot with slices of pork brisket, tightly packed side by side so as to make a complete envelope for the meats.
- Add 1 layer of rabbit and pork meat. Top this with a layer of carrots, onions, garlic, thyme, crushed bay leaf, parsley, and salt and pepper to taste. Top with another layer of pork and rabbit. Put the veal foot or knuckle on top. Add the white wine. Cover the dish.
- Preheat oven to 350°F., 180°C. or 5 Regulo.
- Make a stiff dough with water and flour and seal the pot and lid together with this dough, leaving only 1 inch of the rim uncovered for steam to escape.
- Bake the terrine in the preheated oven for 1 hour. Then reduce heat to 300°F., 150°C. or 4 Regulo, and let cook for another 1½ hours.
- When the cooking time is over, remove the pot from the oven and let it cool without opening it.
- When cold, open the lid. Remove the veal foot. Refrigerate the terrine overnight.
- Unmold on a chilled platter. Serve with a green salad.

RABBIT IN ROQUEFORT SAUCE
(Lapin des Causses)

The Roquefort cheese should be white and regularly veined with blue. When greenish-gray it is too ripe for good taste. Watch the salt seasoning; Roquefort is quite salty.

- Easy
  6 servings
  Very affordable
  1¼ hours
  Best season: year around

  2 medium-size onions
  US 2 TB, UK 1 TB, oil (1 TB)
  US 4 TB, UK 2 TB, butter (60 g)
  1 rabbit, 3 to 3½ lbs., cut into serving pieces (1.5 kg) (see note below)
  2 shallots
  salt and pepper
  1½ oz. fresh Roquefort cheese (50 g)
  US ¾ cup, UK ⅔ cup, heavy cream (2 generous dl)
  chopped parsley

- Peel the onions and cut into thin slices. Heat the oil and the butter and sauté the onions until golden. Remove to a plate wth a slotted spoon, pressing on onions to extract all the fat.

- Brown the rabbit pieces well in the same fats, proceeding in several batches so the rabbit pieces brown evenly. Return the onions to the pan.

- Peel and chop the shallots, add them to the pot, and season with salt and pepper. Cover and let cook gently for 30 minutes.

- Mash the Roquefort cheese with a fork, then gradually mix it with the heavy cream and add the mixture to the pot. Mix gently. Cover again and finish cooking for another 20 minutes. Test doneness of the rabbit with a skewer. Correct the seasoning of the sauce.

- Empty the stew into a country-style deep dish and serve sprinkled wth chopped parsley.

USE EITHER
1 young rabbit, cut into 6 serving pieces: 2 shoulders, the rib, the loin and 2 legs; or 1 box of frozen rabbit, 2½ to 3 pounds (1 to 1.5 kg).

If you have no Roquefort cheese, try Danish Blue or Stilton.

RABBIT WITH PRUNES AND RAISINS
(Lapin aux Pruneaux)

Another recipe from northern France. In that part of France called Picardie and Flanders, Dutch gin is often used instead of Cognac. Some people add a "pinch" of prepared Dijon mustard to the sauce when it is finished.

- Relatively easy
  6 servings
  Very affordable
  1 hour and 10 minutes, plus 2 hours to soak the prunes and raisins
  Best season: fall and winter

  20 soft pitted prunes
  1½ oz. light raisins (50 g)
  lukewarm water
  2 onions
  3½ oz. slab bacon (100 g)
  US 4 TB, UK 2 TB, butter (60 g)
  1 rabbit, 3½ lbs. (1.5 kg) (see note, p. 184)
  US 2 TB, UK 1 TB, flour (15 g)
  US 1 cup, UK 1 scant cup, dry white wine (2.5 dl)
  US ½ cup, UK ⅓ cup, water (1 generous dl)
  salt and pepper
  thyme
  bay leaf
  US 3 TB, UK 1½ TB, Cognac (1½ TB)

- Cover the prunes and raisins with lukewarm water and let stand for 2 hours.

- Peel the onions and cut into thin slices.

- Cut the bacon into strips ⅓ x ½ inch. Put them in a cold braising pot to render their fat and cook them until golden. Remove to a plate.

- Add the onions to the fat, brown them until golden, and remove them to the same plate as the bacon, pressing on the onions to extract the fat.

- Add the butter to the fat. Heat well. Brown the rabbit pieces until golden all around; proceed in several batches if need be so the pieces can brown evenly and not overlap each other.

- Sprinkle the meat with the flour and stir well so the flour coats the meat and turns golden.

- Add the onions, bacon, white wine, water, salt, pepper and thyme to taste, and bay leaf. Cover and let cook gently for 30 minutes.

- Drain the prunes and raisins and add them and the Cognac to the pot. Cover and continue to cook for another 30 minutes. Correct seasoning.

- To serve, empty into a deep country-style dish and serve very hot.

KNOW YOUR RABBIT
A young rabbit can be recognized by its thin leg bones, large joints and white fat. Older rabbits have thick, squat legs and yellow fat.

RABBIT HUNTER'S STYLE
(Lapin Chasseur)

For more taste and flavor, flambé the rabbit wth a good ounce of Cognac or other spirit before covering the pot and starting the first part of the cooking.

If you have time on your hands, marinate the rabbit in the aromatics overnight, then dry the rabbit well and cook as above.

In summer replace the tomato paste with 3 or 4 fresh tomatoes, preferably peeled and seeded.

- Relatively easy
  6 servings
  Very affordable
  1 hour and 10 minutes
  Best season: late summer or early fall with fresh tomatoes (see advice)

  ¼ lb. lean bacon (125 g)
  US 4 TB, UK 2 TB, butter (60 g)
  1 rabbit, 3½ lbs., cut into serving pieces (1.5 kg)
  US 2 TB, UK 1 TB, flour (15 g)
  US 1 cup, UK 1 scant cup, dry white wine (2.5 dl)
  US ¼ cup, UK 2 TB, tomato paste (2 TB)
  US 1 cup, UK 1 scant cup, bouillon (2.5 dl)
  bouquet garni
  salt and pepper
  ½ lb. mushrooms (250 g)
  chopped parsley

ARE YOU REALLY IN A HURRY?
Replace the tomato paste and the bouillon by a can of tomato sauce; but keep the aromatics and the white wine.

- Cut the bacon into strips ⅓ x ½ inch. Put them in a cold braising pot and render them slowly until they turn golden.
- Remove the bacon to a plate. Add the butter to the pot and brown the pieces of rabbit on all sides. Proceed in several batches if need be to brown pieces evenly and not overlap in the pan.
- Add the flour and stir well, continuing to cook until the flour coats the meat and has turned golden.
- Add the white wine, tomato paste, bouillon and *bouquet garni*. Add also salt and pepper to taste. Cover and cook for 30 minutes.
- Prepare the mushrooms. Cut them into quarters.
- Add the mushrooms and bacon to the pot. Let cook for another 15 to 30 minutes, depending on the size of the rabbit. Correct the seasoning.
- To serve, empty into a deep country-style dish and sprinkle with chopped parsley. Serve with the rabbit a dish of steamed potatoes or a good dish of pasta.

VENISON CHOPS
(Côtelettes de Chevreuil)

If the frying pan is too small, cook the chops in 2 or 3 frying pans, or if you have only 1 pan cook them in 2 batches, taking care to undercook them and to finish cooking when the sauce is finishing.

The wine served with this dish should be excellent, full-bodied, as old as possible: think of a Pomerol, any of the Chambertin family, or a Châteauneuf du Pape. Expensive and delicious meat deserves expensive and delicious wine.

■ Easy
6 servings
Expensive unless you have shot the animal yourself
20 minutes
Best season: fall to early winter

1 garlic clove
2 TB parsley leaves
US 2 TB, UK 1 TB, oil (1 TB)
US 4 TB, UK 2 TB, butter (60 g)
6 venison chops
salt and pepper
US 1 cup, UK 1 scant cup, bouillon (2.5 dl)
US 2 TB, UK 1 TB, red-wine vinegar (1 TB)
¼ tsp. dried thyme
¼ tsp. crushed bay leaf
1 tsp. flour (5 g)
parsley or watercress bouquets

- Peel the garlic, Chop it fine as well as the parsley to obtain a *persillade*.
- Heat oil and half of the butter in a large skillet or an electric frying pan. Add the chops and brown well on one side. Turn over, salt and pepper the seared side, and cook the second side. Remove the meat to a hot platter, as soon as the blood appears at the surface of the second side. Keep warm.
- Heat the pan very hot to caramelize the meat juices deeply. Discard the fat.

Replace it by the bouillon and deglaze the pan well. Reduce the heat; add the vinegar, thyme and bay leaf. Reduce by one third.

- Meanwhile, mix flour and the remainder of the butter with a fork. With a whisk, gather the mixture and whisk very fast into the simmering liquid. Bring to a boil and remove from the heat.
- Strain the sauce into a small pot. Return the chops to the hot pan and reheat them over high heat for 1 minute on each side, while you add the garlic and parsley to the sauce.
- Put the chops on a heated platter and spoon the sauce over them. Decorate with parsley or watercress bouquets.
- As a vegetable consider well-buttered chestnut purée or well-buttered mashed potatoes. Also, braised celery.

ABOUT VENISON
Deer should be eaten 1 week after it has been shot.

If you have bought the chops and they smell gamey, wash them in lukewarm vinegar, rinse them, dry them well.

FILLETS OF DEER HUNTER'S STYLE
(Filet de Chevreuil Chasseur)

What if you have a leg of deer? The French call it by the cute name of cuissot. *It should also be marinated. Then it is dried, browned in the pork fat, and everything—bouillon and marinade as well as all the aromatics and vegetables—is added to the pot. The pot is covered and the leg cooked until a skewer inserted deep into the leg feels just very warm, but not hot, when removed and applied to the top of the hand.*

■ Relatively easy
6 to 10 servings depending on size
Extremely expensive
45 minutes, plus 2 full days for marinating
Best season: fall to early winter

3 onions
2 shallots
thyme, crumbled bay leaf, parsley stems
US 4 TB, UK 2 TB, oil (2 TB)
US ⅓ cup, UK ¼ cup, red-wine vinegar (1 scant dl)
US 2½ cups, UK 2¼ cups, dry white wine (.5 L)
3 garlic cloves, crushed
10 peppercorns, black and white
1 side of deer fillet (sirloin strip)
3½ oz. fresh pork brisket (100 g)
salt and pepper
US ½ cup, UK ⅓ cup, bouillon (1 generous dl)
US 2 TB, UK 1 TB, butter (30 g)
chopped parsley

- Two days before you cook the dish, *prepare a marinade.* Peel onions and shallots and chop coarsely. Mix with crumbled thyme and bay leaf and chopped parsley stems. Add oil, vinegar, white wine, garlic and peppercorns. Put the meat in this to marinate, and turn it several times while doing so. Store in refrigerator, covered with plastic wrap.

- On the day of your dinner, dry the meat well. Keep it ready to cook on a plate. You may want to cut the fillet into 2 equal strips each about 6 to 8 inches long for easier cooking.

- *Prepare a sauce:* cut the pork brisket into small cubes; render them. Reserve the fat on a saucer to cook the meat.

- Leaving the cubes of bacon in the pan, add the vegetables of the marinade and cook over high heat until they turn golden. Add the marinade and reduce by one half to two thirds.

- Strain this reduction into a bowl through a very fine strainer since it is essential that you keep only the clear liquid.

- Heat the rendered pork fat in a large skillet. Brown the 2 pieces of deer on each side. Salt and pepper each only after it is seared. As soon as the meat is well seared, turn the heat down and cook for 3 to 4 more minutes on each side, depending on the size of the fillet. The meat should remain medium rare; that means, that when you test by pushing with your finger, the finger will go in by about ⅛ inch.

- Set the meat on a plate; keep warm. Add the bouillon to the pan without removing the fat. Reduce until only a very thick mixture is left, 2 to 3 tablespoons. Add the strained marinade, mix well, and boil down for a few minutes. In the boiling whisk in the butter, and add the parsley. Turn the heat off.

- Roll the meat in the sauce for 1 to 2 minutes. Cut it into slices ⅓ to ½ inch thick and serve on a hot platter with the sauce spooned over.

- The very best vegetable is a dish of braised chestnuts.

ONE-POT MEALS
French Regional Specialties
(Les Plats-Repas)

CONFIT AND CASSOULET
(A Languedoc Bean, Duck and Lamb Casserole)

This title cannot be translated into English. It is the name of the greatest specialty of the French Province of Languedoc.

In Languedoc it is said that for the cassoulet to be good, one should let the crust build three times, punch it down three times, and let it build a final time.

- Difficult, a bit long, well worth the time
  6 to 8 servings
  Expensive
  Divide the work over 2 days
  Best season: fall and winter months

  DAY ONE
  1 duck, 4½ to 6 lbs., the larger the better (2 to 3 kg)
  coarse salt
  6 fresh pork hocks
  US 2 cups, UK 2 scant cups, water (.5 L) plus water for soaking beans
  1 lb. dried cannellini beans (450 g)

  DAY TWO
  4 medium-size onions, 2 whole, 2 chopped
  bouquet garni
  6 pieces of lamb stew (neck is best)
  salt and pepper
  5 garlic cloves
  5 sun-ripened tomatoes, peeled, seeded and chopped, or 3 cups canned pear-shaped tomatoes with canning juices
  bread crumbs

DAY ONE
- Cut the duck into 6 pieces: 2 legs and 2 pieces out of each breast. As you cut up the breasts, leave the meat attached to part of the breastbone for better taste and texture.
- Put the pieces of duck in a shallow baking dish and salt them lightly. Do the same with the fresh pork hocks. Cover with a plastic wrap and let stand for 4 hours.

- Meanwhile, remove all the pads of fat from the skin and carcass of the duck left after you have boned it. There will be 1 to 1½ cups of solid fat; also, cut the skin into small pieces.
- Put the water in a pot. Cut the fat into small cubes and drop them into the water together with the pieces of skin. Simmer. By the time the duck has finished salting the fat will be rendered.
- Wipe the salt off the duck pieces. Put them in a large pot where they will not overlap one another. Pour the clear liquid duck fat over them and heat the pot over medium heat until the meat starts sizzling in the fat. Transfer the dish to a 325°F., 165°C. or 4 to 5 Regulo oven, and bake until the meat is tender to the skewer test (p. 304). Cool and refrigerate. This is a *confit*.
- Soak the beans in water overnight.

DAY TWO
- Rinse the beans and the pork hocks well. Put them in a large pot. Cover them with water, then add US 2 cups, UK 2 scant cups, water (.5 L) more. Bring to a boil slowly. Add the 2 whole onions and the *bouquet garni* and cook for 1 to 1½ hours.
- Drain hocks and beans and reserve the cooking juices. Chop the hocks; discard the bones. Mix the meat with the beans.
- Remove enough duck fat from the dish

containing the duck to make a ¼-inch layer on the bottom of a braising pot. In this fat, brown the lamb pieces very well on all sides. Salt and pepper the pieces well. Remove them to a plate as soon as they are nice and brown.

- In the same fat, add the 2 chopped onions, 4 garlic cloves, crushed, the fresh tomatoes or the canned pear-shaped tomatoes, mashed, and their canning juices, and the lamb. Bring to a simmer, add the cooking juices of the beans, and let cook, covered, over low heat until the meat is three quarters done, or about 1 hour. Correct seasoning very well.

- The last step is the best:
Use a deep dish of thick earthenware, at least 3- to 4-quart capacity. Rub this dish with the remaining garlic clove, then rub it with some duck fat. Add half of the beans and hock meat and one third of the cooking sauce of the lamb. Then add the pieces of lamb and duck, all in one layer. Top with the remainder of the beans and the remainder of the sauce. Sprinkle with a good layer of dry bread crumbs and bake until a nice crust forms on the surface, produced by the sauce bubbling over into the crumbs.

- Serve piping hot with a good Corbières or Cahors red wine.

WHERE TO FIND WHAT
Pork hocks and cannellini beans (long and white): at any Italian neighborhood market. You can use dried navy beans if you cannot find cannellini.

WHAT TO DO WITH
the crisp duck skins and cracklings: enjoy them salted with a glass of beer.

Keep the fat; the duck cooked in its own fat is called confit, *and you can prepare more of it to enjoy it by itself once you discover how delicious it is.*

DAUBE PROVENÇALE
(This dish is the star stew of Provençale cuisine.)

This dish may seem terribly long to prepare, but once it bakes, there is nothing more to do really. And the result is well worth the waiting.

■ Needs care
8 servings
Relatively expensive
7 hours, with 2 hours for the marination
Best season: fresh tomato season

3½ lbs. beef chuck, cut into cubes
   (1.5 kg)
1 bottle of dry white wine
US ½ cup, UK ⅓ cup, dry white Port (1
   generous dl)
1 oz. Cognac (1 TB)
US 3 TB, UK 1½ TB, olive oil (1½ TB)
¾ lb. pork brisket (375 g)
coarse salt
1 piece of pork rind, 6 to 8 inches
water
2 lbs. carrots (1 kg)
4 large onions
4 garlic cloves
6 oz. black olives in brine (180 g)
6 sun-ripened tomatoes
1 lb. fresh mushrooms (500 g)
thyme, bay leaf and parsley, all to your
   taste
¼ tsp. saffron or 2 dozen crumbled
   stigmas
salt and pepper
flour
8 Red Bliss potatoes

• Put the cubes of beef into a dish. Cover them with a mixture of white wine, Port, Cognac and olive oil and let marinate for 2 hours.

• Cut the brisket into pieces ⅓ x ½ inch and sprinkle them with coarse salt. Set them in the salt for the same 2 hours as the beef marinates.

• Add the pork rind to a pot of cold water. Bring slowly to a boil and let the rind get tender and absorb as much water as possible. Cool and cut into ½-inch cubes. Add to the marinade.

• Peel carrots, onions and garlic. Slice the carrots, chop the onions coarsely, and crush the garlic.

• Pit the black olives and blanch them for 2 minutes. Cut the tomatoes into quarters. Prepare the mushrooms as usual (see p. 300). Quarter them. Mix all the vegetables together.

• Preheat oven to 400°F., 220°C. or 6 Regulo as soon as the 2 hours of marinating are finished.

• Rinse the brisket, quickly pat dry. Mix

brisket and beef pieces. Drain the marinade into a bowl.

- In a large braising pot, put a layer of meat and pork rinds and a layer of vegetables mixed together. On each layer of vegetables add thyme, a tiny piece of bay leaf, chopped parsley, a pinch of saffron. Repeat until meats and vegetables have all been used. Salt and pepper the marinade and pour over the stew.
- Make a flour and water paste and seal the pot well all around except for 1 inch long to let steam evaporate.
- Put the pot in the oven to bake for 1 hour; then turn the heat down to 275°F., 130°C. or 2 to 3 Regulo. Bake for another 4 to 5 hours.
- Half an hour before serving, peel the potatoes and cook them in salted water or steam them.
- Serve the stew in the cooking vessel.

THE BEST INGREDIENTS AND WHERE TO FIND THEM

Beef: the best piece is the so-called blade roast bought in one piece and cubed.

Pork rinds are sold in all Italian neighborhood markets, all cleaned and cut into sheets.

Black olives are better also bought in an Italian market and blanched.

Saffron comes ground to a powder, or whole, the dried stigmas of the saffron crocus. With whole saffron you are sure to have the real spice; powders are easily adulterated.

POTÉE AUVERGNATE

At the beginning of this century, each French Province still had its own potée or boiled dinner. This version is from the Auvergne.

These cabbage leaves, stuffed, or even a whole cabbage stuffed, are known over several southwestern Provinces of France as Le Farci.

■ Easy
  6 to 8 servings
  Very affordable
  3 hours, plus 48 hours for salting
  Best season: fall to early spring

  1½ lbs. pork brisket (750 g)
  coarse salt

  FORCEMEAT
  3 slices, ⅛ inch thick, genuine prosciutto
  2 shallots
  1 garlic clove
  chopped fresh herbs (parsley, chives)
  3 slices of white bread, without crusts
  milk for soaking
  5 oz. sausage meat (150 g)
  2 egg yolks
  salt and pepper
  6 to 8 large cabbage leaves

  POTÉE
  8 carrots
  3 onions, each stuck with 1 clove
  5 leeks, white and light green parts only
  5 small white turnips
  2 small center ribs of celery
  2 to 3 garlic cloves
  the heart of the cabbage
  1 fresh shoulder of pork (picnic ham)
  water
  bouquet garni
  6 to 8 Red Bliss boiling potatoes

- Two days before cooking this potful of good food, put the brisket of pork in a dish and salt it all around with coarse salt. On the day you plan to cook the potée, rinse it and dry it.

- *Prepare the forcemeat:* Chop the prosciutto, shallots, garlic and herbs. Soak the bread in milk and squeeze it dry. Mix all these ingredients with the sausage to obtain a homogenous mixture. Add the egg yolks, mix well, and season.

- Remove the wilted outside leaves of the cabbage. Detach the leaves one by one. Select 8 large pretty leaves. Blanch them in boiling salted water for 3 minutes.

- Remove the hard rib of each cabbage leaf. Wrap equal amounts of forcemeat in the leaves. Tie with a thick thread. Refrigerate until ready to use.

- *Potée:* Peel and trim all the vegetables. Cut the remainder of the cabbage into quarters.

- Put the brisket, the pork shoulder and all the vegetables in a large stockpot. Add 3 to 4 quarts of water and the *bouquet garni.* Cover and bring to a boil. Reduce the heat and cook gently for 2 to 3 hours.

- When the soup has been cooking for about 1 hour, add the stuffed cabbage leaves.

- Peel the potatoes. Half an hour before the end of the cooking, add them to the pot. Stop the cooking as soon as they are done.

- To serve, slice the meats and present them on a large platter. Surround them with the vegetables, the potatoes and stuffed cabbage leaves. Serve in soup plates. Serve the bouillon in a tureen. Slices of country bread are the best complement.

WITH THE SAME METHOD
You can prepare a few of the *potées* made in other provinces.

Potée Basque: The meats are a hen or heavy chicken; a piece of beef such as shin with the bone in; a hock of prosciutto. Add to the vegetables 7 ounces (200 g) chick-peas, soaked overnight before cooking them.

Potée Bretonne: Add to the vegetables ½ pound dried beans (250 g), precooked 1 hour before adding them to the pot.

Potée Lorraine: Replace the brisket by the same weight of bacon and add 2 Italian smoked sausages.

Potée Parisienne: This was prepared in all the villages around Paris until the beginning of this century. Add 7 to 8 ounces slab bacon (200 to 250 g), 2 smoked Italian sausages and, at the end of the cooking, ½ pound shelled fresh peas (250 g) or frozen baby peas if you have to save time.

POTÉES
never quite get that country taste if they are cooked in a pressure cooker. The taste is worth the difference in time.

CHOUCROUTE ALSACIENNE

In Alsace a nice big jar of mustard and dense country bread always comes with the choucroute. Use either Dijon or Düsseldorf mustard, both available anywhere in the world.

Also, if you prefer to do as one does in Colmar, remove the potatoes from their blanching water and finish cooking them with the sauerkraut.

- A bit difficult
  6 to 8 servings
  Medium expensive
  3 hours, 1 hour in pressure cooker
  Best season: winter

  3½ to 4 lbs. sauerkraut (1.5 to 2 kg)
  water
  US ⅓ cup, UK 3 TB, lard or goose fat (3 TB)
  1 lb. slab bacon (500 g)
  1 smoked whole rib of pork known by butchers as "Kasseler Rippchen"
  15 juniper berries
  ½ bottle of Sylvaner, Riesling or Traminer wine
  bouillon as needed
  6 to 8 frankfurters
  6 to 8 small Red Bliss boiling potatoes

CHOOSE YOUR INGREDIENTS CAREFULLY

Sauerkraut must be processed without a trace of sugar. Read the label!

Use Sylvaner, Riesling or Traminer from Alsace as cooking and drinking wine.

- Wash the sauerkraut twice in cold water. Blanch it in boiling water for 2 minutes, then rinse it in cold water and press out water with your hands.

- Melt half of the fat in a large oval braising pot and add half of the sauerkraut, piling it loosely. On top, put the slab bacon, the smoked pork ribs and the juniper berries. Add remaining sauerkraut, again loosely piled over the meat. Add the chosen wine and enough bouillon to cover the sauerkraut. Bring to a boil, cover, and bake in a very slow oven, 325°F., 165°C. or 4 Regulo. Let bake until done.

- The dish should be cooked in a maximum of 3 hours. During the last 10 minutes of cooking add the frankfurters.

- Meanwhile, cook the potatoes in boiling salted water.

- To serve, remove the frankfurters, pick the sauerkraut up with a fork and pile it on a large heated platter. Correct the salt and pepper.

- Arrange the potatoes around and slice the bacon and smoked rib. Put the slices of meat and the frankfurters on top of the sauerkraut.

Your frankfurters should be the natural kind without chemical additives.

All good butchers have smoked pork chops in one large train of ribs.

FONDUE SAVOYARDE

This dish is a specialty of the Savoie mountains, where it has a few other local names also. It is mostly made with local Beaufort cheese melted or fondue into hot white wine.

Do as the French do: Enforce the rule that whoever drops bread into the pot, pays for the next bottle of wine. Either there is not enough wine or the whole company feels very, very happy by the end of the meal.

- A bit difficult
 6 to 8 servings
 Medium expensive to expensive
 15 minutes
 Best season: winter

 1 or 2 loaves of light, unseeded rye bread
 2 lbs. Gruyère cheese (see Note) (1 kg)
 1 garlic clove
 1 bottle of dry white wine (see Note)
 US 3 TB, UK 1½ TB, Kirschwasser (see Note) (1½ TB)
 1 tsp. cornstarch
 coarsely ground white pepper

CHEESE CHOICE
It is a good idea to have 1 pound (500 g) each of Gruyère and Emmental.

Have plenty of wine on hand; choose Crépy, Muscadet or Alsatian Riesling.

There is Kirschwasser and Kirschwasser. Choose one imported from Germany, France or Switzerland. It is expensive but it goes a long way.

- Cube a good loaf of dense rye bread.
- Cut half of the cheese into slivers and grate the remainder.
- Peel the garlic clove, crush it, and with it rub the fondue pot.
- Into this pot put the white wine. Heat it slowly until it starts bubbling but not boiling. Gradually add the cheese; stir until homogenous.
- Some of the wine will remain un-homogenized and mixed with some of the cheese butterfat. To remedy this, mix the Kirschwasser with the cornstarch and stir into the fondue, which will immediately thicken. Add white pepper from the mill to your taste.
- Light the fondue alcohol heater (or Sterno) and set the pot over it. Each guest will dip bread cubes into the fondue.

FONDUE BOURGUIGNONNE

This is a misnomer since nothing here is melted or allowed to fondre. The name comes from the fact that one dips the meat into hot fat as one dips bread into hot cheese as in the preceding recipe.

A good plentiful salad is the best table companion to this type of dinner.

■ Easy
  6 servings
  Expensive
  15 minutes
  Best season: year around

  3 to 3½ lbs. roast beef, cut of your choice
  (1.5 kg)

MAYONNAISE
1 egg yolk
1 tsp. vinegar
salt and pepper
1 tsp. dry mustard
US 1¼ cups, UK 1 generous cup, oil (.25 L)
1 tiny garlic clove
1 tiny hot red pepper
fine fresh herbs of your choice, chopped
pickles of your choice, chopped
tomato paste
US 1½ cups, UK 1¼ cups, butter (300 g)
US 1¼ cups, UK 1 cup, oil (300 g)
tomato ketchup or other fancy sauces that can be bought ready made, if you like

- Cut the beef into ½-inch slices and the slices into cubes.

MAYONNAISE
- Put the egg yolk in a bowl with the vinegar, salt and pepper to taste and a good teaspoon of mustard. Mix well. Gradually whisk in the oil (see details, p. 62).
- Divide the mayonnaise into 3 small bowls. In the first add a good pinch of garlic; in the second, a tiny mashed hot pepper; in the third add herbs and pickles to your taste as well as a bit of tomato paste.
- Melt the butter in a saucepan over high heat. Heat the oil in the fondue pot. Lift the solids at the surface of the butter; discard them. Then spoon the liquid butterfat into the hot oil. Discard the white liquid whey at the bottom of the butter pan (see Clarified Butter, p. 294).
- Heat the mixture until it bubbles a bit, then transfer it to an alcohol heater (or Sterno) in the dining room.
- Each guest will cook his own cubes of meat and help himself or herself to any sauce.

THE CUT OF BEEF
It can be sirloin strip, tenderloin, or rib: very expensive. It can also be true eye of the round or top sirloin: less expensive.

PASTA AND RICE
(Les Pâtes et le Riz Salé)

HOW TO KEEP PASTA RIBBONS AND
RICE GRAINS FROM STICKING TOGETHER

Pasta, noodles, macaroni and rice, cooked in a large amount of water: You will notice that all recipes using this method instruct the cook to rinse the cooked pasta or rice under running warm water. This is the reason:

1. The warm water, being cooler than the boiling water in which the pasta or rice was cooked, will stop the cooking by dropping the temperature of the pasta or rice by 50° to 60°F. (10° to 15°C.).

2. Cold water would not be as good because at the surface of all just-cooked pasta and rice there is a soft layer of semiliquid starch. The warm rinsing water will rinse this layer away. Cold water, on the contrary, would recoagulate somewhat this outside layer, but, since it would not coagulate completely, the grains of rice or the ribbons of pasta would stand a fair chance of sticking together.

GREEN PASTA TIMBALE
(Timbale de Macaroni au Vert)

Serve the macaroni in the baking dish. This dish is nutritious enough to be a main course. Round up the meal with a good salad and a pleasant fruit dessert.

■ Requires some care
6 servings
Affordable
50 minutes
Best season: cold days and months

water
salt
½ lb. macaroni of your choice (250 g)
US 4 TB, UK 2 TB, butter (60 g)
US 3 TB, UK 1½ TB, flour (20 g)
US 2 cups, UK 2 scant cups, hot milk (scant .25 L)
1 package (10 oz.) frozen baby peas (300 g)
½ lb. boiled ham in 1 thick piece (250 g)
¼ lb. prosciutto (125 g)
pepper
a small bundle of tarragon leaves
US ½ cup, UK ⅓ cup, heavy cream (125 g)
US 6 TB, UK 3 TB, bread crumbs (3 TB)

• Bring a large pot of water to a boil. Add 1½ teaspoons salt per quart of water just before you add the macaroni. Stir and let simmer the amount of time required by the manufacturer.

• While the macaroni cooks prepare the sauce: Melt half of the butter in a saucepan, add the flour, and cook the obtained *roux* (see p. 303), until golden. Whisk in the hot milk, bring to a boil, and let simmer for a few minutes.

• Quickly defrost frozen baby peas under running cold water. Add them to the sauce. Do not season now; wait until the ham has been added.

• Dice both kinds of ham; add to the sauce. Stop cooking the sauce but keep it hot. Add pepper to taste. Chop the tarragon, add it to the cream, and put both in a large pot.

• Drain the macaroni and rinse under running warm water until the water runs clear. Heat the cream to the boiling point, salt and pepper it, and toss the macaroni in it.

• Butter a baking dish, preferably of glass. Fill the baking dish with alternating layers of macaroni and sauce, ending with a layer of macaroni. Sprinkle with the crumbs. Dot with pieces of butter and put under the broiler to become crusty and golden.

NOODLES
and all forms of pasta are energy-producing foods and do not in themselves represent a balanced meal, unless they are supplemented with meat to supply proteins, raw vegetables and fruits to supply vitamins.

PASTA AU GRATIN AUVERGNE STYLE
(Gratiné de Nouilles à l'Auvergnate)

When you cook noodles bought in a package, follow the directions on the package carefully, but remember that while the pasta is being seasoned and dishes are put together the cooking process goes on, so you may want to keep the pasta a bit firmer so all this can happen without overcooking.

- Easy
  6 servings
  Medium expensive
  20 minutes
  Best season: a side dish for the cold months

  water
  salt
  ½ lb. egg pasta of your choice, in the shape of your choice (250 g)
  US 1 cup, UK 1 scant cup, heavy cream (225 g)
  pepper
  1 small bundle of chives, chopped
  US 6 TB, UK 3 TB, butter (90 g)
  ¼ lb. Saint-Nectaire or Cantal cheese (125 g)

THIS DISH CAN BECOME
much cheaper, if instead of the expensive Saint-Nectaire or Cantal cheeses, you use a good natural cheese local to your area; try any local one with a lot of punch, such as Cheddar.

- Bring a pot of water to a boil. Add 1½ teaspoons salt per quart of water just before you add the pasta. Stir and simmer until tender to your taste (see advice).

- While pasta cooks, put the heavy cream in a large skillet and quickly boil it down by one third. Salt and pepper it. Chop the chives; reserve them on a small plate.

- Drain the cooked pasta in a colander; rinse it under running warm water until the water runs clear. Add the pasta immediately to the hot cream.

- Reheat very well. Add the chives and one third of the butter. Season well.

- Using another third of the butter, butter a 2-quart baking dish. Pour the seasoned noodles into the dish. Dot the surface of the pasta with the remainder of the butter.

- Preheat the broiler.

- Grate the cheese directly over the top of the pasta, building a thin even layer.

- Slide under the broiler until the cheese melts and turns golden. Letting the cheese darken too much would be a disaster; be careful.

- Excellent with all roasts of white or red meats.

PILAF OF VERMICELLI SAVOY STYLE
(Pilaf de Vermicelle Savoyard)

This is a noodle pilaf. You may want to remember that a noodle pilaf is always made with equal volumes of pasta and liquids.

- A bit difficult
  6 servings
  Medium expensive
  25 minutes
  Best season: during cold seasons

  ¾ lb. vermicelli in spools (375 g)
  1 onion
  US ½ cup, UK 4 TB, butter (120 g)
  bouillon, prepare 2 US cups (.5 L)
  2 garlic cloves, chopped
  ¼ cup chopped parsley (2 TB)
  ½ of a Reblochon cheese, cut into ¼-inch cubes
  salt and pepper

YOU CAN USE
all kinds of differently shaped pasta to the great joy of children. "Bows" are particularly popular.

- Break the vermicelli and let them fall into a 1-quart measuring cup. The volume of vermicelli you need is the same as the volume of bouillon that you will need to cook them (see advice).
- Chop the onion finely.
- Heat two thirds of the butter and in it sauté the onion until golden. Add the broken vermicelli and brown it so some of the threads turn golden brown. Mix well.
- Heat the same volume of bouillon as the measured amount of vermicelli. Pour over the vermicelli.
- Cover the pot and cook over low heat until the bouillon has been almost all absorbed. Add the garlic and parsley and turn the heat off. The pasta will absorb the remainder of the bouillon.
- With the remainder of the butter, coat a baking dish. Sprinkle the Reblochon cubes in it. Add the hot pasta and stir well. Correct the seasoning. Serve in the baking dish.
- Excellent with all rabbit stews and sautéed veal and chicken dishes.

KNEPPS AU LARD FUMÉ
(A noodle dish from the Lorraine, with bacon and poppy seeds)

If you prefer, use only butter and fresh herbs of your choice. These quick, no-knead, no-cut noodles are much beloved by children; do not hesitate to prepare a double portion. Leftovers garnish soups very well.

- Requires care
  6 servings
  Very affordable
  20 minutes
  Best season: the cold months

  6 rashers of thick-sliced bacon
  US 6 TB, UK 3 TB, butter (90 g)
  US 2 cups, UK 2 scant cups, unsifted flour
    (250 g)
  6 eggs
  US ⅔ cup, UK ½ cup, milk (2 scant dl)
  salt and pepper
  nutmeg
  water
  US 2 TB, UK 1 TB, poppy seeds (1 TB)

ABOUT THIS DISH
It is found both in Lorraine under the name of Knepps *and in Alsace under the name of* Knepfle, *otherwise known in Germanic countries as* Spaetzle. *The poppy seeds in Lorraine are called* Semsen.

- Cut the bacon into pieces ¼ x 1 inch. Render them slowly in a large skillet. When they are golden, add the butter to the skillet. Reserve. Keep over low heat.

- Put the flour in a bowl, make a well, and add the eggs. Stir until all the flour has been incorporated. Add the milk, and salt, pepper and nutmeg to taste. Stir until smooth.

- Bring a pot of water to a boil. Add salt. Reduce to a simmer.

- Pour about ½ cup of the batter on the bottom of a cake pan that you hold inverted in your left hand. Slant the cake pan over the water and with a long metal cake spatula, shave, one at a time, ¼-inch-wide strips of the batter into the boiling water. The batter will fall to the bottom of the pan, then slowly rise to the surface.

- As the "noodles" rise to the surface, lift them with a slotted spoon and deposit them in the frying pan containing the bacon. Repeat until all the batter has been cooked. Heat the pan slowly.

- Toss well; the mixture will appear a bit sticky at first but as the butter heats slowly the noodles will coat with butter and dry nicely. Just before serving, toss in the poppy seeds and correct the seasoning.

NOUILLES DU VIEUX CANNES

(Diverse versions of this dish can be found in many of the small restaurants in the old city of Cannes.)

French cooks are so attached to butter that they do not hesitate to add a good slab of butter to the whole mixture.

- Easy
  6 servings
  Affordable
  1 hour with the sauce
  Best season: summer with sun-ripened tomatoes

SAUCE
US ⅓ cup, UK ¼ cup, olive oil (1 scant dl)
2 onions, chopped
3 garlic cloves, mashed
2 lbs. sun-ripened pear-shaped tomatoes, peeled (1 kg)
salt and pepper
bouquet garni
US 1 TB, UK ½ TB, chopped fresh mint (½ TB)

PASTA
¼ lb. egg noodles (125 g)
¼ lb. spinach noodles (125 g)
salt
butter
12 small oil-cured olives, chopped

CHEESE
grated Romano cheese (preferably Pecorino from Italy)

- *Prepare the sauce:* Heat the olive oil. Add the onions and brown well without burning. Add the mashed garlic and stir it into the onions. Turn the heat down and let brown gently.
- Add the tomatoes, cut into quarters. Add salt and pepper to taste, a *bouquet garni* and half of the mint. Toss well, cover, and let cook for 30 minutes.
- Bring a pot of water to a boil. Add salt and put the noodles to cook according to package directions. Drain; rinse under running warm water until the water runs clear.
- Toss the noodles into the tomatoes. Add butter to taste. Add the remainder of the mint and the chopped olives. Correct the seasoning (watch the salt for the cheese is salty). Serve in a deep country-style dish sprinkled with the Pecorino-Romano cheese.

IN CANNES
the cheese used in the best little places is a very hard-to-find, hard grating cheese from Corsica known as Niolo.

CREOLE STYLE RICE
(Riz à la Créole)

Is your rice not Converted? Then before cooking the rice put it in a strainer and immerse the strainer in successive baths of cold water until the water does not cloud anymore.

Instant rice is not as tasty. Even if you prefer unconverted rice, use regular rice.

■ Easy
  6 servings
  Thrift recipe
  20 minutes
  Best season: year around

  water
  salt
  1½ cups uncooked Converted rice
  butter
  pepper

THIS COOKING METHOD
is the fastest and to be used only for Converted rice. Always rinse the rice under warm water after it is cooked (see p. 200).

See advice for other types of rice.

- Bring 2 to 3 quarts of water (2 to 3 L) to a boil. Add 1 teaspoon salt per quart of water.
- Add the rice and stir until the water comes back to a boil. Keep boiling, not simmering, or the rice will fall down to the bottom of the pan and fail to cook evenly. The boil will keep the rice in suspension and have it cooked in 14 minutes.
- Empty the cooked rice into a colander and rinse it under running warm, not hot, water until the water runs clear.
- For better and drier texture, butter a baking dish lightly and put the rice in the dish; let the rice sit in a 250°F., 120°C. or 3 Regulo oven for approximately 30 minutes to evaporate the water. Stir occasionally, fluffing upward with the tines of a fork, not a spoon. Salt and pepper the rice during the last fluffing.

WITH THE SAME METHOD
You can prepare rice for the following dishes:
Stews, sautés or ragouts of beef, lamb, veal, poultry or kidneys, or sauced fish dishes.
Salads: prepare the rice as described, and let it cool completely before using it.
Creole rice can be served with Béchamel, Mornay, Aurore, Dieppe, Ravigote and Tomato sauces.

INDIAN-STYLE RICE
(Riz à l'Indienne)

This recipe came to France from Martinique and Guadaloupe, the two French overseas Départements which have a rather large East Indian population.

- A bit difficult
  6 servings
  Affordable to medium expensive
  Best season: year around

  1½ cups converted rice

INDIAN SAUCE
1 coconut
2 onions
US 6 TB, UK 3 TB, butter (90 g)
1½ tsps. curry powder
US ¼ cup, UK 2 TB, cashews (2 TB)
US ¼ cup, UK 2 TB, raisins (2 TB)
salt and pepper
pinch of ground cinnamon
2 whole cloves

WHITE RICE
If you want a super white rice, add the juice of a lemon to the cooking water.

- Cook the rice Creole style following instructions in the preceding recipe.

INDIAN SAUCE
- Punch 2 holes in the coconut and let the juice escape into a 1-quart measuring cup. You need US 1½ cups, UK 1¼ cups (.35 L) of coconut milk, approximately, for the sauce. If you do not have that much, scrape some of the meat from the coconut and chop it. Put it in a blender. Add as much boiling water as you need to make the needed 1½ cups. Blend. Strain, pushing hard on the pulp to release the coconut milk.

- Peel the onions and slice them thinly. Heat the butter in a saucepan. Add the onion slices and brown them lightly. Remove them to a plate with a slotted spoon, squeezing well to press out the butter. Add curry powder to the pan and cook it for 2 to 3 minutes. Add the cashews, raisins, coconut milk, salt and pepper to taste, the cinnamon and the cloves (crush the heads only into the sauce). Bring to a boil and simmer for 3 to 4 minutes. Correct the seasoning.

- Serve the rice in a vegetable dish and the sauce in a sauceboat, both heated well.

- Excellent with plain roasted duck, roasted chicken, panfried veal, lamb chops.

RICE AND MUSSELS
(Riz aux Moules)

Just before serving you can add on top of the rice approximately ½ cup of scalding heavy cream and some chopped parsley.

This dish is excellent to accompany broiled fish which is cooked without sauce.

- Easy
  6 servings
  Thrift recipe
  35 minutes
  Best season: September to April

  2 quarts mussels (2 L)
  1 onion, chopped
  US ½ cup, UK 4 TB, butter (120 g)
  ½ tsp. curry powder
  1½ cups uncooked rice
  US 3 cups, UK 2¾ cups, mussel juice and
     water mixed (see recipe text) (.75 L)
  very little salt
  pepper

ABOUT THIS DISH
It can be transformed into a full meal by adding flaked, cooked fish fillets, shrimps, scallops, etc.

- Clean the mussels and wash them well (see p. 300 for instructions).
- Put the mussels into a covered pot over high heat. Shake the pot every second minute to mix the mussels. In about 8 minutes, all mussels will be opened. Remove from the heat.
- Shell the mussels; filter their juices through a coffee filter or a double layer of cheesecloth, setting the filter over a 1-quart measuring cup.
- Peel and chop the onion.
- Heat the butter in a braising pot or large saucepan. Brown the onion in the butter. Add curry powder and cook for a few minutes. Add the rice; stir until hard and very white.
- Add enough water to the mussel juices to obtain exactly twice as much volume of liquid as you have rice. Pour the liquid mixture into the rice. Cover with paper towels and the pot lid. Bring to a boil, reduce to a simmer, and cook for 20 minutes. You may need very little salt. Pepper well.
- Gently toss the mussels into the rice and serve.

RICE PILAF
(Pilaf de Riz)

If you want to obtain a two-color rice dish, toast one third of the rice very deeply in the butter so it browns visibly; do not burn the rice.

Molded rice is very attractive. Butter a ring mold, pack the rice well into it, and unmold. In the center, you can serve any stew or sauced dish.

- Easy
  6 servings
  Thrift recipe
  30 minutes
  Best season: year around

  US 3 cups, UK 2¾ cups, bouillon of your choice, or water (.75 L)
  US 4 TB, UK 2 TB, butter (60 g)
  1½ cups uncooked rice
  salt and pepper

- Bring bouillon or water to a boil.
- Heat the butter in a pot until it starts browning lightly. Add the rice and toss it in the butter until you can see the grains turn white and dry (see advice).
- Add the whole amount of liquid at once. Bring heat to a low simmer. Stretch several layers of paper toweling over the opening of the pot to catch the steam and close the pot lid. Let cook for 18 to 20 minutes.
- If you use bouillon, correct the seasoning after you finish the cooking. If you use water, season before cooking.

ABOUT THE RICE

In this recipe, the rice used is Converted. All kinds of rice can be used as well. Nonconverted rice molds better.

The rice is better measured by volume than by weight. Note that the volume of liquid used to prepare a pilaf is always twice that of the rice.

WITH THE SAME METHOD

French-Style Rice: Reduce the amount of liquid used by one fifth and add 7 to 8 ounces of sliced raw mushrooms (200 to 250 g) to the pot. Toward the end of the cooking, add 3½ ounces boiled ham (100 g), diced.

Hungarian-Style Rice: Season the pilaf with sweet or hot paprika. Excellent with a ragout or stew of beef.

Rice with Bacon: Render 3½ ounces bacon (100 g), cut into small cubes. In the fat, sauté 2 chopped onions. Remove to a plate. Add some butter to the pan. Sauté the rice and finish the pilaf as above. Add bacon and onions to the pot before covering.

Mediterranean Rice: Sauté the rice in olive oil. Add a large pinch of saffron to the bouillon. At the end of the cooking, add a few chopped olives of your choice (see p. 301).

Oriental-Style Rice: To the butter used to sauté the rice, add as much curry powder as you like. Excellent for poultry dishes, veal and lamb dishes.

Pilaf with Fish Court-Bouillon: To serve with fish, prepare the pilaf either with fish court-bouillon (p. 295) or with fish stock (p. 30).

Tomato Pilaf: Replace half of the water by 3 average tomatoes, peeled and quartered, which will be cooked with the rice.

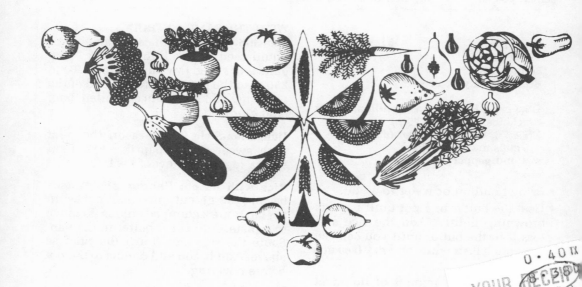

VEGETABLES
(Les Légumes)

FRICASSEE OF ARTICHOKES AND MUSHROOMS
(Artichauts Fricassés)

Prosciutto ham being quite expensive, you may replace it by 3 rashers of thick-sliced bacon, cut into ¼-inch dice. In that case, render the bacon before you add the mushrooms to the pot and discard half of the fat. Use only half as much olive oil and no butter.

- Relatively easy
  6 servings
  Very expensive
  45 minutes
  Best season: May to September when artichokes are plentiful

  2½ doz. baby artichokes, the smaller, the better
  2 onions
  3 garlic cloves
  ¾ lb. mushrooms (375 g)
  US 2 TB, UK 1 TB, olive oil (1 TB)
  salt and pepper
  1 lemon
  US 1 cup, UK 1 scant cup, bouillon (3 dl)
  ¼ lb. prosciutto (125 g)
  US 1 TB, UK ½ TB, butter (½ TB)
  chopped parsley

NO FRESH ARTICHOKES?
Frozen artichoke hearts will save the day; all you have to do is buy 3 boxes (10 oz. or 300 g each), recut the tips of their leaves, and add them to the pan.

- Cut off the stems of the artichokes. Remove the dark green leaves until you are left with little corklike hearts, about ¾ inch wide. Cut ⅓ inch off the top and cut the hearts lengthwise into halves. Let artichokes soak in lemon water.

- Bring a pot of water to a boil and blanch artichokes for 5 minutes.

- Meanwhile, chop the onions and garlic. Clean the mushrooms (see p. 300) and cut them into ¼-inch-thick slices.

- Heat the olive oil in a skillet. Sauté onions and garlic until onions are translucent, then add mushrooms, salt and pepper to taste and lemon juice. Sauté over high heat for a few minutes. Reduce the heat, cover, and let the mushrooms lose their juices.

- Add the blanched artichokes and the bouillon. Simmer together, uncovered, until the artichokes are tender (use the skewer test, p. 304). Toss gently at regular intervals.

- Add the prosciutto, cut into cubes. Mix well. Turn the heat off and let steep together. Reheat well; add the butter. Add salt only if needed, a little pepper and some chopped parsley.

- Empty into a vegetable dish. Excellent especially with chicken, veal and ham.

ASPARAGUS COUNTRY STYLE
(Asperges à la Paysanne)

How about these tiny threadlike green asparagus? They are strictly for salad. They are never peeled, but are blanched in boiling salted water for not more than a few seconds.

Steaming asparagus is fine for the white species. The green ones will discolor badly.

■ Easy
  6 servings
  Expensive
  35 minutes
  Best season: April to June

  3 dozen large asparagus, white or green
  6 eggs
  butter
  salt and pepper

WHICH TYPE OF ASPARAGUS?
Any one growing in your area: the green ones (Belle de Lauris breed); the pure white ones (Argenteuil, Cavaillon or Vineuil breeds); the white ones with purple tips (Italian breed). But always buy them as large and as squat, meaty and thick as possible.

• Bring a large pot of water to a boil. Add 1½ teaspoons salt per quart.

• To prepare the asparagus: holding the stalk between thumb and index finger of both hands, bend stalk until it breaks by itself. It breaks exactly where the fibers stop being edible. Peel the asparagus with a knife or a potato peeler. Wash it well. Tie asparagus in bundles of 6 stalks each.

• Add bundles to the boiling water. Bring back to a boil and boil *hard* for no more than 7 minutes. Remove to a colander. Immediately put the eggs to cook in the same water for no more than 4 minutes.

• Serve the asparagus on a platter lined with a fresh napkin. Serve the eggs in egg cups. Each guest will add butter, salt and pepper to his egg and dip each asparagus into the yolk before eating.

• Excellent as a first course. Otherwise, plain asparagus, without the boiled eggs but well buttered or with hollandaise sauce, goes well with all red meats, all white meats, all fish and shellfish.

CREAMED FRESH SHELL BEANS
(Haricots Frais à la Crème)

Combine any leftover beans with their own cooking liquid, a bit of bouillon and cream, and 2 or 3 onions, chopped and sautéed, and you will have an excellent soup.

- Easy
  6 servings
  Thrift recipe
  45 minutes, 35 minutes in pressure cooker
  Best season: July to September

  4 lbs. shell beans in pods (2 kg)
  2 medium-size onions
  2 garlic cloves
  water
  salt
  chopped parsley
  chopped chervil
  US ⅔ cup, UK ½ cup, heavy cream (150 g)
  pepper

- Shell the beans; peel onions and garlic cloves.
- Bring a pot of water to a boil. Add salt, the beans, onions and garlic. Bring back to a boil, reduce to a simmer, and cook for 20 to 30 minutes, depending on the kind and size of the beans.
- Drain the beans, reserving the cooking water (see advice).
- Chop parsley and chervil. Mix them into the cream. Add a few tablespoons of the bean cooking water and season well. Reheat beans and sauce together without boiling and turn into a vegetable dish.
- Excellent with all types of lamb—sautéed, braised, panfried or roasted.

CHOOSE WELL
Choose the beans with smooth and taut shells.

Two pounds of shell beans yield approximately 12 ounces (375 g) beans, ready to eat.

GREEN BEANS IN LEMON AND PARSLEY BUTTER
(Haricots Verts Maître d'Hôtel)

Leftovers? Heat a couple of tablespoons or so of vinegar with salt and pepper and in it toss the leftover beans; an excellent warm salad.

- Easy
  6 servings
  Medium expensive
  20 minutes
  Best season: June to September

  2 lbs. green beans, as fine as possible (1 kg)
  US ½ cup, UK ⅓ cup, fresh butter (120 g)
  salt and pepper
  lemon juice
  chopped parsley

CHOOSE WELL

A good green bean is always small, from ⅙ to ¼ inch wide. Beans ⅓ inch wide are already starting to grow too old. To check the quality, break one in the center; it should be full of juicy pulp. Large seeds and tough outsides come in older beans.

- String the beans. Break them into halves crosswise. Wash them and let them stand in cold water.
- Meanwhile bring to a boil a large pot of water, 3 quarts at least. Salt the water with 1½ teaspoons salt per quart.
- Add the beans by handfuls, so the water barely stops boiling. *Do not cover the pot.* Boil for 7 to 8 minutes, depending on the size. The beans must remain slightly crunchy and bright green.
- Meanwhile prepare the butter. Cream it with a spoon, fork or electric mixer. Add salt, pepper, lemon juice and parsley to taste. Set aside.
- Drain the beans. Heat a skillet, add the beans, and toss them in the hot skillet to evaporate their water. Remove beans from the heat, let cool for a minute, and toss in the butter, tablespoon by tablespoon. Correct salt and pepper and turn into a vegetable dish.
- Excellent with lamb—chops, leg or shoulder.

SAUTÉED BRUSSELS SPROUTS
(Choux de Bruxelles Sautés)

The double blanching of the sprouts is essential to sweeten the taste and for the assimilation by the human machine.

■ Easy
6 servings
Thrift recipe
25 to 30 minutes
Best season: during the cold months

2½ lbs. Brussels sprouts (1 kg)
6 rashers of thin-sliced bacon
US 4 TB, UK 2 TB, butter (60 g)
salt and pepper

- Bring 2 large pots of water to a boil.
- Clean the Brussels sprouts, remove the wilted outside leaves, and cut the stem ends neatly. Cut a small cross in each stem end for even cooking.
- Add salt to the first pot of water (1½ teaspoons per quart), then add the Brussels sprouts and blanch them for 5 minutes.
- Meanwhile cut the bacon into small pieces and start rendering it in a frying pan.
- After 5 minutes have elapsed, add salt to the second pot and transfer the Brussels sprouts to it to finish cooking for another 7 to 8 minutes.

- Meanwhile, crisp the bacon well and remove it to a plate. Discard half of the rendered fat and add the butter to the pan. Heat butter until golden.
- Drain the Brussels sprouts and add them to the frying pan. Bring the heat high enough so they brown lightly on all sides. Just before serving, add the bacon. Correct the seasoning.

WITH THE SAME METHOD
Brussels Sprouts Auvergne Style: Open a jar of whole chestnuts and heat them with the sprouts for a few minutes after they have browned.

Brussels Sprouts au Gratin: When the sprouts are golden, empty them into a dish. Sprinkle them first with the bacon, then add a thick layer of grated Gruyère cheese and pass under the broiler to melt the cheese. Excellent with pork, venison and game.

CHOOSE WELL
Your sprouts should be very green, crisp and compact.

BRAISED CABBAGE
(Chou Braisé)

This dish can become a thrifty one-pot dinner, if you bury in the cabbage 12 Italian sausages during the last 45 minutes of cooking and set 6 potatoes to cook on top of the cabbage during the last half hour of cooking.

■ Easy
6 servings
Thrift recipe
2½ hours, 1½ hours in pressure cooker
Best season: a cold weather dish

1 large green cabbage
water
salt
6 rashers of thin-sliced bacon
1 onion, stuck with 1 clove
pepper
bouillon, approximately 2 cups (.5 L)
US 4 TB, UK 2 TB, butter (60 g), optional

THE CABBAGE
If you prefer a white cabbage, use that instead; it also tastes delicious but the leaves may break more easily.

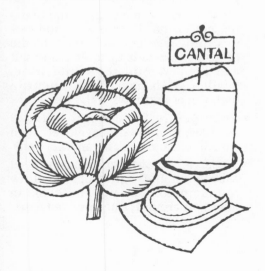

- Discard the wilted outside leaves of the cabbage. Remove the large outside leaves one by one and cut out the rib. When you reach the heart of tight leaves, cut it into 4 quarters.

- Bring a large pot of water to a boil. Add 1½ teaspoons salt per quart and add the cabbage. Blanch for 5 minutes. Drain well. As soon as the cabbage has cooled, press out most of the water.

- Arrange the rashers of bacon in crisscross pattern on the bottom of a pot. Add the cabbage in successive layers, salting very lightly; on the last layer, add the onion cut into halves and stuck with the clove. Season well with pepper. Finally add enough bouillon to reach the level of the cabbage leaves.

- Bring to a boil, cover, reduce heat, and let cook very gently for about 2 hours, 1 hour in pressure cooker.

- The cabbage must be very well done and almost candied in its own juices. If you wish, add the butter now, mixing it into the vegetables. The bacon will have fallen apart during the cooking.

- Excellent with all pork dishes, game and venison.

STUFFED CABBAGE
(Chou Farci)

This is more of a thrifty main dish than a vegetable accompaniment. Round up the meal with a good soup and a good salad. End it with a piece of cheese.

With the removed heart of the cabbage, cut finely, make yourself a small healthy salad for lunch. Since it will not be overcooked, it still will be full of vitamins. Unfortunately braised vegetables lose most of their vitamins.

■ Difficult
6 servings
Thrift recipe
2¾ hours, 1¾ hours in pressure cooker
Best season: during the cold months

1 large cabbage
2 shallots
3 onions
1 garlic clove
2 carrots
chopped parsley
1 lb. sausage meat (500 g)
1 egg
salt and pepper
3 slices of white bread, crusts removed
a few TB milk
US 4 TB, UK 2 TB, butter (60 g)
US 1 cup, UK 1 scant cup, dry white wine (2.5 dl)
US 1 cup, UK 1 scant cup, bouillon (2.5 dl)
bouquet garni

- Half-fill a pot of water. Bring to a boil and add 1½ teaspoons salt per quart of water.
- Cut the stem of the cabbage flush to the leaves; discard the wilted leaves. Wash cabbage and leave it whole. Put it to blanch in the rapidly boiling water. As soon as the water comes back to a boil, remove the cabbage upside-down to a colander and let it cool so you can handle it.
- Peel and chop the shallots, 1 onion, and the garlic. Slice the other 2 onions and the carrots.

- Put the chopped vegetables in a bowl. Add some parsley, the sausage meat, the egg, and salt and pepper to taste. Soak the bread in the milk, squeeze it dry, and add it to the other ingredients. Mix into a homogenous forcemeat. Test the forcemeat (see p. 298).
- Cross 2 kitchen strings on the kitchen table or counter; put the cabbage at the center and pull apart the outer leaves gently. Remove the center leaves and core by grabbing it firmly with your working hand and twisting it off (see advice). Replace the removed cabbage heart by half of the forcemeat. Close 2 or 3 leaves and add more forcemeat. Continue this way until all the forcemeat has been used. Tie the cabbage into a neat package, using the prepared strings.
- Melt the butter in a large round braising pot. Sauté sliced onions and carrots until nice and golden. Add the cabbage, stem side up at first, and salt and pepper. Add the white wine, bouillon and *bouquet garni*. Bring to a boil. Cover and reduce the heat.
- Cook gently for 1 hour. Using 2 spatulas, turn the cabbage over, stem side down, and cook for another hour.
- To serve, remove the strings and set cabbage at the center of a shallow round platter. Empty the cooking juices all around. Cut into wedges.

CREAMED CARROTS
(Carottes à la Crème)

Baby carrots are even better this way. Brush them well under running cold water. Cook them whole without slicing. In French kitchen terms, a baby carrot is barely 1 inch long and ½ inch wide, never bigger. If your carrots are bigger, cut them into small pieces.

■ Easy
6 servings
Thrift recipe
25 minutes, 10 minutes in pressure cooker
Best season: late spring and summer

1½ lbs. carrots (750 g)
salt
US 3 TB, UK 1½ TB, butter (45 g)
pepper
US ⅔ cup, UK ½ cup, heavy cream (150 g)
lemon juice
chopped parsley

- Bring a large pot of water to a boil. Add salt.

- Meanwhile, peel the carrots and cut them with a knife, a slicer, or a food processor into ⅛-inch slices.

- Immerse the carrot slices in the boiling water, bring back to a boil, and boil hard for 3 to 4 minutes. Drain.

- Heat the butter over high heat until it turns golden. Toss the carrots in the butter, add salt and pepper to taste, and let the carrots brown a little bit.

- Off the heat, add the cream and lemon juice to your taste. Empty into a vegetable dish and sprinkle with parsley. Correct the seasoning.

CARROTS
are rich in vitamins A, B and C and contain a lot of good iron. Excellent to keep your eyes in good shape.

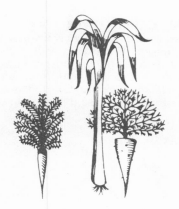

WITH THE SAME METHOD
Carrots Flavored with Port: When the carrots are cooked, heat the butter until it browns lightly, then add US ⅓ cup, UK 3 tablespoons, Port (3 TB) and boil hard together for 1 minute. Toss the carrots into the Port and butter and add the cream. Add a tiny dash of nutmeg. Excellent with all birds and all veal dishes.

CAULIFLOWER COUNTRY STYLE
(Chou-Fleur de Campagne)

Do you know that a piece of dry bread added to the cooking water of the cauliflower will keep the cooking smell from permeating your home? Try it.

Also, now is the time to be thrifty and to prepare a small soup with all the peelings and stems cooked in the cooking water of the cauliflower.

- Easy
  6 servings
  Thrift recipe
  35 minutes
  Best season: year around

  1 large cauliflower
  vinegar
  2 eggs
  US ½ cup, UK 4 TB, butter (125 g)
  salt and pepper
  parsley
  US ⅓ cup, UK ¼ cup, dry bread crumbs (4 to 5 TB)

- Bring a potful of water to a boil and add 1½ teaspoons salt per quart.

- Clean and trim the cauliflower. Peel all the stems quickly (it is easy) and cut into as many small flowerets, about ½ inch across, as possible. Rinse in vinegar water.

- Add cauliflowerets to the boiling water and cook for 7 to 8 minutes. Vegetables must remain slightly crunchy for this presentation to work.

- At the same time add the 2 eggs to hard-boil them for 10 minutes. To retrieve them easily, simply empty the water (see advice first) after you have removed the cauliflower and rinse the eggs under cold water so they peel well. Cool completely.

- Heat half of the butter in a frying pan. Toss the cauliflower in the butter until hot. Season with salt and pepper.

- Arrange the cauliflowerets, stem ends up, in a 1-quart bowl; pack in well. Keep hot in the oven.

- Chop the shelled eggs and the parsley. While you do so, heat the dry bread crumbs in the remaining butter until golden.

- Invert the cauliflower on a shallow soup plate. Sprinkle with the chopped eggs and parsley mixed, then with the buttered crumbs.

- Excellent with veal, rabbit, chicken, etc.

ABOUT CAULIFLOWER
A good cauliflower is snow white with very tight flowers. It will keep well in its green leaves if stored in the crisper of your refrigerator. Slugs love cauliflower and hide well in its complex structure; that is why you are instructed to rinse it in vinegar water.

EGGPLANT FLAN WITH TOMATO SAUCE
(Flan d'Aubergines à la Tomate)

Eggplants should not be too large. They must have a dark purple, very smooth and taut skin without spots or pitting. All kinds of eggplants may be used: the regular eggplant; the green Caribbean eggplant with purple streaks; the tiny Italian eggplant.

■ Requires care
6 servings
Affordable
1½ hours, approximately
Best season: fall for best eggplants, but feasible year around

2½ lbs. eggplant (1.2 kg)
salt
3 garlic cloves
2 onions
US ⅔ cup, UK ½ cup, olive oil (2 scant dl)
pepper
dried thyme and bay leaf
3 eggs
2 cups tomato sauce, homemade or canned (.5 L)

• Wash the eggplants, cut them into ½-inch cubes, and put them in a shallow dish. Salt them and let them stand to bleed for approximately 30 minutes. Stir occasionally.

• Peel and chop the garlic cloves and onions.

• Drain the eggplants, rinse them well, and dry them well in paper or tea towels.

• Heat all the oil in a braising pot (it will all be needed, for the eggplant will and must absorb it for goodness' sake).

• Brown the onions and garlic lightly.

Add the eggplant cubes and stir well. Add only a little salt, some pepper, thyme and crushed bay leaf; mix well. Cover and cook for approximately 30 minutes.

• Preheat oven to 400°F., 200°C. or 6 Regulo.

• Beat the eggs into an omelet batter; add a pinch of salt and pepper.

• At the end of 30 minutes, whisk the eggplant cubes to a very coarse purée. Remove from the heat, cool a bit, and mix in the eggs. Stir until homogenous.

• Butter heavily a 6-cup charlotte mold. Pour the flan batter into it.

• Bring a kettle full of water to a boil. Set the charlotte mold in a shallow pan and set the pan on the oven rack. Pour the boiling water into the lower pan. Bake for about 35 minutes, or until a skewer inserted three quarters of the way to the center of the loaf comes out clean.

• Meanwhile, prepare a tomato sauce (see p. 61) or, if you prefer, open a can of ready-made sauce. Unmold the flan and spoon the sauce over it. Serve very hot.

BRAISED ENDIVES
(Endives Braisées)

For added welcome taste render a few chopped rashers of bacon and use some of the bacon fat with less butter. Also, a sautéed chopped onion can be a good addition.

■ Easy
6 servings
Very expensive
40 to 45 minutes
Best season: November to April

12 beautiful endives
US 4 TB, UK 2 TB, butter (60 g)
juice of 1 lemon
same amount of water
salt
pepper
US 6 TB, UK 3 TB, heavy cream (90 g)

• Remove the tip of the leaves of the endives, any wilted or stained leaf, then remove the center part of the root by digging around with your knife to excise a small cone which can be bitter. Leave the endives whole.

• Wash endives quickly by running cold water directly from the spigot through their leaves. Press them to extract the water.

• Melt the butter in a sauteuse pan; add the lemon juice, a few tablespoons of water and endives; salt and pepper the endives.

• Cover and cook, turning at regular intervals. If the endives brown too much keep adding water, never bouillon. The length of the cooking varies with the size: medium-size endives need 20 to 25 minutes, large ones need 30 to 35 minutes.

• The endives must look translucent and be tender to a skewer test (see p. 304). When they are cooked, add the cream and reheat very well. Serve in a heated vegetable dish.

WITH THE SAME METHOD
Braised Lettuce: Remove any wilted outside leaves. Cut lettuces lengthwise into halves, wash them well, and prepare little bundles by enclosing the white center leaves in the tightly closed outside leaves. Use only a few drops of lemon juice. Bouillon is permissible in small quantity since lettuce is full of water.

GRADES OF ENDIVES IN EUROPE
There are many. Those exported are always the largest and best. Spotless and of uniform size, they are sold in their own blue-paper-lined wooden boxes. Do not buy them out of a supermarket tray; they will be bitter. The use of the blue paper is to keep them sweet by keeping out the light; light lets chlorophyll develop and consequently a bitter taste.

ENDIVES WITH HAM AU GRATIN
(Endives au Jambon Gratinées)

This dish is plentiful enough to be a main course. Complete the menu with a soup, a salad and cheese.

■ Easy
6 servings
Expensive
40 minutes
Best season: November to May

12 endives

SAUCE
US 2 TB, UK 1 TB, butter (30 g)
US 2 TB, UK 1 TB, flour (15 g)
US 1¼ cups, UK 1 generous cup, milk (.25 L)
salt and pepper
nutmeg
3½ oz. Gruyère cheese, grated (100 g)
6 slices of boiled ham

- Braise the 12 endives as indicated in the preceding recipe.
- *Sauce:* Melt the butter in a saucepan; add the flour to make a *roux*. Add the hot milk to bind, using a whisk, and stir until the sauce boils. Add salt, pepper and nutmeg to taste. Add two thirds of the cheese and let cook for a few more minutes.
- Cut the slices of ham into halves and wrap each endive in a piece of ham.
- Butter a baking dish. Add one third of the sauce, the ham-wrapped endives, and top with the remainder of the sauce. Top with the remainder of the Gruyère and broil until golden. Serve in the baking dish.

WITH THE SAME METHOD
Leeks and Ham au Gratin: The recipe is exactly the same. Use only the white part of the leeks. Use the remainder of the leeks to prepare a soup. Braise the leeks without lemon juice but with bouillon.

REMEMBER
never to soak endives, or they will turn bitter.

LEEKS AU GRATIN
(Poireaux au Gratin)

Only large leeks available? Cut them across into slices about ⅓ inch thick and proceed with the recipe.

- Easy
  6 servings
  Thrift recipe to expensive, depending on availability of leeks
  40 minutes
  Best season: with new leeks, August to October

  12 good leeks
  US 6 TB, UK 3 TB, butter (90 g)
  salt and pepper
  US 1 cup, UK 1 scant cup, water (3 dl)
  6 oz. Gruyère cheese, grated (180 g)
  US ½ cup, UK ⅓ cup, dry bread crumbs (5 TB)

CHOOSE WELL
If possible, choose small leeks no more than ¾ inch in diameter.

- Cut off the roots of the leeks. Remove the green tops, keeping only the very light green and white parts. Cut each leek lengthwise into halves without cutting all the way through the root end. Wash the leeks by letting the water run from the spigot between their leaves. Shake them to drain them well.

- Heat the butter in a frying skillet and brown the leeks well, turning them over several times. Salt and pepper them, add the water, cover, and let cook until tender. The leeks should be done in approximately 25 minutes.

- Preheat the broiler. Butter a baking dish.

- Put 1 layer of leeks, 1 layer of cheese, and so on, ending by a layer of cheese and bread crumbs mixed.

- Meanwhile, reduce the water in the skillet to a very thick jelly and pour it all around the side of the dish, so it flows under the leeks. Dot top with butter and put under the broiler to melt and become golden.

BROILED MUSHROOM CAPS BORDELAISE
(Champignons Grillés à la Bordelaise)

All mushrooms need heavy seasoning and are able to make big wines such as Pomerol, Médoc and St. Émilion show all their potency and goodness.

■ A bit difficult
6 servings
Expensive to very expensive
20 minutes
Best season: whenever you feel like it with cultivated mushrooms; July to September with Boleti

18 mushrooms, large if cultivated, smaller if wild
3 garlic cloves
1 bouquet of parsley
olive oil as needed
salt and pepper

OTHER MUSHROOMS
This recipe can also be applied to all wild edible Boleti such as Boletus Edulis, Boletus Mirabilis, Boletus Badius. In one word, all Boleti, the stems of which are also edible and with no red coloring of the tubes.

- Clean the mushrooms (see p. 300). Cut off the mushroom stems. Chop them as well as the garlic and the parsley.
- Pour a tablespoon or so of olive oil into a frying pan. When it is very hot, add the chopped mixture and cook it for a few minutes until the juices have escaped from the mushroom stems, then evaporated again. Sprinkle with salt and pepper.
- Heat the broiler. Brush the caps with oil and broil them for a few minutes on each side. The length of the broiling depends on the size of the mushrooms. Salt and pepper well.
- Put the caps, hollow side up, on a heated platter. Fill the caps with equal amounts of the mushroom hash.
- Excellent with red meats, squab, lamb roasts and roasted chicken.

MUSHROOMS À LA PROVENÇALE
(Champignons à la Provençale)

When fresh mushrooms are not very good because of the heat (July and August), replace them by wild mushrooms or canned mushrooms. Use either first quality caps or sliced mushrooms, not the broken pieces.

■ Easy
6 servings
Medium expensive
15 minutes
Best season: year around

1½ lbs. fresh button mushrooms (750 g)
3 garlic cloves
a good bouquet of parsley leaves
US 3 TB, UK 1½ TB, olive oil (1½ TB)
salt and pepper
3 slices of white bread
US ¼ cup, UK 2 TB, butter (60 g)

WILD MUSHROOMS
This recipe can also be prepared with the following wild mushrooms:
all Boleti (see p. 225);
chanterelles (Cantharellus cibarius, Craterellus cornucopioides);
mousseron (Marasmius oreades or fairy ring mushrooms);
true morels (Morchella esculenta deliciosa and anguticeps);
false morels (Verpa conica and Gyromitra Gigas).

• Clean the mushrooms (see p. 300); leave them whole if you have button mushrooms, quarter them if they are large.

For the wild mushrooms:
• Chanterelles must be washed as little as possible and cut into smaller quarters.

• Mousseron/Meadow mushrooms can be left whole; their stems are tough and must be discarded.

• Morels must be washed quickly for they harbor "guests" in their folds.

• Chop garlic and parsley. Heat the olive oil. Add the mushrooms, and salt and pepper them. Let them lose all their moisture, then over high heat let moisture evaporate. Add garlic and parsley and sauté mushrooms until brown.

• While the mushrooms brown in one skillet, cut the crusts off the slices of bread and cut each slice into 2 triangles. Fry the triangles in the butter.

• Spoon the mushrooms over the croutons and set on a platter.

• Excellent with eggs, all white and red meats.

MUSHROOMS IN WHITE SAUCE
(Champignons en Sauce Blanche)

Are guests delayed? If these mushrooms must wait, keep the saucepan in a hot water bath.

■ Sauce is a bit difficult
6 servings
Expensive
30 minutes
Best season: year around

1½ lbs. fresh mushrooms (750 g)
US 4 TB, UK 2 TB, butter (60 g)
salt and pepper
1 lemon
US ½ cup, UK ⅓ cup, dry white wine (1 generous dl)
1½ tsp. cornstarch
US 6 TB, UK 3 TB, heavy cream (90 g)
1 egg yolk
3 slices of white bread
oil for browning croutons
chopped parsley

• Prepare the mushrooms as described on page 300. Cut them into quarters or halves, depending on their size.

• Melt and heat the butter; add the mushrooms, salt and pepper to taste and lemon juice. Toss over high heat for a few minutes and cover to extract the juices.

• After 5 minutes, add the white wine and reheat very well, boiling hard for a few minutes. Remove the mushrooms to a soup plate or a shallow dish.

• Mix the cornstarch with one third of the cream and stir into the cooking juices of the mushrooms. Let simmer for 5 minutes, adding all the juices that will have escaped from the mushrooms.

• While the sauce simmers, mix the egg yolk and the remainder of the cream. Set aside. Remove crusts from bread and cut the slices into 6 triangles. Brown them in the oil. Keep warm.

• Return the mushrooms to the saucepan and reheat very well. Remove about ¼ cup of the sauce and whisk it very quickly into the yolk and cream mixture (see p. 299, *liaison*). Add to the panful of mushrooms, mix well, and stir until one little boil appears at the center of the pot.

• Empty the mushroom ragout into a dish and decorate with croutons and chopped parsley.

• Excellent with chicken, plainly broiled or roasted, with plain veal steaks and escalopes, with steaks and roasts of beef.

FOR CULTIVATED MUSHROOMS
only, or if you find the species called Agaricus *or* Psalliota Arvensis, *or meadow mushroom, from which our cultivated mushroom descends.*

BABY PEAS IN THE FRENCH MANNER
(Petits Pois à la Française)

■ Easy
6 servings
Affordable
45 minutes
Best season: June through August

3½ lbs. fresh peas in pods (1.5 kg)
12 silverskin onions
1 head of soft-leaf lettuce (preferably Boston lettuce)
US ⅓ cup, UK ¼ cup, water (1 scant dl)
parsley sprigs
salt and pepper
US 8 TB, UK 4 TB, butter (120 g)

- Shell the peas. Peel the onions. Clean the lettuce, then tie it.
- In an enameled cast-iron pot, put water, onions, lettuce, as much parsley as you like, salt and pepper to taste, the peas and three quarters of the butter. Cover and let cook gently for 20 to 30 minutes. The cooking time depends on the size of the peas, and this style of cooking always results in well-done peas by tradition. If the peas are not well done, they do not taste the way they should.
- Remove the parsley. Empty the peas into a vegetable dish. Add the remainder of the butter. Cut the lettuce into 6 wedges and add to the peas.

CHOOSE WELL
Choose good peas with shiny, taut shells without stains or traces of dehydration. Peas retain all their sugar and lovely taste if they are shelled just before cooking.

STUFFED POTATOES EN PAPILLOTES
(Pommes de Terre Farcies en Papillotes)

You can vary this dish by changing the herbs and aromatics with the season.

■ Easy
6 servings
Thrift recipe
1 hour and 10 minutes
Best season: cold weather

8 baking potatoes
½ lb. thin-sliced bacon (250 g)
4 shallots
chopped parsley
US ½ cup, UK ¼ lb., butter (125 g)
salt and pepper

- Preheat oven to 400°F., 220°C. or 6 Regulo.
- Peel the potatoes, wash them, and cut off a small slice on the bottom so the potato will stand in a baking dish.
- Cut off a 1½-inch slice at the top to be used as a lid. With a melon baller, remove about 3 tablespoons of pulp from inside the potatoes. Chop this pulp coarsely. Rinse it in 3 successive waters.
- Chop the bacon and the shallots. Render the bacon slowly until golden. Add the shallots and toss in the hot fat until golden. Add some chopped parsley.

- Remove the chopped potato to a tea towel and pat dry. Add half of the butter to the pan and add the chopped potato pulp. Over high heat toss all ingredients together. Salt and pepper them. Fill the cavities of the potatoes with the mixture. Put the lid of each potato on.
- Cut 6 large squares of aluminum foil, butter them, and wrap 1 potato in each square. Place packages on a baking sheet. Bake in the preheated oven for 1 hour.
- This dish is plentiful enough to make a whole meal if a nice green salad and cottage cheese flavored with fresh herbs is served with it.
- As a plain vegetable it is excellent with roast beef and all roasted meats, roast turkey and capon, etc.

CHOOSE WELL
The best potatoes for this dish are mealy baking potatoes that will readily absorb all fats and tastes.

SAUTÉED POTATOES LYON STYLE
(Pommes de Terre Sautées à la Lyonnaise)

If your onions are too strong toward the end of winter, blanch them before sautéing them (see p. 293).

■ Easy
6 servings
Thrift recipe
40 minutes
Best season: year around

2 lbs. waxy potatoes for boiling (1 kg)
6 onions
US 4 TB, UK 2 TB, butter (60 g)
US 4 TB, UK 2 TB, oil (2 TB)
salt and pepper
chopped parsley

- Wash the potatoes. Put them in a large saucepan, cover with cold water, and bring to a boil. Add salt, reduce to a simmer, and cook for 20 minutes, *10 minutes in pressure cooker.*

- Peel the onions; slice them.

- Heat the butter in a large skillet and sauté the onions over very moderate heat, stirring often. The onions will soften first, then start browning.

- Peel the potatoes and cut into ⅙-inch slices.

- Heat the oil in a second skillet, add the potatoes, and sauté them over high heat until they are golden on all sides. Let them color well on one side before you turn them over. When the potatoes are done, lift them with a slotted spoon and add them to the skillet containing the onions; mix both vegetables well. It is essential that you leave all the oil in the potato skillet, discarding it once all the potatoes have been removed. Salt and pepper the vegetables and sprinkle them with parsley. Serve.

WITH THE SAME METHOD
Lorraine Potatoes: Before you cook the onions, cut 3½ ounces slab bacon (100 g) into pieces ⅓ x 1 inch and render them. Sauté the onions partly in the bacon fat, partly in butter.

CHOOSE WELL
Choose waxy potatoes; Red Bliss would be fine.

GRATIN DAUPHINOIS
(One of the multiple versions of the baked potato dish of the French Alps in the Dauphinois)

Do you feel like splurging? Omit the eggs and replace the hot milk by the same amount of heavy cream. Calorific but a treat once in a while.

- Easy
  6 servings
  Thrift recipe
  1 hour
  Best season: year around

  4 large baking potatoes
  2 cups milk (.5 L)
  1 garlic clove
  salt and pepper
  nutmeg
  2 eggs
  3½ oz. Gruyère cheese, freshly grated (100 g)

CHOOSE WELL
The best grated cheese is the cheese you grate yourself, using a food processor, a mixer attachment or a hand grater.

- Peel and slice the potatoes. Wash them, put them in a pot, and cover them with cold milk. Bring to a boil and simmer for 5 minutes.
- Peel the garlic clove and rub it well all over the bottom and sides of a 1-quart baking dish.
- Preheat oven to 325°F., 165'C. or 4 Regulo.
- Transfer the potatoes to the baking dish in successive layers. Season each layer with salt and pepper and also sprinkle with a dash of nutmeg.
- Beat the eggs with the cooled milk and half of the grated cheese and pour the mixture over the potatoes. Cover with the remainder of the Gruyère. Bake for 40 to 45 minutes, or until the top is golden.
- Excellent for all veal and red meat dishes.

RATATOUILLE
(The ancestral dish of mixed Mediterranean vegetables, a specialty of the Riviera and Provence)

Be careful, an old eggplant can spoil a ratatouille. If you have only huge, old eggplants full of seeds, bleed them first with salt, rinse them well, pat them dry before frying them.

■ Easy
6 servings
Affordable
2½ hours
Best season: summer when all vegetables are cheap and plentiful

3 eggplants
3 baby zucchini (marrows or courgettes)
3 onions
5 tomatoes
2 peppers, 1 green, 1 red
2 garlic cloves
bouquet garni
US ½ cup, UK ⅓ cup, olive oil (1.5 dl)
salt and pepper
chopped parsley

- Cut eggplants and zucchini into ½-inch cubes.
- Peel the onions; dice them coarsely. Quarter the tomatoes. Split the peppers, remove seeds and ribs, and cut into 1½-inch squares. Peel the garlic cloves and crush them. Prepare a *bouquet garni*.
- Heat the olive oil in a large enameled cast-iron braising pot. Add the eggplants and zucchini and coat them well with oil. Let them brown a bit.
- Add then the peppers, onions, garlic, *bouquet garni*, and salt and pepper to taste. Cover and let cook for 30 minutes.
- Add the tomatoes, cover, and let cook for another 30 minutes. During these last minutes, if the liquid in the pot appears too abundant, leave the pot uncovered.
- To serve, remove the *bouquet garni*. Empty the vegetables into a country-style dish, correct the seasoning, and sprinkle with chopped parsley.

WHAT TO DO WITH LEFTOVERS OF RATATOUILLE
Rice Crown: Mold a pilaf of rice into a ring mold (see p. 209) and put reheated ratatouille in the center.

Omelette Niçoise: Cook leftover ratatouille until all juices have evaporated, and stuff it into the center of an omelet.

Pasta and Ratatouille: Add any style of noodle to leftovers of ratatouille and serve with Parmesan cheese.

ABOUT RATATOUILLE
Ratatouille is good hot, lukewarm and cold so do not hesitate to prepare plenty ahead of time.

Ratatouille needs a good spirited seasoning; do not undersalt or underpepper.

GRATIN OF SPINACH AND EGGS
(Epinards aux Œufs)

If you are in a hurry, you can prepare the same dish with 3 boxes (10 oz. or 300 g each) frozen leaf spinach, previously defrosted and sautéed in a small pat of butter to reheat.

■ Easy
6 servings
Thrift recipe
50 minutes
Best season: summer

4 lbs. spinach (1.75 kg)
US 3 TB, UK 1½ TB, butter (45 g)
US 2 TB, UK 1 TB, flour (15 g)
US 1¼ cups, UK 1 generous cup, milk, scalding (.5 L)
salt and pepper
nutmeg
3 eggs
US ½ cup, UK ⅓ cup, yogurt, natural, unflavored, unsweetened (½ container)
¼ lb. Gruyère cheese, grated (125 g)

CHOOSE WELL
Good spinach has whole shiny leaves, crisp and dark green.

- Wash the spinach in several waters. Remove the large ribs from the leaves.
- Bring a large pot of water to a boil. Salt it.
- Blanch the spinach as follows: Put a handful of spinach in a large conical strainer, immerse in the water; count 1 as you dip and at the count of 6, empty the wilted spinach into a bowl. Repeat until all spinach has been blanched. It will take no more than 3 to 4 minutes.
- Prepare the sauce: make a white *roux* with two thirds of the butter and all the flour. Bind with the scalding milk and thicken, stirring constantly. Add salt, pepper and nutmeg to taste. Simmer for 5 minutes.
- Beat the eggs, yogurt and Gruyère together with a pinch of salt and pepper.
- Press the spinach between your hands to get rid of the water, and chop it very coarsely.
- Mix the spinach with the sauce you have made. Butter a fireproof dish and empty the mixture into it. Pour the egg-yogurt-cheese mixture over the spinach and pass under the broiler until the mixture is set.

SWISS CHARD AU GRATIN
(Bettes au Gratin)

If you are short of time, cook the chard a day ahead. Next day, reheat it in butter, build the dish with cheese, and broil.

How about the green parts? Please use them; they contain a lot of good blood-strengthening iron. Sauté them in butter like spinach leaves, cut into chiffonnade, use in a salad, or add to a spinach or watercress soup.

■ Easy
 6 servings
 Thrift recipe
 50 minutes, approximately
 Best season: late spring to summer

 water
 salt
 1 lemon
 2 lbs. Swiss chard (1 kg)
 US 6 TB, UK 3 TB, butter (90 g)
 6½ oz. Gruyère cheese, grated (195 g)
 salt and pepper
 US ⅔ cup, UK ½ cup, dry bread crumbs (5 TB)

YOU SHOULD KNOW THAT
Swiss chard is recommended as a diet food and a good "thinner." To be effective as a diet food it should be eaten without sauce and with very little butter.

- Bring a large pot of water to a boil; add salt and lemon juice.
- While the water heats, clean the chard. Remove the thin skin and strings from the ribs, cut the ribs into 1-inch-long pieces. Wash them well. Save greens for another meal (see advice).
- Immerse the ribs in the boiling water and cook until tender, varying with width of the ribs, from 8 to 15 minutes.
- Butter a 1-quart baking dish. Drain the Swiss chard.
- Fill the baking dish with alternate layers of chard and grated cheese; do not forget to sprinkle lightly with salt and pepper also, and end with a layer of cheese.
- Top the cheese with bread crumbs and pour remaining butter, melted, over to cover the whole surface of the crumbs.
- Keep hot in the oven. At the last minute, put under the broiler to brown the top well.

STEWED PEAR-SHAPED TOMATOES
(Tomates à la Cocotte)

In this recipe, any gravy left over from any roast added just before serving would be a marvelous addition.

■ Easy
6 servings
Affordable
35 minutes
Best season: late July to late September

12 pear-shaped tomatoes
1 onion
3½ oz. brisket of pork (100 g)
1 garlic clove
US 2 TB, UK 1 TB, butter (30 g)
pinch of thyme
tiny piece of bay leaf, crumbled
chopped parsley
bouillon if needed
salt and pepper

• Wash the tomatoes.

• Peel the onion; slice it. Cut the pork brisket into pieces ⅓ x 1 inch. Peel and mash the garlic.

• Slowly render the pork. Discard half of the fat, add some butter to remaining fat, and sauté the onion until translucent.

• Remove onion and pork to a plate. Replace them by the tomatoes. Brown tomatoes on all sides, then add mashed garlic, thyme, bay leaf and parsley.

• Return onion and pork to the pot. Cover and let cook for 10 to 15 minutes.

• If the pot appears too dry, gradually add a bit of bouillon. Correct the seasoning and serve.

CHOOSE WELL
The tomatoes you need for this preparation are Italian pear-shaped fruits which do not fall apart easily.

STUFFED TOMATOES
(Tomates Farcies)

Children absolutely love this dish. To make it even more attractive, add around the tomatoes all the scooped-out tomato pulp plus 1 cup of rice, precooked in boiling water for 5 minutes.

The best instrument to remove tomato seeds is actually one of your fingers.

- A bit difficult
  6 servings
  Affordable
  50 minutes to 1 hour
  Best season: late July to late September

  12 medium-size tomatoes
  salt and pepper
  3 slices of white bread, crusts removed
  milk for soaking
  1 onion
  1 garlic clove
  chopped parsley
  ½ lb. sausage meat (250 g)
  1 egg
  US 3 TB, UK 1½ TB, butter (45 g)

THE TOMATOES
This recipe is for medium to large tomatoes. If you have only huge tomatoes, cut them crosswise into halves and fill each half.

- Preheat oven to 400°F., 220°C. or 6 Regulo.
- Remove the stems of the tomatoes. Cut a lid in each stem end and with a teaspoon scoop out all the insides (see advice). Sprinkle insides with salt and pepper. Turn the tomato shells upside down on a plate so they can lose their juices.
- Soak the bread in the milk and squeeze dry. Peel and chop the onion and garlic. Chop the parsley. In a bowl, mix the sausage, egg, soaked bread and all the aromatics above, plus salt and pepper to taste. Mix very well to homogenize.
- Fill the tomatoes with the forcemeat. Put a small pat of butter over each and top them with their lids. Put the tomatoes in a baking dish.
- Bake for 40 to 50 minutes, depending on size.

TOMATOES PROVENÇALE
(Tomates Provençales)

Serve these tomatoes with eggs, all chops, with rice or even green beans.

- Easy
  6 servings
  Affordable
  20 minutes
  Best season: late July to late September

  6 large sun-ripened tomatoes
  1 shallot
  1 garlic clove
  US ½ cup, UK ⅓ cup, chopped parsley (6 TB)
  US ⅓ cup, UK ¼ cup, olive oil (1 scant dl)
  flour
  salt and pepper

RIPE TOMATOES
They are essential, but they should still be firm or they will sag badly.

- Preheat oven to 400°F., 220°C. or 6 Regulo.
- Wash the tomatoes. Cut them crosswise into halves. Remove the stem scar. With your index finger, remove all the seeds.
- Peel and chop the shallot and garlic extremely fine together with the parsley.
- Heat the olive oil in a large skillet. Dip the cut side of each tomato into flour and sear in the oil over very high heat. Using a spatula, turn the tomatoes over. Sear the second side. Remove to a heated baking dish.
- To the hot oil and juices in the pan, add the chopped aromatics. Toss them very fast. Spoon an equal amount over each tomato half. Season tomatoes with salt and pepper.
- Finish baking in the hot oven for 5 to 8 minutes.

SMOTHERED ZUCCHINI
(Courgettes Étuvées)

For added flavor, at the same time as you sauté the onion, you could also sauté a few slices of fresh pork brisket or bacon.

■ Easy
   6 servings
   Thrift recipe
   30 minutes
   Best season: summer when squash is young, small and seedless

   12 tiny zucchini (baby marrows or courgettes)
   salt
   1 onion
   2 garlic cloves
   US 2 TB, UK 1 TB, olive oil (1 TB)
   US 2 TB, UK 1 TB, butter (1 TB)
   pepper
   chopped parsley

● Wash the small zucchini very well. Cut them into ⅓-inch slices. Salt the zucchini slices and let them stand for 15 minutes, mixing occasionally.

● Peel and chop onion and garlic. Heat the olive oil and butter; in it sauté the onion until translucent. Add the garlic and toss well.

● Rinse the zucchini and pat dry. Add them to the pan. Sprinkle with salt and pepper. Toss well in the oil and cover. Cook, gently stirring occasionally, until the zucchini are translucent green.

● Correct the salt and pepper and sprinkle with parsley.

● Excellent with all meats, especially white meats and poultry.

CHOOSE WELL
Zucchini or courgettes are best when they are small, shiny and firm. They should be barely 1 inch in diameter, no more than 5 inches long and still seedless.

SALADS
(Les Salades)

CHICORY SALAD MARSEILLES STYLE
(Salade de Chicorée Marseillaise)

To make this salad more plentiful and nourishing, add 1 hard-boiled egg per person.

■ Easy
6 servings
Thrift recipe
15 minutes
Best season: winter, early spring

1 large head of chicory, curly type
2 slices of French bread
2 garlic cloves

DRESSING
salt
1 tsp. prepared Dijon mustard
US 2 TB, UK 1 TB, vinegar (1 TB)
pepper
US 6 TB, UK 3 TB, olive oil (3 TB)
4 flat anchovy fillets

● Clean the chicory, remove and discard the hard external leaves. Wash it in several waters, drain well, and roll in a towel to dry very well. Cut leaves into bite-size pieces.

● Dry the bread slices under the broiler for a few minutes. Rub the slices with a peeled clove of garlic. Cut bread into 12 cubes.

● *Prepare the dressing* in a salad bowl. Dissolve a little salt and the mustard in the vinegar. Add pepper to taste and gradually add the oil.

● Cut the anchovy fillets into small pieces and add them to the dressing.

● Put the chicory pieces over the dressing and drop the garlic croutons on top. Toss the salad just before serving.

ABOUT ANCHOVY FILLETS
Rinse them under water to eliminate some of the salt used in preserving.

CAULIFLOWER SALAD
(Salade de Chou-Fleur)

Remember that little invisible slugs have a predilection for cauliflowerets; a 10-minute stay in vinegar water will pull them out of hiding.

Tastes vary on the texture of cauliflower. The French tend to like it a bit on the overdone side. It is better slightly crunchy.

■ Easy
   6 servings
   Affordable
   50 minutes
   Best season: summer

water
juice of 1 lemon
1 cauliflower
3 eggs
salt
1½ lbs. fresh peas in pods (750 g), or 1 box (10 oz.) frozen baby peas (300 g)
1 head of Boston lettuce
3 sun-ripened tomatoes, peeled if desired

DRESSING
US 6 TB, UK 3 TB, small-curd creamed cottage cheese (3 TB)
juice of 1 lemon
salt and pepper
US ½ cup, UK 4 TB, oil of your choice (4 TB)
chopped fresh herbs of your choice

GOOD PRODUCE
A good cauliflower is tight, very heavy and very white, with green leaves.

- Bring a large pot of water to a boil and add the juice of 1 lemon.
- Separate the cauliflower into small flowerets. Wash the flowerets well and cook them in the lemon water for 8 to 10 minutes, or as long as you prefer (see advice).
- When you have removed the cauliflowerets from the water, put the eggs and salt to taste in the pot and continue simmering for 10 minutes. Rinse eggs under cold water and peel.
- Shell the peas if need be and place the fresh or frozen peas in a large strainer. Immerse in the boiling water for 2 minutes.
- Line a shallow antipasto bowl (1½ quarts) with the lettuce leaves at regular intervals. Arrange the tomatoes, washed and cut into quarters, alternately with the eggs, also cut into quarters, around the edge of the bowl.
- *Prepare the dressing:* Put the cottage cheese, lemon juice, salt and pepper to taste in a blender container. Gradually add the oil and process until smooth. Turn into a small bowl and add the chopped fresh herbs. Correct the seasoning.
- Mix cauliflowerets and peas and toss together with salt and pepper. Put at the center of the lettuce and cover with the dressing.

RICE, RAISIN AND ALMOND SALAD
(Salade de Corinthe)

To this salad you can also add any leftover chicken, veal, pork, lamb or thin slices of smoked tongue, cut into ⅓-inch strips.

■ Easy
6 servings
Affordable
15 minutes
Best season: summer and fall

2 oz. dark raisins (60 g)
1 red pepper
1 green pepper
1 head of escarole
1 generous cup of cooked rice, Creole style (see p. 206).
2 oz. chopped blanched almonds (60 g)

DRESSING
fines herbes of your choice
salt and pepper
US 2 TB, UK 1 TB, vinegar (1 TB)
US 4 TB, UK 2 TB, mayonnaise (2 TB) (see note below)
US ⅓ cup, UK 3 TB, oil (3 TB)

MAYONNAISE
can be homemade or purchased, according to how much time you have and how important it is for you to use completely fresh ingredients.

- Wash the raisins; let them soak in warm water in a cup for 15 minutes.
- Cut the 2 peppers into ⅛-inch julienne after discarding all the seeds and ribs. If you prefer to peel the peppers, broil them for a few minutes first to be able to pull off the skin.
- Clean the escarole carefully, wash in several waters, drain it, pat it dry in one or several tea towels, and cut it into bite-size pieces.
- *Prepare the dressing:* Wash, dry, and chop the *fines herbes.* Put salt and pepper to taste and the vinegar in a bowl. Mix well and add the mayonnaise (see p. 62). Finally add the oil very gradually. Add the herbs. Correct the seasoning.
- Mix rice, drained raisins, escarole leaves and peppers in a large bowl. Pour the dressing over, correct seasoning, and serve sprinkled with the almonds. Toss just before serving.

ENDIVE AND HAM SALAD
(Salade d'Endives et Jambon)

Another way to prepare the endives: Cut the core out of the root end of each endive, cut ⅛ inch off the root end itself, and cut the whole endive into quarters.

- Easy
  6 servings
  A bit expensive
  10 minutes
  Best season: September to May

  6 endives
  2 acid apples
  2 slices of boiled ham, each ⅛ inch thick
  2 red beets, cooked
  US ½ cup, UK 4 TB, shelled walnuts (4 TB)

  DRESSING
  salt and pepper
  1 tsp. prepared strong Dijon mustard
  US 2 TB, UK 1 TB, wine vinegar (1 TB)
  US 6 TB, UK 3 TB, oil of your choice (3 TB)

CHOOSE WELL, WORK WELL
You need an acid apple such as Greening or Granny Smith.

Use excellent wine vinegar.

Remember, never soak Belgian endives or leave them exposed to the light, or they will turn bitter.

- Loosen all the endive leaves. Wash them *very rapidly* and dry them well in a tea towel. Cut them into 4 pieces each (see advice).
- Peel and core the apples; cut into thin slices.
- Chop the ham very finely.
- Peel the beets and cut them into ¼-inch cubes.
- *To prepare the dressing,* put salt and pepper to taste and the mustard in a bowl; add the vinegar and the oil.
- Mix all the ingredients in a salad bowl and correct the seasoning. Sprinkle the walnuts on top. Serve.

WITH THE SAME METHOD
Endive and Cheese Salad: Replace the ham with 2 ounces Gruyère, Edam or Saint-Paulin cheese (60 g), cut into small cubes.

Endive and Celery Salad: Replace the red beets with celery ribs taken from the tender center heart and cut across into ⅛-inch-thick slices. Add a bit of Roquefort to the dressing.

GREEN-BEAN SALAD
(Salade de Haricots Verts)

Do you want a mellower potato? Slice them while they are hot and sprinkle them with ½ cup or so of dry white wine (1 generous dl). Add the dressing afterwards.

■ Easy
6 servings
Medium expensive
35 minutes
Best season: summer to fall

**1½ lbs. green beans (750 g), fine
    ¼-inch-wide beans**
water
salt
5 boiling potatoes (Red Bliss)
3 eggs
4 tomatoes
18 large basil leaves, scissored

DRESSING
1 garlic clove
1 shallot
salt and pepper
chopped parsley
US ¼ cup, UK 2 TB, vinegar (2 TB)
US ¾ cup, UK ⅔ cup, oil (2 dl)
grated Parmesan cheese

YOU CAN
when beans of first quality and fresh basil are out of season, use frozen beans and dried basil to prepare the salad. It will not be as good, but it will be acceptable.

- String the green beans; break them into halves crosswise. Wash them.
- Boil the green beans in salted water for 8 to 10 minutes. Drain them and cool under running cold water.
- Boil the potatoes in their jackets in the same boiling water for 20 minutes.
- During the last 10 minutes of cooking the potatoes, add the eggs to the water and hard-boil them.
- When both eggs and potatoes are cooked, rinse them under cold water and peel them all immediately.
- Wash the tomatoes. Cut them into quarters.
- Put the green beans into an oval or rectangular deep dish and salt them lightly. Slice the potatoes and arrange them at the center of the dish. Garnish all around with quarters of tomatoes and quarters of eggs.
- Sprinkle the finely cut basil leaves over the potatoes.
- *Prepare the dressing:* Rub a small bowl with the garlic clove. Chop the shallot very finely, put it in the corner of a towel, and squeeze to extract all the juices. Add to the garlic. Add salt, pepper and chopped parsley to taste. Add vinegar and oil and mix well. Correct the seasoning.
- Spoon the dressing over the beans and potatoes and finally sprinkle with as much cheese as you like.

APPLE AND BOSTON LETTUCE SALAD
(Salade de Laitue aux Pommes)

For delicate stomachs the best dressing is always lemon juice and olive oil.

■ Easy
6 servings
Affordable
10 minutes
Best season: fall, in apple season

2 oz. dark raisins (60 g)
**3 apples, preferably Greening or Granny
  Smith**
1 lemon
2 oz. walnut halves (60 g)
1 large head of Boston lettuce

DRESSING
salt and pepper
US 2 TB, UK 1 TB, tomato ketchup (1 TB)
juice of 1 lemon
US ⅓ cup, UK 4 TB, oil (4 TB)

- Soak the raisins in lukewarm water for 15 minutes to plump them.
- Peel the apples, cut them into thin slices, and sprinkle them with lemon juice to prevent them browning.
- Chop the walnuts coarsely.
- Trim the lettuce, wash it, and dry it well in a tea towel.
- Put the lettuce into a salad bowl and over it sprinkle the apples, walnuts and raisins.
- *Prepare the dressing:* Mix salt and pepper to taste, ketchup, lemon juice and oil.
- Toss the salad with the dressing, correct the seasoning, and serve.

ROMAINE OR ESCAROLE
can also be used in this salad.

TONGUE SALAD
(Salade de Langue)

To make the salad more substantial add 1 hard-boiled egg per person.

- Easy
  6 servings
  Thrift recipe
  20 minutes
  Best season: tomato season

  1 large head of lettuce
  leftover cooked tongue, or 12 oz. smoked
  **   tongue (375 g)**
  2 potatoes, cooked
  6 sour pickles
  5 tomatoes
  6 celery ribs (preferably from the center of
  **   the stalk)**

  MAYONNAISE
  1 egg yolk
  US 1 TB, UK ½ TB, vinegar (½ TB)
  salt and pepper
  US ¾ cup, UK ⅔ cup, oil (2.5 dl)
  1 garlic clove

- Trim the lettuce, wash it, and blot it dry in a tea towel. Line a bowl with the larger leaves. Cut the other leaves into ¼-inch julienne.
- Trim all fat from the tongue, if you are using a leftover tongue. Cut the tongue into ¼-inch cubes.
- Peel the potatoes and cut them into small cubes.
- Chop the pickles. Cut the tomatoes into quarters.
- Peel and trim the celery ribs, wash them, dry them, and cut them into ¼-inch sticks.
- *Prepare the mayonnaise* with the egg yolk, vinegar, salt and pepper to taste, the oil, plus the well-mashed garlic clove (see p. 298).
- Mix all ingredients and fill the prepared bowl. Correct the seasoning. Serve.

LEFTOVERS
Any leftover meat can be used, such as boiled beef, or corned beef.

SPRING SALAD
(Salade de Mai)

Do you know that green leaves from radishes, a few potatoes, and a bit of cream will give you a fresh-tasting spring soup?

■ Easy
  6 servings
  Thrift recipe
  20 minutes
  Best season: spring to September for the best leaf lettuce

  2 small heads of leaf lettuce, 1 red, 1 green
  2 large beets, cooked
  1 bunch of fresh red radishes with leaves on
  5 oz. Pyrénées cheese (150 g)
  6 scallions
  1 small bunch of fresh fines herbes of your choice

  DRESSING
  US 2 TB, UK 1 TB, vinegar (1 TB)
  US 6 TB, UK 3 TB, oil (3 TB)
  salt and pepper

ABOUT THE INGREDIENTS
Use very fresh radishes with the leaves on; it is essential for freshness.

Pyrénées cheese is to be found in all cheese shops and many supermarkets as well. It is recognizable by its removable brown plastic shell.

- Trim the heads of lettuce, wash them, and pat them dry.
- Peel and cube the beets; cut into ⅓-inch cubes.
- Clean the red radishes; remove greens (see advice) and roots. Wash them and slice them. If they are strong, sprinkle them with salt and let stand for 10 minutes.
- Cut the cheese into ⅓-inch cubes.
- Wash the scallions and cut them into ¼-inch-thick slices, using scissors where the leaves are tubular and a knife where the stem is compact, white and juicy.
- Wash and chop the *fines herbes.*
- *Prepare the dressing* by mixing vinegar, oil, and salt and pepper to taste.
- Marinate the beets and cheese cubes in the dressing for 30 minutes. Just before serving, toss in all the other ingredients. Correct the seasoning and serve.

DANDELION SALAD
(Salade de Pissenlit)

About wilting: Wild dandelions that have wilted a bit during transport will be revived when washed in very lukewarm water.

■ Easy
   7 servings
   Thrift recipe
   15 minutes
   **Best season: spring, with young field
      dandelions**

   1 lb. dandelions greens (500 g)
   6 rashers of thick-sliced bacon
   3 potatoes, cooked

   DRESSING
   1 lemon
   salt and pepper
   US 6 TB, UK 3 TB, olive oil (3 TB)

WILD DANDELIONS
They are bright green and tougher than cultivated dandelions, but they are tastier and richer in vitamins and minerals. Excellent for the health of your liver and gall bladder. Pick wild dandelions no later than the middle of July.

- Cut off the root end of the dandelions. Discard the tough outside leaves and wash the others several times. Drain them and pat them dry. They should never soak.

- Cut the bacon into pieces ⅓ x 1 inch and render them in a skillet. When done, drain in a paper towel. Reserve the pan. Meanwhile, peel and slice the potatoes.

- *Prepare the dressing* by mixing lemon juice with salt and pepper to taste. Add the oil and mix well.

- Discard the fat in the frying skillet. Add the dressing to the pan to scrape and deglaze. Add the bacon pieces.

- Mix potatoes and dandelions in a bowl and pour the dressing and bacon over the salad. Toss just before serving.

NORTHERN FRENCH CHICKEN SALAD
(Salade de Poulet du Nord)

Another reason, besides prettiness, for sprinkling dishes with parsley: it is one of the best sources of vitamins A and C.

■ Easy
6 servings
Affordable
10 minutes
Best season: year around

1½ cups leftover cold boneless chicken
(½ chicken, 2 legs or 2 breasts)
6 oz. Mimolette cheese (180 g)
1 large head of lettuce

DRESSING
US 2 TB, UK 1 TB, vinegar (1 TB)
mustard
salt and pepper
US 6 TB, UK 3 TB, oil (3 TB)
chopped parsley

- Cut the chicken into large slivers.
- Cut the Mimolette into cubes about ⅓-inch size.
- Trim the lettuce, wash it, and dry it. Cut the leaves into bite-size pieces.
- Mix lettuce, chicken and cheese.
- Prepare the dressing by mixing the vinegar with mustard, salt and pepper to taste. Add the oil and chopped parsley. Mix well.
- Dress the salad and toss it just before serving. Correct the seasoning.

ABOUT MIMOLETTE
This cheese is to be found in all cheese stores. It is made in Northern France. If you cannot find any, use Dutch Edam from Holland, or domestic.

SHRIMP SALAD AS IN MARTINIQUE
(Salade de Crevettes au Rhum)

Is the dressing a bit too rich? Prepare it using yogurt as a base (about ½ cup) and use half as much oil and no lemon.

■ A bit difficult
6 servings
Expensive
30 minutes
Best season: spring, summer or early fall

SALAD
24 large shrimps in the shell, cooked
3 eggs
1 head of soft-leaf lettuce
3 grapefruits
3 avocados
US 2 TB, UK 1 TB, dark rum (1 TB)
chopped parsley

DRESSING
1 egg yolk
1 tsp. mustard
US ⅔ cup, UK ½ cup, oil (2 scant dl)
salt
US 1 TB, UK ½ TB, lemon juice
large pinch of cayenne pepper
US 2 TB, UK 1 TB, ketchup (1 TB)
US ⅓ cup, UK ¼ cup, heavy cream,
whipped (50 to 55 g)

- Shell the shrimps.
- Hard-boil the eggs (p. 72) in salted boiling water for 10 minutes.
- Wash the lettuce leaves, keep them whole, and dry them well with paper towels.
- Cut the grapefruits crosswise into halves; remove the pulp in chunks. Reserve the shells.
- Peel the avocados, cut them lengthwise into halves, and cut the flesh into pieces the same size as the grapefruits.

- Toss avocado and grapefruit into the rum.
- Cut 18 of the shrimps into 1-inch-long pieces and add to the fruit mixture. Keep refrigerated, covered with clear plastic wrap.
- *Prepare the dressing as you would a mayonnaise (p. 62) with the yolk being mixed with the mustard and the oil gradually added to those ingredients. Add the salt dissolved in the lemon juice, the ketchup and cayenne pepper. Finally, fold in the heavy cream. Correct the seasoning.*
- Mix about two thirds of this dressing into the fruit and shrimp mixture; mix well.
- Scrape all the membranes out of the reserved grapefruit halves and line each with a lettuce leaf. Divide the salad among the prepared shells. Spoon one sixth of the remaining dressing over the salad and top each one with 1 large shelled shrimp and ½ hard-boiled egg. Sprinkle with some chopped parsley.

LANGOSTAS
If you live where langostas can be found, either fresh or frozen, use those instead of shrimps; lobster pieces or slices would also be very good, as well as poached scallops.

DESSERTS
(Les Desserts)

FLAMBÉED BANANAS
(Bananes Flambées)

Use your fondue set. Light the small alcohol or Sterno stove in the dining room; cook the bananas in the kitchen and bring the pan to the dining room to flambé at the table, using the fondue stove as a source of heat.

■ Easy
6 servings
Medium expensive
10 minutes
Best season: all through the winter months

6 bananas
US 6 TB, UK 3 TB, butter (90 g)
US ⅓ cup, UK 6 TB, sugar (100 g)
US ⅓ cup, UK ¼ cup, rum of your choice (1 scant dl)

- Since the cooking time is extremely short, prepare all ingredients and implements first.
- Peel the bananas; leave them whole.
- Heat the butter in a large skillet until it turns hazelnut brown. Add the bananas. When they are golden on one side, turn them over to brown on the other, turning with a metal spatula. The heat should remain medium low at all times to allow the bananas to heat to the center without falling apart.
- Sprinkle the bananas and the butter with sugar and let the sugar melt and lightly caramelize. Remove the pan from the heat.
- Heat the rum in a small saucepan without letting it boil.

- Return the skillet to the heat. With a large sauce spoon dip out some of the hot rum. Ignite the rum with a match and pour into the pan of bananas. While the rum is flaming, dip out some of the syrup with the same sauce spoon and keep basting the bananas with it until the flames die out. Serve immediately.

WITH THE SAME METHOD
Flambéed Pineapple: Use fresh or canned pineapple slices and follow the same method. You can also prepare a mix of bananas and pineapple.

Flambéed Peaches: Use fresh or canned peaches. Follow the same method, but instead of rum, use Grand Marnier, Triple Sec or Curaçao.

ABOUT BANANAS
They are best when they are small and when they have a moderate amount of ripeness spots. Such a banana in France is called tigrée, or tiger banana, because of the similarity of colors between the animal and the fruit.

RUM
It can be white or dark according to your personal taste.

COMPOTE OF APRICOTS
(Compote d'Abricots à la Vanille)

Use preferably a stainless-steel or enameled pan.

Do not discard the pods of vanilla beans after using the seeds. Add the pods to a small jar of sugar to obtain vanilla sugar. Also, store the unused part of the vanilla bean in the same jar.

- Easy
  6 servings
  Medium expensive
  20 minutes
  Best season: July

  2½ lbs. fresh apricots (1 kg)
  few tablespoons of water
  sugar
  1 vanilla bean

- Wash the apricots; cut them into halves.

- Break 10 apricot pits with a mallet. Extract the almonds within the pits, peel them, and add them to the pot as soon as the apricots start to cook.

- Do not cover the pan at any time. Add a few tablespoons of water to a large sauteuse pan and a few tablespoons of sugar. Add the apricot halves, skin side down. Cook over gentle heat, then turn over, one by one, to cook the second side.

- In about 8 minutes, the apricots will show signs of falling apart. Remove the pan from the heat. Cut a 1-inch-long piece of a vanilla bean, open it on the side, and scrape the vanilla seeds from both sides into the compote. Empty the compote into a serving dish. Refrigerate or keep at room temperature, whichever you prefer. Serve with a small bowl of sugar.

- The almonds of the apricots may be left in or removed from the compote as you prefer.

WITH THE SAME METHOD
Plum Compote: Wash 2½ pounds plums, cut them into halves, and pit them. Cook slowly with only sugar; plums have so much juice that they require no water. Remove from the heat and pour into a serving dish as soon as the plums collapse.

Rhubarb Compote: Use 2½ pounds rhubarb. Cut ¼ inch of the stalks at each end, pulling to remove the skins in both directions. Cut the stalks into 1½-inch chunks. Put the rhubarb in a pot with a lot of sugar and a few drops of water. Do not cover and cook slowly. As soon as the pieces seem about to collapse, remove the compote to a serving dish.

ABOUT APRICOTS
The acidity of the apricots intensifies as they cook, so use a bit of sugar while cooking and serve a bowl of sugar or honey with the compote.

All fruit compotes can also be accompanied by a dish of Crème Chantilly (see p. 260).

STRAWBERRIES—A FEW IDEAS
(Les Fraises ...)

The sparkling wines you can use include also California "Champagne"; Asti Spumante; Vouvray Mousseux.

Should you be using frozen strawberries, use only those packed loosely in plastic bags and start the maceration while they are still frozen. By the time the strawberries defrost, they will be ready to eat.

■ Easy
6 servings
Medium expensive
10 minutes
Best season: June 1st to July 15th

1 quart strawberries (500 g)
sugar to your taste and according to the natural taste and sweetness of the berries
lemon juice to your taste

- Put the strawberries in a basin of cold water and toss them gently to discard all dirt and sand.
- Drain the strawberries in a colander, hull them, and carefully remove any rain or mold spots with a paring knife.
- Put the strawberries in a bowl. Cut the larger ones lengthwise into halves, or even into quarters if they are very large.
- Sugar the berries and sprinkle them with lemon juice. Let macerate in the refrigerator for no more than 2 hours.
- Divide the berries into 6 dessert dishes or glasses of any style you like. Serve.

WITH THE SAME METHOD
Strawberries in Champagne: Prepare the berries as above, using only a few drops of lemon juice. Pour over them a small cup of Champagne of your choice (2.5 dl), extra dry, Brut, white or pink, or any Vin Mousseux that you like (see advice).

Strawberries Chantilly: Prepare the berries as above, using sugar and either Grand Marnier, Curaçao or Kirschwas-ser. Put the berries in the cups and cover with Crème Chantilly (p. 260).

Strawberries and Orange: Macerate the strawberries with sugar, the juice of 2 oranges and 1 ounce of orange liqueur (1 TB). Decorate with a slice of orange straddling the edge of the glass.

Strawberries in Wine: Macerate the berries with sugar, a small cup of red wine (2.5 dl) mixed with the juice of 1 orange and 1 ounce Cognac or whisky, for 2 hours.

Strawberries with Vanilla Cream: Macerate the strawberries with Kirschwasser and sugar for 2 hours. Meanwhile prepare a light vanilla cream by mixing US 1 tablespoon, UK ½ tablespoon, cornstarch (½ TB) with US 1 cup, UK 1 scant cup, heavy cream (3 dl) and US ¼ cup, UK 2 tablespoons, sugar (2 TB). Bring to a boil, stirring until thickened. Cool completely. Whip another ½ cup cream with the seeds of ½ vanilla bean and a bit of confectioners' sugar and fold into the cold vanilla cream.
Divide the berries and their juices into 6 serving dishes and pour an equal amount of vanilla cream over each dish of berries.

WASHING STRAWBERRIES
How you wash them is important. Wash them before you stem them to prevent water entering the fruit and diluting its natural juices.

PEACHES IN RASPBERRY PURÉE
(Pêches à la Purée de Framboises)

If you prefer, cook the peaches in a syrup made of equal amounts of water and sugar for 7 to 8 minutes; chill.

Also, frozen raspberries may be less expensive than fresh ones. Use 2 packages (10 oz. or 285 g each) and reserve the packing syrup to make sherbet (see p. 288).

■ Easy
  6 servings
  Expensive
  10 minutes
  Best season: July and August

  6 ripe peaches
  1 lemon
  1 pint fresh raspberries (250 g)
  sugar
  Kirschwasser and Curaçao
  pistachios for garnishing

- Peel the peaches and rub them with the lemon.
- Arrange peach halves upside down in a crystal dish. Refrigerate.
- Put the raspberries in a blender and purée them. Add sugar to your taste and a mixture of Kirsch and Curaçao to your taste. Strain the purée over the peaches.
- Cover the peaches with plastic wrap and let them macerate for 2 hours.
- Sprinkle chopped blanched pistachios over the dish just before serving.

TO PEEL PEACHES
If the skin does not come off by itself, bring a pot of water to a boil and immerse the peaches in the water for 2 minutes. Cool under cold water and peel.

CHANGE YOUR FRUIT, YOU CHANGE YOUR DESSERT
Strawberries in Raspberry Purée: Proceed exactly as described above, using strawberries instead of peaches.

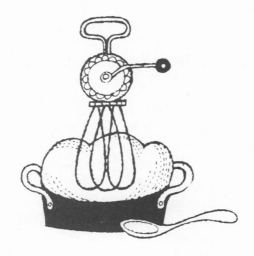

PEARS POACHED IN RED WINE
(Poires au Vin)

These pears keep very well for several days, in the refrigerator or even unrefrigerated.

■ Easy
6 servings
Medium expensive
1 hour
Best season: August and September

1 bottle of dry red wine
½ lemon
US 2 cups, UK 2 scant cups, sugar (450 to 500 g)
pinch of ground cinnamon
pinch of freshly grated nutmeg
12 firm pears, Bartlett or Bosc

DO NOT
use very soft "melting" pears for this dessert; choose pears that are not quite ripe but still quite firm.

A country wine from France, California or any other origin with 10.5 to 11% alcohol will be perfect.

- Empty the wine into a stainless-steel or enameled pot. Add the lemon, cut into thin slices, the sugar, cinnamon and nutmeg. Bring to a boil. Simmer while you peel the pears.

- Peel the pears. Small pears should be left whole with the stem on and core removed. Larger pears should be cut lengthwise into halves and cored. Remove the seeds, using a melon baller.

- Add the pears to cook in the wine, cover, and reduce the heat to very low. Cook the pears extremely slowly. They will be done when a large darning needle goes into the fruit and comes out without difficulty.

- Transfer the cooked pears to a deep dish. Reduce the cooking syrup until it coats the back of a spoon.

- Pour the syrup over the pears, let cool, and refrigerate.

APPLES IN PAPILLOTES
(Pommes en Papillotes)

The alcohol contained in brandies and liqueurs evaporates during the cooking process. When it is added before the cooking starts or by flambéing, only the aroma of the brandy remains.

■ Easy
6 servings
Thrift recipe
50 minutes
Best season: cold months

US 4 TB, UK 2 TB, butter (60 g)
6 slices of white bread
6 large Cortland apples
2½ oz. chopped almonds (75 g)
6½ oz. granulated sugar (195 g)
US ½ cup, UK 4 TB, heavy cream (125 g)
US 2 TB, UK 1 TB, brandy or Calvados (1 TB)

BAKING APPLES
must be chosen for this dessert. The brandy can be any one you have, but applejack or Calvados would be best.

• Preheat oven to 400°F., 220°C. or 6 Regulo.
• Butter the slices of bread on one side only.
• Cut 6 sheets of foil 9 inches square.
• Put each slice of bread, buttered side down, on a sheet of foil.
• Peel the apples and core them generously.
• Mix the chopped almonds and the sugar and process in the blender to obtain a powder.
• Empty the mixture into a bowl. Add the cream and chosen spirit. Spoon an equal amount of the mixture into each apple and put an apple on each slice of bread.
• Close the foil packages. Put them on a jelly-roll pan. Set the pan on the medium rack of the oven and cook them for 30 to 40 minutes. The exact cooking time depends on the size of the apples.
• Serve warm, lukewarm or cold. Each guest can open his own *papillote*. You can, if you want, present a small pitcher of cream and some sugar in a bowl.

APPLE AND FRUIT FRITTERS
(Beignets aux Pommes et aux Fruits)

An electric fryer is a wise investment for many reasons: it is reasonably priced; it sits securely on a counter; it has a thermostat that prevents overheating of the oil. Follow the manufacturer's direction for temperatures.

■ Easy
6 servings
Thrift recipe
1 hour
Best season: fall and winter

FRYING BATTER
US 1 cup, UK 4 oz., sifted flour (125 g)
1 large egg, separated
pinch of salt
US 2 TB, UK 1 TB, oil (1 TB)
US 1 cup, UK 1 scant cup, milk (.25 L)

5 large apples
granulated sugar
US ⅓ cup, UK 3 TB, rum (3 TB)
oil bath for frying

- *Prepare the frying batter first.* Put the flour in a bowl, make a well in it, and add the egg yolk, salt and oil to the well. Using a whisk, slowly bring the flour into the egg yolk. Add the milk as you go along. Beat the mixture well; there should not be any lumps. Strain the batter into another bowl and let stand for at least 30 minutes.

- Peel the apples. Remove the cores and cut apples into ¼-inch-thick slices. Put the apple slices in a bowl, sprinkle them with a bit of sugar and the rum, and let macerate until you are ready to cook the fritters.

- Heat the oil bath to 375° to 400°F., 200° to 220°C. or 6 Regulo.

- Beat the egg white into a not-too-stiff foam and fold it into the fritter batter. Dip the apple slices into the batter. When the oil bath has reached the frying temperature, add a few slices of apples at a time. When each fritter is golden on one side, turn it over with a slotted spoon and fry the other side.

- Drain the fritters on a plate geneously lined with crumpled absorbent paper toweling. Sprinkle with sugar. Serve while you put another batch of fritters into the oil.

WITH THE SAME METHOD
Dried Apricot Fritters: Soak 1 pound dried apricots (500 g) in water overnight. Cook them with a bit of water and sugar for a few minutes. Drain, and coat with batter.

Pineapple Fritters: Canned pineapple must be dried. Coat with batter and fry. Fresh pineapple should be cleaned, cut into slices, and macerated in rum and sugar. Drain before dipping into batter.

Prune Fritters: Pour boiling tea over 1 pound pitted prunes (500 g). Let stand for 1 hour, drain, and dip into the batter.

WINTER FRUIT SALAD
(Salade de Fruits d'Hiver)

Oranges are ready to use when the rind and the underlying white pith are removed together and the pulp appears bright and juicy.

- Easy
  6 servings
  Medium expensive
  30 minutes
  Best season: October to April

  6½ oz. dried figs (200 g)
  1½ oz. dark raisins (45 g)
  1½ oz. dark rum (1½ TB)
  1½ oz. water (1½ TB)
  3½ oz. granulated sugar (100 g)
  3 bananas
  2 apples
  1 lemon
  5 oranges
  2½ oz. chopped shelled walnuts (80 g)
  2½ oz. shelled hazelnuts (80 g)

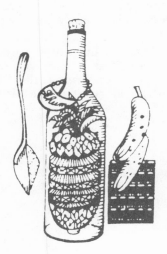

- Split the work over 2 days.

DAY ONE
- Cut each fig into 4 pieces. Macerate them and the raisins in rum and an equal amount of water plus about 1½ ounces of granulated sugar (45 g).

DAY TWO
- Peel the bananas and the apples. Slice them into a bowl. Sprinkle them well with lemon juice. Peel 3 oranges to the pulp; cut them also into slices and add them to the bananas. Add the chopped walnuts (see Almonds, p. 292) and the remainder of the sugar. Add the whole peeled hazelnuts (p. 299).
- Squeeze the juice from the other 2 oranges. Add it to the figs and raisins and empty the whole mixture over the fresh fruits. Cover with plastic wrap and refrigerate. Do not toss the fruit salad.

WHAT TO USE
You can use 2 types of bananas, the ordinary yellow ones or the delicious red, short ones. Both should be firm and not overripe so as not to fall apart. The lemon juice will prevent oxidation.

WHIPPED CREAM
(Crème Chantilly)

Heavy creams vary widely from one country to another. In France and England, for example, cream is so thick that it must be thinned with cold milk before being whipped to prevent the cream turning into butter. In the U.S., on the contrary, the cream called heavy cream or whipping cream is more liquid and can be whipped without the addition of cold milk.

- Easy
  6 servings
  Medium expensive
  10 minutes
  Best season: year around

  **US 1 cup, UK 1 scant cup, whipping
  cream (250 g)**
  US 2 TB, UK 1 TB, cold milk (1 TB)
  **US 2 TB, UK 1 TB, confectioners' sugar (1
  TB)**
  1 tsp. pure vanilla extract

USES
Whipped cream is used plain for fresh fruit desserts. It can be also flavored with coffee, chocolate, liqueur. It can also be a decoration for cakes and puddings when piped through a pastry bag fitted with a star tip.

- Have the cream ice cold before you whip it. If need be, put the bowl containing it in the freezer.
- If you beat the cream by hand with a wire whisk, use a round-bottom bowl; if you use the electric mixer, use the small narrow mixer bowl.
- Put the cream in the well-chilled bowl, add milk if needed (see advice), and sugar and vanilla. Whip slowly at the beginning and increasingly quickly as the thickening progresses.
- Stop beating as soon as the cream holds its shape and forms soft peaks on the beaters. Do not overbeat the cream or it will separate into whey and butter.
- Should the cream be used to decorate a cake, beat it as long as you can and until the cream forms a "flag" directly pointing at right angles from the whisk.

PASTRY CREAM
(Crème Pâtissière)

Another way to prevent the formation of a skin at the surface of a cream is to sprinkle it lightly with sugar.

- Easy
  6 servings
  Inexpensive
  15 minutes
  Best season: year around

  3 eggs
  US ⅔ cup, UK 6 oz., sugar (150 g)
  US 4 TB, UK 2 TB, flour (30 g)
  US 2 cups, UK 2 scant cups, milk (.5 L)
  flavoring to suit your taste

PASTRY CREAM
can be used as is for dessert, or it can fill cream puffs or éclairs, or can be the base for a fruit tart, in a pastry shell.

- Break the eggs into a bowl. Add the sugar and ribbon well together. Beat in the flour on low speed of your mixer, then little by little add the milk.
- Turn into a saucepan. Still using the electric mixer, or a wire whisk, put the pot over medium heat and bring to a boil, stirring constantly.
- Remove from the heat as soon as 1 or 2 boils are visible at the center of the cream.
- Add the flavoring. Flavorings can be: 3 ounces chocolate (90 g), melted and added to the finished cream: 1 tablespoon pure vanilla extract; 1 tablespoon instant coffee powder; 2 to 3 tablespoons any spirit or liqueur.

FRANGIPANE CREAM
(Crème Frangipane)

You can use your electric beater all through the cooking if you have a plug within reasonable reach; this way you will have less work and no lumps in the cream.

■ Easy
6 servings
Medium expensive
30 minutes, plus 2 hours for milk infusion
Best season: year around

2 cups milk (.5 L)
1 vanilla bean, or finely grated rind of 1
    lemon
1⅓ oz. chopped blanched almonds (50 g)
2 whole eggs
3 extra egg yolks
6 oz. sugar (90 g)
pinch of salt
US 8 TB, UK 4 TB, flour (60 g)
1⅔ oz. unsalted butter (50 g)
¼ tsp. bitter almond extract

USES
Use to fill tartlet shells, crêpes, génoise cake, jelly roll.

- Scald the milk. Add the vanilla bean or the grated lemon rind. Cover, let cool, and steep for 2 hours.
- Put the almonds in the container of a blender. Strain the milk over them and blend until perfectly smooth.
- Using an electric beater, ribbon (see p. 302) the whole eggs, the extra egg yolks and the sugar together well. Add a pinch of salt, then slowly add the flour, and gradually add the almond milk.
- Turn the cream into a large saucepan, put over medium heat, and cook, stirring constantly, until 1 or 2 boils appear at the center of the pot and the cream is thickened.
- Remove the pot from the heat and add the butter, whipping it in bit by bit. Also add the bitter almond extract. Cool completely before using.

STIRRED CUSTARD
(Crème Anglaise)

The cooking method used here is fast and efficient. It works extremely well on gas heat. On electric heat you may have to be a little more careful lest the high heat of the electric element coagulate the custard too fast at the bottom. Stir fast, using a square-ended spatula; cover the whole bottom of the pan steadily in a regular sweeping pattern.

■ Requires care
  6 servings
  Affordable
  15 minutes
  Best season: year around

  12 egg yolks
  US 1 cup, UK ½ lb., sugar (250 g)
  pinch of salt
  1 tsp. vanilla extract
  1 quart milk, scalded (1 L)

ABOUT STIRRED CUSTARD
It is mostly a dessert sauce, but is also used in desserts such as molded rice puddings, ice creams, etc. You can prepare it in smaller quantities.

• Put the egg yolks, sugar, salt and vanilla in a thick-bottomed saucepan. Mix well until completely blended.

• Gradually add the scalded milk, adding very little at a time until half of the milk has been added, then pour in the remainder in 2 or 3 additions. Mix well.

• Set the pot over high heat. Stirring very fast with a wooden spoon, look for the foam to disappear. Remove the pot from the heat as soon as only 2 or 3 big bubbles remain and whisk very fast and very quickly to cool the custard (see advice).

• Immediately strain the custard into a bowl.

WITH THE SAME METHOD
Coffee-Flavored Stirred Custard: Add 1 teaspoon instant coffee powder per cup of custard after custard has finished cooking.

Chocolate-Flavored Stirred Custard: Melt chocolate to your taste and gradually blend in the scalded milk; use only ¾ cup sugar (6 oz. or 190 g).

Liqueur-Flavored Stirred Custard: Use US 2 tablespoons, UK 1 tablespoon (1 TB) liqueur of your choice for each cup of finished custard.

Orange- or Lemon-Flavored Stirred Custard: Infuse the fine-grated rind of 1 orange or 1 lemon in the milk.

UPSIDE-DOWN CUSTARD
(Crème Renversée)

The choice is yours: When the cream is oven-baked, if you like a crust on the top, do not cover it with anything. If you would rather not have a crust, cover the mold with aluminum foil and expect the cooking time to be a bit longer.

■ Requires attention
 6 servings
 Thrift recipe
 1¼ hours, 25 minutes in pressure cooker

US 2 cups, UK 2 scant cups, milk (.5 L)
1 vanilla bean or 1 TB vanilla extract
US ¾ cup, UK 6 oz., sugar (180 g)
pinch of salt
water
lemon juice or vinegar
US 1 TB, UK ½ TB, unsalted butter (15 g)
3 whole eggs

• Scald the milk. Cut open the vanilla bean and scrape all the seeds into the hot milk. Let stand for 5 minutes. Add half of the sugar and a pinch of salt. Stir until the sugar has completely dissolved.

• Put a dash of water, a drop of lemon juice or vinegar and the other half of the sugar in a frying pan. Set the pan over medium heat and cook to a dark caramel.

• Pour the caramel directly in the center of a 1-quart mold. Holding the mold by both handles, turn it in all directions to cover it as completely as possible with a ⅛-inch layer of caramel. Turn the mold upside down and let cool.

• Butter every bit of the surface of the mold not covered by the caramel.

• Bring a kettle full of water to a boil.

• Now, finish the custard. Beat the eggs until well liquefied and gradually beat in the sugared milk. Strain the custard into the prepared mold.

• Preheat oven to 300°F., 130°C. or 2 to 3 Regulo.

• Set the mold in a baking dish and put the dish on the oven rack. Pour boiling water into the dish around the mold. Bake for 50 to 60 minutes. The custard is done when a skewer inserted two thirds of the way to the center comes out clean and hot.

• Remove baking dish from the oven and let custard cool in the water bath.

• *To bake in the pressure cooker:* Set the mold in the metal basket of the pressure cooker and lower the basket into the cooker. Cover the mold with a sheet of aluminum foil. Fill the cooker with boiling water up to ½ inch from the rim of the mold. Seal the cooker and count 8 minutes of cooking as soon as the pressure is reached. Open the cooker as soon as the custard is done.

• Chill the custard before you unmold it; this way you can rest assured that it will not break or collapse. To unmold, pass the tip of a flexible knife blade all around the mold and turn the cream over. The melted caramel becomes a delicious sauce.

USE
either a 1-quart charlotte mold with smooth sides, or 1-quart ring mold. In the ring mold the custard will cook in half the time.

EGGS IN THE SNOW
(Œufs à la Neige)

Many variations can be prepared by flavoring the stirred custard with lemon or orange rind, instant coffee, liqueur of your choice, etc.

- Difficult
  6 servings
  Medium expensive
  30 to 40 minutes
  Best season: year around

  STIRRED CUSTARD (Crème Anglaise)
  6 egg yolks
  US ⅔ cup, UK 6 oz., sugar (150 g)
  pinch of salt
  US 2½ cups, UK 1 generous pint milk (.5 L), scalded
  seeds of 1 vanilla bean

  MERINGUE EGGS
  4 egg whites
  US ½ cup, UK 4 oz., sugar (125 g)

THE TEMPERATURE
of the eggs is important. Eggs cook and foam best when they have been sitting at room temperature for 4 hours.

STIRRED CUSTARD

- Proceed exactly as described in the basic recipe on page 263. As a flavoring, scrape the seeds of a cut-open vanilla bean into the egg-yolk and sugar mixture. Strain the custard into a deep crystal bowl.

MERINGUE EGGS

- Beat the egg whites until they can carry the weight of a raw egg in its shell, then fold in the sugar.

- Bring a skilletful of water to a boil. Reduce to a bare simmer. Shape 4 meringue eggs at a time, using 2 sauce spoons, and drop them into the water. Let poach for 2 minutes, then flip the eggs over, using a slotted spoon. Cook for 2 more minutes. Drain on a cake rack placed over a tea towel. Repeat the operation until all egg whites have been used.

- When all meringue eggs have been poached, transfer them to the bowl of custard where you will float them on top of the custard. Refrigerate for several hours before serving.

WITH THE SAME METHOD
Ramekins of Snow in Coffee Cream: Flavor the stirred custard with a teaspoon or so of instant coffee powder. Pour the custard into individual ramekins. Float 1 large meringue egg on each ramekin of custard and sprinkle with grated chocolate.

CHOCOLATE CREAM
(Crème au Chocolat)

Do you need more portions? Add about 2 more tablespoons of sugar to the basic cream. Whip 2 to 4 egg whites and fold them into the cream while it is still lukewarm.

Would you like a richer cream? Beat ½ cup heavy cream to the Chantilly stage with a tablespoon or so of rum and a tablespoon of confectioners' sugar. Fold it into the cream after cream has cooled completely.

Would you like a chic decoration? Prepare the whipped cream but do not fold it in; put it in a pastry bag and pipe it on top of the cold chocolate cream.

- Easy
  6 servings
  Medium expensive
  30 minutes
  Best season: colder months

  1 quart milk (1 L)
  6 oz. best available chocolate (180 g)
  4 egg yolks
  US ½ cup, UK 4 TB, sugar (4 TB)
  US 2 TB, UK 1 TB, cornstarch (1 TB)
  US 1 TB, UK ½ TB, unsalted butter, very cold (½ TB)

- Heat 3 cups of the milk with the chocolate and stir well until the chocolate has completely melted.

- Mix egg yolks and sugar, stirring until a good foam forms. Strain the cornstarch into the yolk and sugar mixture and mix until homogenous. Finally, gradually stir in the remainder of the cold milk.

- Slowly add the chocolate milk to this mixture, then pour the mixture into the saucepan.

- Slowly heat the cream over medium-low heat, stirring constantly, until the mixture coats a wooden spoon and shows 1 or 2 bubbles at the center (see Creams, p. 296).

- Strain the cream into a pretty serving dish. Stick the cold butter on the tines of a fork. As soon as the cream has cooled for 2 to 3 minutes, slide the pat of butter all over the surface of the custard. The film of butter will prevent formation of a thick skin.

WITH THE SAME METHOD
Brazilian Cream: In the hot milk add a teaspoon or so of instant coffee powder.

Mocha Cream: Replace the chocolate by US 4 tablespoons, UK 2 tablespoons, instant coffee powder (2 TB).

Caramel Cream: Use twice as much sugar. Cook the sugar to caramel and dissolve it with 3 cups of the milk, scalded. Do not use any chocolate.

CHOOSE WELL
Your choice of chocolate is important. The better the chocolate, the better the cream. Best results are obtained with Swiss bittersweet chocolate, but be prepared to find it expensive.

CHOCOLATE MOUSSE
(Mousse au Chocolat)

You can change the basic taste with 1 teaspoon instant coffee powder added to the sugar syrup, or 2 to 3 tablespoons of any liqueur of your choice added to the yolks while they ribbon (see p. 302).

■ Relatively easy
  6 to 8 servings
  Expensive
  20 minutes
  Best season: cooler months

  4 eggs
  pinch of salt
  US ½ cup, UK 2½ oz., confectioners' sugar (125 g)
  US ⅓ cup, UK ¼ cup, water (1 scant dl)
  8 oz. unsweetened chocolate (250 g)
  US ½ cup, UK 4 oz., unsalted butter (125 g)

FOR A CHANGE
omit the butter and replace it by US ½ cup, UK 4 ounces, heavy cream (125 g), whipped quite soft and folded into the mousse after the egg whites.

- Separate the eggs. Drop the yolks into a bowl with a pinch of salt.
- Melt the sugar and water together. Bring the syrup to a boil.
- Start beating the yolks and while you beat add the boiling syrup to them. Beat until a very heavy foam is obtained.
- Melt the chocolate and butter together over hot water. Cool this mixture and add to the egg yolks.
- Beat the egg whites until the foam can carry the weight of a raw egg in its shell. Mix about one quarter of the whites into the chocolate base and fold in the remainder.
- Turn into a crystal serving dish or into individual crystal dishes and keep refrigerated for several hours before serving.

WITH THE SAME METHOD
Coffee Mousse: Use US ½ cup, UK 4 ounces, regular sugar (125 g) and add to the foamed yolks 1½ teaspoons unflavored gelatin dissolved in 6 ounces prepared double-strength coffee, boiling hot. Beat until cold. Fold in the egg whites and US ½ cup, UK 4 ounces, heavy cream (125 g), whipped quite soft.

RICE DESSERT WITH PRUNES AND RAISINS
(Riz Sucré aux Pruneaux)

This dessert becomes a marvelous treat if you serve a Stirred Custard (Crème Anglaise, p. 263).
flavored with rum with it. Both can easily be done a day ahead and kept refrigerated.

- Easy
  6 to 8 servings
  Very affordable
  1 hour, plus 3 hours for chilling
  Best season: cold months

  18 soft pitted prunes
  lukewarm water
  US ⅓ cup, UK ¼ cup, dark raisins (50 g)
  US ¼ cup, UK 2 TB, rum (2 TB)
  oil
  salt
  6½ oz. round-grain rice (Arborio rice)
  (200 g)
  US 1½ qts., UK 1¼ qts., milk (1.25 L)
  1 TB pure vanilla extract (15 g)
  2 tsp. unflavored gelatin
  US ¾ cup, UK 6 oz., sugar (175 g)
  US 1 cup, UK 8 oz., heavy cream (250 g)

ABOUT THE RICE
*It is important here to use round-grain very
starchy rice (Italian Arborio, for example)
which cooks to a creamy texture. Converted
rice never develops the mellowness necessary for the proper texture of this dessert.
Italian rice is on sale in all Italian markets
and easy to find in other stores.*

- Put the prunes in a bowl, cover them
  with lukewarm water, and let them
  plump while you cook the rice. Also
  cover the raisins with the rum.
- Lightly oil a 2-quart charlotte mold.
- Bring a large pot of water to a boil. Add
  a little salt and the rice, cover, and
  cook at a rapid boil for 10 to 12 minutes. Drain rice in a colander.
- Bring the milk to a boil. Add the vanilla and a pinch of salt. Add the rice,
  and let it cook very slowly until it has
  absorbed most of the milk. This may
  require as much as 45 minutes.
- At 15 minutes before the end of the
  cooking, dissolve the gelatin in approximately ½ teacup of the prune
  soaking water. Add gelatin solution to
  the rice. Also add the drained raisins.
- When the rice is cooked, add the rum
  and the sugar; stir until the sugar has
  dissolved. Let cool completely but
  keep at room temperature.
- Whip the cream to a semistiff texture
  and fold it into the rice (see p. 297 for
  Folding).
- Turn half of the rice into the prepared
  mold. Add all the prunes, packing
  them tightly against one another in a
  single layer and leaving ½ inch of rice
  showing at the edge all around the
  mold. Pour in the second layer of rice,
  enclosing the prunes completely in
  rice.
- Chill the rice for several hours. Unmold on a platter.

CRÊPES
(The French idea of a pancake)

A crêpe pan of cast iron is a lifetime investment. See page 301 on how to condition a cast-iron pan so you never have to use butter or oil when cooking crêpes.

■ Relatively easy
6 to 8 servings
Thrift recipe
1 hour
Best season: cold months

US 2 cups, UK ½ lb., sifted flour (250 g)
3 large eggs
large pinch of salt
US ¼ cup, UK 2 TB, rum (2 TB)
US 6 TB, UK 3 TB, oil (3 TB)
US 2 cups, UK 2 scant cups, milk (.5 L)

• Put the flour into a bowl and make a well in the center. Drop the eggs, salt, rum and oil into the well. Mix well, slowly incorporating the flour into the eggs. Start adding the milk also gradually. As soon as the batter flows from the beaters in a continuous ribbon, add all the remainder of the milk and mix very well.

• Strain the batter into a clean bowl and let stand for 30 to 40 minutes.

• Heat a crêpe pan. Lift the pan forward so it is at a 45-degree angle with the burner. Pour US 2 tablespoons, UK 1 tablespoon, crêpe batter (1 TB) into the lip of the pan and slowly bring the pan back to level, at the same time tilting it from left to right and vice versa. The batter will spread to cover the whole bottom of the pan. Let the pancake cook on its first side until you can see bubbles of butter forming, then flip the pancake over or turn it with a spatula. Let cook for 1 minute on the other side. Invert the crêpe onto a plate resting over a pan of simmering water, to keep the crêpes hot.

WITH THE SAME METHOD
Chestnut Crêpes: Combine ⅔ cup French candied chestnut spread with ⅓ cup heavy cream flavored with a bit of Kirschwasser. Spread on the crêpes, roll them, and serve hot. Candied chestnut spread is available in all specialty stores.

Pastry Cream Crêpes: Prepare Pastry Cream (p. 261) while the batter rests. As soon as each crêpe is done, spread it with a layer of pastry cream. Fold each crêpe in quarters.

Orange Crêpes: Replace the rum in the crêpe batter by the finely grated rind of 2 oranges. Squeeze the juice of the oranges. Cook the crêpes, sugar them lightly, and roll them. Keep them hot. Before serving heat the juice of the oranges with US 4 tablespoons, UK 2 tablespoons, sugar (2 TB). Pour the syrup over the hot crêpes.

Crêpes with Orange Marmalade: Spread crêpes with orange marmalade and arrange them in a baking dish. Sprinkle with sugar and put under the broiler to caramelize. Heat some orange liqueur in a small pot and ignite. Pour flaming over the crêpes.

TO USE LEFTOVER CRÊPE BATTER
Bananas in Cloaks: Peel 6 bananas and brown them in butter in a frying pan. Roll each banana in a crêpe. Return the wrapped bananas to the frying pan and sprinkle with sugar. Heat some rum in a small pan, ignite it, and pour flaming over the bananas.

CLAFOUTIS
(A specialty fruit pancake-pie from the Limousin)

Proportions of eggs, milk and flour are liable to vary enormously in Clafoutis. Clafoutis is a typical example of woman's cooking where what is at hand is used for the sake of economy and thrift. For example, you can omit eggs and replace by a large tablespoon or so of flour. Whatever you use, you will see the clafoutis swell and rise immensely, to "fall" finally and brown. All clafoutis will do that by the nature of the basic ingredients.

- Easy
  6 servings
  Thrift recipe
  55 minutes
  Best season: with fresh summer fruits

  1 to 1½ lbs. black cherries (500 to 750 g)
  US 2 TB, UK 1 TB, butter (30 g)
  US 1 cup, UK 4 oz., flour (125 g)
  US ½ cup, UK 3½ oz., granulated sugar (100 g)
  pinch of salt
  3 eggs
  US 1¼ cups, UK 1 generous cup, milk (3.5 dl)
  1 tsp. vanilla extract
  granulated or confectioners' sugar

- Preheat oven to 350°F., 190°C. or 5 Regulo.
- Wash the cherries, and remove the pits if you like, but the cake is more flavorful with the pits.
- Butter generously the bottom of a 9- to 10-inch baking dish.
- Put the flour in a bowl and make a well in the center. Drop the sugar, salt and eggs into the well and mix, slowly gathering in the flour. Add the milk and vanilla extract. Strain the batter into a clean bowl.
- Pour 1 ladleful of the batter into the buttered baking dish and bake for 5 minutes, or until solid. This provides a "bottom" for the cake and prevents the fruit sticking to the bottom of the dish.
- Add all the fruit to the dish and pour remaining batter over.
- Bake on the middle rack of the oven for 40 to 45 minutes.
- The *clafoutis* is served lukewarm or cold. Sprinkle the top with granulated or confectioners' sugar before serving.

WITH THE SAME METHOD
Clafoutis with Dried Apricots: Use 5 ounces dried apricots (75 g), soak for 2 hours, and cut them into 2 or 3 pieces.

Clafoutis with Peaches: Use 6 ripe peaches.

Clafoutis with Pears: Use 4 ripe Bartlett pears.

Clafoutis with Apples: Use 4 apples.

VANILLA EXTRACT
It not only adds flavor to a batter but also it lessens the strong egg-yolk taste in all types of batter. There is pure vanilla extract and imitation vanilla extract made with vanillin, a manufactured chemical with almost the same taste as natural vanilla.

GÉNOISE
(A whole-egg spongecake)

Génoise freezes extremely well; wrap in aluminum foil; also, this cake keeps at room tempera-ture, wrapped in plastic, for several days without drying out. Génoise is the base of multiple cakes, some filled with cream, others with jams, etc.

■ Difficult
8 to 12 servings
Thrift recipe
1 hour, plus 30 minutes for cooling
Best season: year around

US 1 TB, UK ½ TB, raw butter (½ TB)
flour for the pan
US 5 TB, UK 2 oz., butter (75 g)
US 1 cup, UK 4 oz., flour (110 to 120 g)
4 eggs
US ½ cup, UK 4 TB, sugar (125 g)
large pinch of salt
flavoring of your choice (see note below)

ABOUT THIS GÉNOISE
This batter will fill either an 8-inch-square cake pan or a 9-inch round cake pan.

The cake is difficult; it must be super light and fluffy. Please understand well the terms Ribbon and Fold before you start working.

The flavoring can be 1 tablespoon vanilla extract, or finely grated lemon or orange rind, or 2 tablespoons liqueur of your choice.

● Preheat oven to 325°F., 160°C. or 4 Regulo.

● Butter the pan with the first amount of butter in the list of ingredients. Flour only the bottom of the pan.

● Melt and cool the second portion of butter. Sift the flour.

● Break the eggs into a bowl. Set the bowl over another bowl or pot of hot water. Add sugar and salt to the eggs. With an electric mixer, beat until you have a large bowl of whitish foam that falls into a heavy ribbon when the beaters are lifted from the bowl (see Ribbon, p. 302).

● Resift the flour. Add the flavoring to the batter and beat for 1 more minute.

● Pour the flour into a conical strainer. Sift one third of the flour over the egg foam and fold it in (see Folding, p. 297). Repeat twice, with the second and third portions of the flour.

● Immediately pour the whole amount of melted butter on the batter and fold until the batter is completely blended.

● Turn the batter into the prepared pan. Bake on the lowest rack of the oven for 40 minutes.

● The cake is done when it shrinks from the sides of the pan and when a skewer inserted at the center comes out dry and is too hot to be tolerated on the top of your other hand for more than a split second.

JELLY-ROLL CAKE
(Biscuit Roulé)

Possible fillings are any jelly that you like; whipped cream flavored with a liqueur or mixed with berries of your choice; pastry cream or frangipane cream; chocolate or mocha cream, etc.

■ Requires care
6 servings
Affordable
30 minutes
Best season: year around; change the fillings with the season

US 5 TB, UK 2½ TB, butter (75 g)
1 tsp. vanilla extract
4 eggs, separated
US ½ cup, UK 4 oz., granulated sugar (125 g)
pinch of salt
US 1 cup less 2 TB, UK 3½ oz., sifted flour (100 g)
½ tsp. baking powder
confectioners' sugar
Filling (see advice)

- Preheat oven to 350°F., 190°C. or 5 Regulo.
- Melt 4 tablespoons of the butter (60 g) in a small pot; let it cool.
- Grease a jelly-roll pan, 13 x 17 inches, and line it with parchment paper. Butter the paper with the remainder of the butter.
- Soak several layers of paper toweling and squeeze them dry.
- Put the vanilla, egg yolks, granulated sugar and the pinch of salt into the mixer bowl, and beat until the mixture forms a heavy ribbon (see p. 302).
- While this is happening, mix the flour and baking powder.
- Beat the egg whites until they can carry a raw egg in its shell without sinking more than ¼ inch into the batter.
- As soon as the ribbon stage is reached in beating the yolks, pour the cooled, melted butter over them and add one quarter of the egg whites. Fold these ingredients together.
- Slide the remainder of the whites over the yolks, sift the flour mixture over them, and fold again until the batter is homogenous.
- Turn the batter into the jelly-roll pan, and bake in the preheated oven for 12 to 14 minutes.
- While the cake is baking, sprinkle a tea towel with confectioners' sugar. As soon as the cake is done, invert it onto the towel. Peel off the paper from the cake, and cover the cake with the prepared wet towels. Cool completely.
- Once the cake is cold, cut off ⅓ inch all around to remove the crisp edges. Fill the cake (see advice), roll it up, and sprinkle with more confectioners' sugar.

CREAM PUFFS, ÉCLAIRS, PROFITEROLES

Are you worried about your cream puffs failing? Then add ½ teaspoon baking powder to the flour and the recipe will become failproof.

■ Requires care
8 to 12 servings
Medium expensive
20 minutes
Best season: year around

CREAM PUFFS
US 1 cup, UK 1 scant cup, water (2.5 dl)
pinch of salt
US 1 TB, UK ½ TB, sugar (½ TB)
US ½ cup, UK 4 oz., butter (125 g)
US 1 cup, UK 4 oz., sifted flour (125 g)
5 small eggs
1 tsp. vanilla extract

CONFECTIONERS' GLAZE
US 2 cups, UK 2 scant cups,
  confectioners' sugar (200 g)
1 to 2 TB liqueur of your choice, colored
  with 1 drop of red or green food
  coloring, or 1 to 2 TB prepared
  double-strength coffee

• Put water, salt, sugar and butter, cut into small pieces, in a 2-quart saucepan. Bring slowly to a boil.

• As soon as the mixture foams up like milk, remove the pot from the heat and add all the flour at once. Stir well until a large ball forms.

• Return the pot to medium heat and stir and flatten the ball of dough for 2 or 3 minutes so as to evaporate some of the moisture. Remove from the heat again.

• Add the eggs, beaten, one by one, stirring well after each addition, until you have a stiffish deep yellow batter, which baked will give cream puffs. Add vanilla.

• Put the batter into a pastry bag (see p. 301) fitted with a ¾-inch plain nozzle. Pipe out the dough.

Cream Puffs: Pipe 1½-inch balls at 2-inch intervals. Bake for 25 to 30 minutes. Yield: 2 to 3 dozen puffs.

Éclairs: Pipe 4-inch-long sticks at 2-inch intervals. Pass the tines of a fork over the surface without going into the batter by more than ⅛ inch. Yield: 18 to 20 éclairs.

Profiteroles: Pipe ½-inch balls at 1½-inch intervals. Bake for 12 to 15 minutes. Yield: 36 to 42 profiteroles.

• In all cases bake on the middle rack of the oven until dark golden, nice and dry.

• To fill, punch a hole at the bottom of each puff and shoot the filling, stuffed into a pastry bag, straight into the puff. Éclairs are filled by pushing a hole at each end of the éclair. For filling use Whipped Cream (p. 260) or Pastry Cream (p. 261).

Glaze: Mix confectioners' sugar with liqueur and food coloring, or with lukewarm coffee. Stir until you have a smooth glaze. Brush it or spoon and spread it on the top of the pastries.

CHILDREN'S FUN
Encourage your youngsters to help you; they love the excitement of the "cream-puff" miracle.

ICE CREAM PROFITEROLES WITH CHOCOLATE SAUCE
(Profiteroles Glacées au Chocolat)

About the sauce: Should it "seize" or harden during dinner, add some boiling milk to it until it regains the consistency you like.

■ Easy
8 servings
Medium expensive
15 minutes
Best season: fall and winter

40 profiteroles (p. 273)
1½ quarts French vanilla ice cream (1.5 L)

CHOCOLATE SAUCE
½ lb. unsweetened chocolate (250 g)
US ⅔ cup, UK ½ cup, hot milk (2 dl)
US 4 TB, UK 2 oz., unsalted butter (60 g)

- Before dinner, slit the sides of 40 profiteroles.
- Shape 40 balls of vanilla ice cream with a melon baller and put them on a jelly-roll pan. Keep them solidly frozen.

CHOCOLATE SAUCE
- Break the chocolate into a pot. Add the milk and butter and slowly stir over low heat until the mixture forms a sauce. Keep hot in the top pan of a double boiler over hot water during dinner.
- Just before serving, have a friend or child help you slip 1 ice-cream ball into each puff. Pile them on a large serving platter.
- Serve the hot sauce in a heated bowl on the side.

CREAM PUFFS
They freeze well. Put them in plastic bags, well sealed. When ready to use them, set them solidly frozen on a baking sheet in a medium oven for 7 to 8 minutes; they will taste as if you had just baked them.

SWEET PASTRY DOUGHS
(Pâtisserie, Pâtes de Base, Sucrées)

Be aware that flours vary in their starch and protein contents. Add just enough flour to make a dough that will remain tender. American flours are harder than European flours so that you may need less flour in America.

To roll out these sweet pastries, keep the pastry between 2 layers of plastic wrap to which it will never stick. Sweet pastries heat very quickly; always work with them as cold as possible.

All these pastries freeze well. Defrost them in the refrigerator 24 hours before you plan to use them.

SWEET PASTRY WITH EGG YOLK
US 6 TB, UK 3 TB, unsalted butter (90 g)
US ¼ cup, UK 2 TB, sugar (60 g)
pinch of salt
1 egg yolk
1 tsp. vanilla extract (optional)
US 1 cup, UK 4 oz., flour, sifted (125 g)

- Cream the butter with an electric mixer. Add the sugar, salt, egg yolk, and vanilla if used. Beat until fluffy. With a spatula flatten in the flour until an homogenous dough is obtained.
- Put the dough in plastic wrap. Flatten it into a disc 1 inch x 6 inches. Refrigerate for 1 hour. Yield: pastry for one 10-inch pie.

SWEET PASTRY WITH WHOLE EGG
US ¼ lb., UK 4 TB, unsalted butter (125 g)
US ¼ cup, UK 2 TB, sugar (60 g)
pinch of salt
1 egg
1 tsp. vanilla extract (optional)
US 2 cups, UK ½ lb., sifted flour (250 g)

- Cream the butter with an electric mixer. Add the sugar, salt, egg, and vanilla if used. Beat until fluffy. With a spatula flatten in the flour until a smooth pastry dough is obtained.
- Put the dough in plastic wrap. Flatten it into a disc ½ inch x 8 inches. Refrigerate for 1 hour. Yield: pastry for one 10-inch pie.

PASTRIES
All pastries prepared 1 day ahead and refrigerated overnight have a better texture and are easier to handle and roll out.

UNSWEETENED PASTRY DOUGHS
(Pâtisserie, Pâtes de Base non Sucrées)

Important! All pastries freeze very well. Make as much of any pastry as you have time for and freeze it. Defrost in the refrigerator 24 hours before you plan to use it.

SHORT PASTRY (PÂTE BRISÉE)
US 1½ cups, UK 6 oz., flour, sifted (180 g)
US ½ cup, UK 3½ oz., butter (120 g)
pinch of salt
US 2 TB, UK 1 TB, sugar (2 TB) (optional)
US 4 TB, UK 2 TB, water (2 TB)

For a more tender pastry, you may use US 9 TB, UK 4 oz., butter (135 g)

• Make a well in the flour. Add the butter, very cold, cut into tablespoons. Add the salt, and the sugar if used. Flatten the butter into the flour until a meal is obtained with lumps of flour and butter paste about ⅓ inch across.

• Add the water, tablespoon by tablespoon, working it into a dough. With the heel of the hand work lightly into a dough. Flatten into a cake ½ inch x 6 inches. Refrigerate for 30 minutes before using. Yield: pastry for one 10-inch pie.

PUFF PASTRY (PÂTE FEUILLETÉE)
US 2 cups, UK ½ lb., sifted flour (250 g)
US 1 cup, UK ½ lb., unsalted butter (250 g)
US ⅓ cup, UK ¼ cup, water (1 scant dl)
½ tsp. salt

STEP ONE
• Make a well in the flour. Cut the butter into 1½-tablespoon chunks. Mix them with the flour, flattening the butter into the flour until you have pieces of butter and flour about ½ inch across.

• Add the water with the salt dissolved in it and gather the dough into a ball. Flatten into a rectangle 5 x 7 inches and ½ inch thick. Refrigerate for 20 minutes.

STEP TWO
• Remove pastry from refrigerator. Starting from the center of the pastry and with 1 stretch in each direction, roll out the dough 4 inches forward, away from you, and 4 inches toward you. Fold into thirds to re-form a rectangle 5 x 7 inches. *Now be careful:* turn this rectangle to give it a 90-degree turn so that it will look like a closed book ready to be opened. Repeat the same rolling you did before, 4 inches away from you, 4 inches toward you. Again fold into thirds to make a rectangle 5 x 7 inches. Refrigerate the dough.

STEPS THREE AND FOUR
- The operation done before must be re-peated another 4 times. This operation is called giving "turns" and the turns are given two by two, each 2 turns at an interval of 30 minutes; during the interval the pastry is refrigerated.
- The most important thing to re-member is that every time you are going to give a turn you must have changed the direction of your pastry by 90 degrees so that it always looks like a *closed book ready to be opened.*

- It is preferable to prepare the dough 24 hours ahead of the time you plan to use it.

ALL PASTRIES
prepared a day ahead and allowed to rest in the refrigerator for 24 hours have a better texture and are easier to handle.

If you prefer ready-made Puff Pastry, it can be purchased made with butter in good spe-cialty shops or made with vegetable shorten-ing in supermarkets.

APRICOT TART
(Tarte aux Abricots)

The best pie plates are made of white porcelain and have a dull unfinished bottom for better heat absorption. Beware of pans with detachable bottoms; the layer of air between the mold and the detachable circle does not allow heat to reach the center of the pie evenly and the bottom remains soggy.

■ Quite easy
6 servings
Medium expensive
50 minutes, with the pastry done ahead
Best season: July and August

1 recipe Sweet Pastry with Egg Yolk (p. 275)

CREAM
1 egg
US ¼ cup, UK 2 TB, sugar (2 TB)
US ¼ cup, UK 2 TB, flour (30 g)
US ⅓ cup, UK 3 TB, milk (3 TB)
US ⅓ cup, UK 3 TB, heavy cream (3 TB)
pinch of salt
US ¼ cup, UK 2 TB, Kirsch (2 TB)

FRUIT
1½ to 2 lbs. ripe fresh apricots (750 g to 1 kg)
US 3 TB, UK 1½ TB, sugar (1½ TB)

- Preheat oven to 400°F., 200°C. or 6 Regulo.
- Roll out the pastry and fit it into a buttered 10-inch pie plate. Fit the pastry with an aluminum-foil liner and fill with beans (see Blind Baking, p. 293).
- Prebake for 10 to 12 minutes.
- Prepare the cream: Mix egg, sugar, flour, milk and cream in a bowl; add a pinch of salt and the Kirsch. Pour this cream into the prebaked pie shell.
- Wash and pit the fruit. Cut them into halves and arrange the halves so they overlap and form concentric circles.
- Bake for about 45 minutes, or until the tops of the apricots are browned.
- Remove from the oven, cool completely, and sprinkle with sugar just before serving.

ABOUT THIS TART
This recipe is for a 10-inch tart and the method is valid for all very juicy fruits such as plums, grapes, cherries. The flour in the cream absorbs the fruit juice to prevent it softening the pie bottom.

FRENCH CHERRY TART
(Tarte aux Cerises Acides)

Do not ever refrigerate cooked pies or tarts; they absorb all the moisture from the refrigerator and become soggy and soft.

- Relatively easy
  6 servings
  Medium expensive
  50 to 60 minutes
  Best season: June and July

  **1 recipe Short Pastry (p. 276), prepared
  the day before**

  FILLING
  1½ to 2 lbs. sour cherries (750 g to 1 kg)
  2 egg yolks
  US ⅓ cup, UK 3½ oz., sugar (90 g)
  pinch of salt
  US 3 TB, UK 1½ TB, flour (1½ TB)
  US 2 TB, UK 1 TB, butter (30 g)
  US 1½ cups, UK 1⅓ cups, milk (3.5 dl)
  US 2 TB, UK 1 TB, Kirsch (1 TB)

- Preheat oven to 375°F., 190°C. or 5 Regulo.
- Roll out the pastry ⅙ inch thick and fit it into a buttered 10-inch pie plate. Refrigerate pastry while you prepare the cherries.
- Pit the cherries.
- *Prepare the custard filling:* Mix egg yolks, sugar, salt and flour. Melt the butter and add the milk. Add butter and milk mixture gradually to the yolk and flour mixture. Flavor with Kirsch.
- Put the cherries in the pie shell. Bake on the bottom rack of the oven for 20 to 25 minutes. Pour the custard over the cherries and finish baking for another 20 to 25 minutes, or until the top is golden.
- Let cool, and lift the tart out of the plate to a rack.

THIS TART
is so good that even prepared a day ahead and kept on a cool shelf it will still be a favorite.

STRAWBERRY TART
(Tarte aux Fraises)

For a finishing touch, do as the pastry chefs do: Melt a jar of red currant jelly and brush it over the berries; the appearance will be professional. Whip some cream to a stiff Chantilly and pipe rosettes among the berries.

■ Relatively easy
  6 to 8 servings
  Medium expensive
  50 minutes
  Best season: May to July

  1½ to 2 lbs. fresh strawberries (750 g to 1 kg)
  US 1 TB, UK ½ TB, sugar (15 g)
  Kirschwasser
  1 recipe Sweet Pastry with Whole Egg (p. 275), prepared the day before

  CREAM
  2 eggs
  US ⅓ cup, UK 2½ oz., sugar (90 g)
  US ⅓ cup, UK 1⅔ oz., flour, sifted (50 g)
  US 1¼ cups, UK 1⅛ cups, milk, cold (3.5 dl)
  US 3 TB, UK 1½ TB, orange liqueur of your choice
  US 2 TB, UK 1 TB, unsalted butter (30 g)

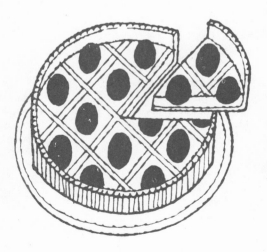

- Wash the berries, drain, and hull them. Macerate them with the sugar and Kirsch to taste in a bowl.

- Preheat oven to 350°F., 180°C. or 5 Regulo.

- Roll out the pastry and fit it into a lightly buttered 9- to 10-inch pie plate. Prick the pastry heavily with the tines of a fork. Line the pastry with foil and fill the foil with beans. Bake for 20 minutes. Let cool completely in the plate before filling it with the cream.

- *Prepare the cream:* Mix in a saucepan the eggs, sugar and flour. Gradually dilute with the cold milk. Thicken, stirring constantly, over medium heat; stop cooking only when you see 1 or 2 boils at the center of the pot. Remove from the heat; add the liqueur and butter. Cool the cream, stirring at regular intervals.

- Spread the cold cream on the bottom of the pie shell. Arrange the berries on top of the cream.

ABOUT THIS METHOD
For a 9- to 10-inch pie plate, this method is best for all berries that are very juicy and lose shape while cooking–raspberries, blueberries, all types of gooseberries and currants, grapes, kiwi fruit.

FLAMBÉED APPLE TART
(Tarte aux Pommes Flambées)

About the cooking of the apples: It is advisable to add water bit by bit and turn the apples at regular intervals so they cook evenly and gradually. These apples, quartered, will cook just right if, when you core them, you cut out the core with a straight line along the length of the apple. You will gain some time as the apples will cook faster and more evenly, even though you will indeed lose a bit of apple pulp.

■ A bit difficult
6 servings
A bit expensive
1 hour, plus 1 day ahead for the pastry
Best season: September through April

1 recipe Short Pastry (p. 276), prepared the day before

FILLING
2 to 2½ lbs. green apples (1 kg)
US ¼ cup, UK 2 TB, unsalted butter (60 g)
ground cinnamon
US ⅓ cup, UK ¼ cup, brown sugar (100 g)
US ¼ cup, UK 2 TB, water (2 TB)
dash of liqueur of your choice

FLAMING AND SERVING
US 1 cup, UK 1 scant cup, heavy cream (125 g) whipped into Chantilly, unsweetened
US 4 TB, UK 2 TB, brown sugar (2 TB)
pinch of ground cinnamon
US ⅓ cup, UK ¼ cup, whisky, Calvados, applejack or Cognac (1 scant dl)

APPLES
Use Greening or Granny Smith apples for tartness and texture.

● Preheat oven to 400°F., 200°C. or 6 Regulo.
● Roll out the pastry. Fit it into a lightly buttered 10-inch pie plate. Prick the bottom of the pastry heavily with the tines of a fork. Fit foil into the shell and fill it with beans. Bake for 12 to 15 minutes.
● Turn the oven off. Remove the beans. Return the pie to the oven and let the shell remain in the dying oven where it will finish cooking and stay warm.
● Peel the apples, core them, and cut them into quarters (see advice).
● Heat the butter in a large skillet. Brown the apples well over high heat. Turn the heat down, add the cinnamon to taste, brown sugar, water and a dash of liqueur. Cover the apples and let them cook until tender.
● Arrange the apples attractively in the pastry-lined pan.
● Whip the cream and put it into an attractive bowl.
● Just before serving, sprinkle the additional brown sugar and cinnamon over the top of the tart. Heat the chosen liqueur in a small pot and pour it flaming over the apples.
● Serve the pie and cream together.

ALMOND TARTLETS
(Tartelettes Amandines)

These tartlets will keep well for at least 3 days if properly stored in a canister.

- Easy
  12 tartlets, 2½ inches across
  Medium expensive
  40 minutes
  Best season: year around

  US 10 TB, UK 5 TB, unsalted butter (150 g)
  US ½ cup, UK 4½ oz., sugar (125 g)
  pinch of salt
  1 tsp. almond extract
  4 eggs, separated
  US 1 cup, UK 4 oz., sifted flour (125 g)
  3½ oz. chopped blanched almonds (100 g)
  1 tsp. baking powder
  unsalted butter to butter 12 tartlet pans,
  **   2½ to 3 inches across**
  confectioners' sugar

TWO TECHNICAL POINTS
Buy almonds, especially if chopped or ground, as you need them for they become rancid easily. Keeping them refrigerated helps.

When making a cake of this type, beware of overworking the batter; see Gluten (p. 298).

- Preheat oven to 325°F., 160°C. or 4 Regulo.
- Cream the butter until very soft. Add four fifths of the sugar and the salt, and beat well. Add the almond extract and the egg yolks, one by one. Leave the electric mixer at medium speed to work on the mixture while you prepare the remainder of the batter.
- Sift the flour twice.
- Put the chopped almonds in a blender container with the rest of the sugar, and process until you have a smooth powder.
- Mix flour, baking powder and almond powder.
- Beat the egg whites until they can carry the weight of a raw egg in its shell; it should not sink into the whites by more than ¼ inch.
- To finish the batter, add the dry ingredients to the yolks and sugar base, flattening the mixture into the soft base with a spatula so as not to develop gluten, which would make the cakes rubbery.
- Finally fold in the egg whites.
- Butter the tartlet molds generously. Spoon the batter into the molds. Bake in the preheated oven for 20 to 25 minutes.
- Unmold as soon as baked. To serve, dust with confectioners' sugar.

EXPRESS TART
(Tarte Express)

Ricotta or any other soft white cheese always contains a large percentage of moisture. To prevent the cheese from oozing water into the crust, add any good whipped cream stabilizer to the cheese as you whip.

- Easy
  6 servings
  Medium expensive
  15 minutes
  Best season: year around

  2 or 3 dry coconut macaroons
  1 lb. ricotta or other fresh white cheese
  (see advice) (500 g)
  US ¼ cup, UK 2 TB, sugar (60 g)
  pinch of salt
  1 baked tart shell, 8 to 9 inches, any style
  1 can (8¼ oz.) pineapple slices (234 g)

OTHER FRUITS
You can use other canned fruits, such as peaches or apricots.

- Crumble the macaroons.
- Beat the ricotta or other cheese with three quarters of the sugar and the salt. Add the crumbled macaroons.
- Spread this mixture evenly on the bottom of the baked pastry.
- Drain the pineapple slices, but reserve the syrup.
- Cut each slice of pineapple into 8 small pieces and cover the filling with them, building a regular pattern.
- Mix together remaining sugar with US ⅓ cup, UK ¼ cup, of the reserved pineapple syrup (1 scant dl). Boil hard for 5 minutes.
- Brush the syrup over the pineapple slices to glaze them. Serve promptly.

PINEAPPLE TART
(Tarte à l'Ananas)

Too much work? If the puff pastry is too much work, use any sweet pastry or short pastry (see pp. 275-277).

■ Pastry handling needs care
6 to 8 servings
Medium expensive
1½ hours
Best season: year around

⅔ recipe Puff Pastry (p. 276).

CREAM
2 egg yolks
US ⅔ cup, UK 6 oz., sugar (150 g)
US 5 TB, UK 2½ TB, flour (2½ TB)
US 1 generous cup, UK 1 cup, cold milk (.25 L)
1 tsp. vanilla extract
US 2 TB, UK 1 TB, Kirsch (1 TB)

FRUIT
2 cans (8 oz. each) pineapple slices (227 g each)
6 oz. apricot jam (180 g)
US 2 TB, UK 1 TB, Kirsch (1 TB)

ABOUT THIS RECIPE
This method works for all canned fruits: peaches, apricots, pears.

A prebaked pastry shell can be purchased if you prefer.

● Roll out puff pastry ⅛ inch thick. Fit it into a lightly buttered 10-inch pie plate. Press the pastry snugly against the plate. Cut the edges neatly with the rolling pin passed quickly but firmly over the rim of the plate. Prick the pastry heavily with a fork and line with foil and beans. Before baking refrigerate for at least 30 minutes.

● Preheat oven to 425°F., 220°C. or 6 Regulo.

● Bake the pastry for 15 to 20 minutes. Remove the beans and foil and bake for another 2 or 3 minutes. Turn the oven off and let the pastry finish cooking in the dying oven for another 5 minutes. Cool on a rack.

● While pastry is baking, prepare the cream. Mix very well the egg yolks, sugar and flour. Dilute with the cold milk. Slowly bring to a boil over medium heat. Remove from the heat as soon as thickened. Cool for a few minutes, then add vanilla extract and Kirsch. Cool completely, stirring at regular intervals.

● Drain the pineapple slices very well. Cut them into quarters. Pour the cold cream into the cold pastry shell.

● Melt the apricot jam, add the Kirsch to it, and strain it. Keep warm.

● Arrange the pineapple pieces attractively on the cream and brush the fruit with the apricot jam.

JAM SOUFFLÉ
(Soufflé à la Confiture)

Any time on your hands? A recipe of stirred custard (crème anglaise), flavored with the appropriate liqueur, would do wonders for this soufflé at a company dinner.

- Easy
  6 servings
  Thrift recipe
  40 minutes
  Best season: year around

  12 oz. jam of your choice (375 g)
  4 egg whites
  US 1 TB, UK ½ TB, unsalted butter (15 g)

- Preheat oven to 400°F., 200°C. or 6 Regulo,
- Heat the jam in a 2-quart saucepan.
- Beat the egg whites, and fold them into the hot jam until the mixture is homogenous.
- Turn into a buttered 6-cup soufflé mold. Bake for 15 to 20 minutes, or until the soufflè is solid at the center.

THIS SOUFFLÉ
is a good way to use leftover egg whites.

FRENCH VANILLA ICE CREAM
(Glace Rapide à la Vanille)

Do you own an ice cream churner? If so, you can replace the heavy cream by milk. Cook the yolks with the milk to make a stirred custard, cool it, and let it freeze in the machine.

- Easy
  6 servings
  Medium expensive
  20 minutes, plus 3 to 4 hours for freezing
  Best season: summer, but year around

  6 egg yolks
  US 1 TB, UK ½ TB, vanilla extract (½ TB)
  US ⅔ cup, UK 5 TB, granulated sugar (5 TB)
  pinch of salt
  US 1⅓ cups, UK 1¼ cups, heavy cream (250 g)

- Ribbon heavily (see p. 302) together the egg yolks, vanilla extract, sugar and salt.

- In another bowl, whip the cream until semisoft. Fold the cream into the vanilla-flavored yolks.

- Pour the cream into ice-cube trays and freeze for 1 hour.

- After an hour, beat the cream with the electric mixer and freeze again. Repeat this operation 2 or 3 times more. To avoid defrosting of the ice cream, put the bowl in which you whip in the freezer in between beatings.

- Serve in glasses or cups with cookies or ladyfingers.

SANITATION
is extremely important; all your ingredients must be absolutely fresh and your utensils cleaned scrupulously since bacteria have a tendency to develop very quickly in this type of uncooked ice cream.

WITH THE SAME METHOD
Coffee Ice Cream: Use only 1 teaspoon vanilla extract and add instant coffee powder to your taste.

Chocolate Ice Cream: Replace the vanilla by 2 ounces chocolate (60 g), melted.

CAFÉ LIÉGEOIS
(A specialty of the City of Liège, adopted by the whole of France)

Would you prefer a chocolate Liégeois? Very simply, replace the coffee ice cream by chocolate ice cream.

- Easy
  6 servings
  Medium expensive
  20 minutes, plus 30 minutes to cool the coffee
  Best season: year around

  6 demitasses of extremely strong dark roast coffee
  sugar
  Cognac
  US 1 cup, UK 1 generous cup, heavy cream (200 g)
  1 recipe coffee ice cream (p. 286)
  cocoa powder

- Prepare the coffee and add sugar and Cognac to your taste. Cool to lukewarm, then pour an equal amount of each into 6 large glasses.
- Put the glasses to refrigerate until you are ready to serve.
- Whip the cream to Chantilly, sweetening to your taste (see p. 260).
- When you are ready to serve dessert, add a scoop or two of ice cream to each portion of coffee, in each glass. Spoon some whipped cream over the mixture. Dust lightly with cocoa powder.

ABOUT SWEETENING
The sweetening of frozen desserts is important. They need more sugar than cold desserts, since the colder a mixture is, the less sweet it seems to the taste buds.

STRAWBERRY SHERBET
(Sorbet aux Fraises)

If you worry about texture and consistency, remember that a sherbet is never hard and can be served quite soft.

- Easy
  6 to 8 servings
  Medium expensive
  30 minutes, plus time for freezing
  Best season: June and July

  US ¾ cup, UK 6½ oz., granulated sugar (200 g)
  US ¾ cup, UK ½ cup, water (2.5 dl)
  1¼ lbs. hulled fresh strawberries (625 g)
  juice of ½ lemon

- Melt the sugar in the water. Bring to a boil. As soon as you have a syrup, remove it from the heat. Cool completely.
- Wash the berries, drain, and hull them. Purée them and add the lemon juice.
- Blend the purée with the syrup and pour into an ice-cube tray.
- Freeze for 1 hour, then remove to a chilled bowl and whip. Freeze again and whip again 2 more times.
- Serve the sherbet in large glasses with or without whipped cream.

NO FRESH BERRIES?
If you have no fresh berries or the fresh ones are too expensive, you can use loose-pack frozen berries packed without syrup.

WITH THE SAME METHOD
Prepare a sherbet with any fruit purée such as raspberry, pineapple, red or black currant.

ORANGE SHERBET
(Sorbet à l'Orange)

Would you like a striking presentation? Take the time to cut a lid in the oranges and after you extract all the juice, remove all membranes with a serrated spoon. Fill the orange shells with the sherbet.

- A bit difficult
  6 servings
  Medium expensive
  30 minutes
  Best season: orange season

  6 large juice oranges, juiced
  juice of 1 small lemon
  1 tsp. finely grated lemon rind
  US 2 cups, UK 6 oz., confectioners' sugar
  (200 g)
  US 1¼ cups, UK 10 oz., evaporated milk
  (285 g)
  1 egg white
  pinch of salt
  toasted almonds, chopped

ALWAYS FREEZE
Freeze ices and sherbets in long flat dishes, where they can freeze rapidly.

- Mix the orange and lemon juices, the lemon rind, three quarters of the confectioners' sugar and the evaporated milk in a bowl.
- Pour the mixture into an ice-cube tray and freeze for 1 hour, or until set.
- Beat the sherbet with the electric mixer for 5 minutes. Return to the ice-cube tray and keep the mixer bowl frozen.
- Beat the egg white, gradually adding to it the remainder of the confectioners' sugar and a pinch of salt.
- Turn sherbet and egg white into the frozen mixer bowl and fold into each other. Refreeze in the ice-cube tray until solid.
- Present the sherbet in glasses topped with chopped toasted almonds.

EXPRESS FRUIT ICE
(Glace Express aux Fruits)

A good idea for a different dessert: With perfect fruit of the same kind as used in the ice, prepare a small compote and flavor it with an appropriate liqueur. For example: peaches and Grand Marnier or strawberries and Kirschwasser. Then top the ice with this fruit compote.

■ Easy
   6 to 10 servings
   Thrift recipe
   5 minutes, plus time for cooling milk and freezing
   Best season: adapt to the fruit being used

   1 can (13 oz.) unsweetened evaporated milk (384 ml)
   2 cups puréed fresh fruit (.5 L)
   US 1 cup, UK 1 scant cup, granulated sugar (250 g)
   dash of lemon juice

- Empty the evaporated milk into a large mixer bowl. Store in freezer compartment until the edges start freezing.
- Meanwhile, purée enough of any ripe fruit to obtain approximately 2 cups.
- Dissolve the sugar in the fruit purée; add a dash of lemon juice.
- Whip the evaporated milk until a stiff foam is obtained.
- Pour the fruit and sugar mixture gradually over the foam, folding it in.
- Turn the mixture into 2 ice-cube trays and freeze.
- Let the ice mellow before serving in glasses or dishes.

THIS IS AN EXCELLENT
recipe for using overripe peaches, strawberries, nectarines, pears. Raspberries are excellent too, but the purée must be strained to discard the seeds.

GLOSSARY

Almonds: These are available in shells; shelled whole, still retaining the brown skin; blanched, with brown skin removed. When blanched, they can be whole, slivered in length, sliced across or chopped. *To blanch* almonds, bring a pot of water to a boil, add the almonds, and turn off the heat. The skin will slip off when the almond is squeezed between thumb and index finger. *To chop* almonds, use a knife or a food processor. *To powder* almonds you must add some sugar to chopped almonds. Process the mixture in a blender or food processor until reduced to powder.

Aluminum foil: Use the heaviest aluminum foil. When you cook in it, the dull side should be on the outside. When you want to protect food from further browning, the shiny side should be on the outside.

Anchovies: Anchovies are packed as fillets either flat or round, canned in oil. They also come packed in salt. In all cases rinse them under cold water before adding to a cooked dish or sauce. For salads, rinse only if necessary for your personal taste.

Anglaise: An *anglaise* is a mixture of 1 egg, 1 teaspoon oil, 1 teaspoon water with a pinch of salt and pepper, beaten until completely liquefied. The mixture is brushed on floured items. These foods or pieces are then coated with bread crumbs and fried in butter or oil. See also BREADING.

Armagnac: A French spirit prepared in the southwestern part of France south of the Garonne river. Its bouquet and aroma make it the perfect companion to all fowl, game birds and venison. It must be reduced or ignited for flambéing. See FLAMBAGE.

Aromatics: All the ingredients that contribute to enhance and develop the flavor and aroma of culinary preparations. Herbs, a *bouquet garni*, carrots, onions, celery, garlic and *persillade* can all be considered aromatics.

The chief aromatic vegetables are onions, carrots and celery cut into the following sizes: ⅛-inch cubes *(brunoise)*; ¼-inch cubes *(mirepoix)*; ⅓-inch cubes *(salpicon)*; ¼-inch strips *(julienne)*; ⅛-inch strips *(paysanne)*.

Bacon: Smoked and salted brisket of pork as known in English-speaking countries. In French, bacon is called *lard fumé*. The fresh brisket of pork in French is called *lard frais*. The French word *bacon* means the meat that is called "Canadian bacon" in English-speaking countries.

Bain-Marie: see WATER BATH.

Baster and gravy separator: A large kitchen syringe used to baste meats with their gravy or other liquids. A baster is also the best lean and fat gravy separator. Pour any gravy into a glass measuring cup; the fat will rise to the top. Squeeze the bulb of the baster tightly, insert the syringe into the lean gravy beneath the fat, release the bulb, and draw up all the lean portion. Pour it off into a saucepan or sauceboat. See GRAVY.

Beurre manié: In English "kneaded butter" is the name given to unmelted, raw butter mixed with an equal volume of raw flour to thicken a sauce or gravy quickly. The *beurre manié* is whisked rapidly into the simmering liquid, which thickens instantly. The sauce or gravy should then immediately be removed from the heat.

Binder, to bind, binding: A binder is a thickener such as flour, starch or egg yolks. To bind means to add a thickener to a liquid or conversely add liquid to a thickener, so that the thickener dilates and thickens the liquid. A binding can be a thickener such as a slurry, a *roux*, a *liaison* or *beurre manié*. See these words.

Blanching: For young fresh vegetables: cooking in boiling, salted water. For pungent old vegetables (e.g., cauliflower, leeks): parboiling in boiling water to lessen their pungency. The blanching water is discarded. For meats: some salted meats such as bacon may also be blanched, but in this case the blanching starts in cold water.

Blender: A food processing machine that grinds, purées and liquefies. Almost a must in any modern kitchen.

Blind baking: A pastry shell is said to be "blind baked" when it is baked empty of filling. The shell is often lined with aluminum foil or parchment paper and this lining is filled with dried beans or rice or metal nuggets, which prevent the pastry lifting from the pan. When pastry is done, the beans are removed as well as the liner; the shell is sprinkled with sugar and left to dry inside the dying oven. Blind-baked pastry shells are used for all pies filled with cream and/or fruit or both.

Boiling vegetables: In French cuisine, boiled or "blanched" vegetables are always cooked in plenty of water salted with 1½ teaspoons (7.5 g) of salt per quart and kept at a rolling boil all through the cooking time. The pot should never be covered or the vegetables will discolor, especially the green ones. Baking soda should *never* be added to the water in which the vegetables will cook or they will become mushy on the outside.

Bouillon: In classic French cuisine the first recipes given in cookbooks were those for stock or bouillon. You can prepare an all-purpose bouillon with a few meaty veal bones, several chicken wings and some aromatics. The bouillon can be frozen in jars and defrosted as needed. You can also use any bouillon left from Chicken Soup (see p. 12) or pot-au-feu (p. 109), or even any vegetable broth from the cooking of vegetable soups.

Bouillon cubes, or semisolid meat extracts, can be added to vegetable broth to obtain a basic, all-purpose bouillon. When using bouillon cubes, be careful not to use too much. Manufacturers' instructions usually give a salty broth and as a result a salty sauce. It is prudent to use half as much as indicated on the wrapper to start with. You can always add a small fraction of a cube or a pea-size piece of meat extract to your finished sauce to balance the final taste. See also MEAT EXTRACT.

Bouquet garni: A small ôr large bundle of parsley stems (for more flavor), a sprig of dried thyme and bay leaf (a piece of leaf or a whole leaf depending on the amount of liquid to be flavored). The three aromatics are tied together and must be left to float freely in whatever sauce or stock they will flavor, so as to release a maximum amount of taste. Wrapping the *bouquet garni* in cheesecloth or attaching it at the pot handle by a string is often advocated by authors who do not strain sauces. The first method is preferred.

Braiser, braising pot: *Braiser* means to cook in a tightly covered pot with just enough liquid barely to cover the meat, in the case of a stew, or to reach halfway to the top of the meat, in the case of a whole piece of meat. The word comes from the French *braise*, which means glowing coal or charcoal. Formerly, when cooking on the hearth, one cooked with charcoal under the pot. More charcoal was put inside of an upside-down lid that was made hollow for that purpose, and the bottom of the lid rested directly on the meat. The meat cooked within two layers of charcoal. Nowadays, braising is done in the oven to reproduce the same enclosed atmosphere as in the old hollow-lid braising pots. Put a large layer of foil on the meat and arrange it flush on the top of the meat so it makes an upside-down lid that will catch any condensation and allow the sauce to concentrate by reduction instead of being constantly rewatered. The meat then "braises" instead of boiling. The best way to convince yourself of the utility of this method is to do a braise once without the upside-down foil and the next time with it. The difference in the texture of the meat and the taste of the sauce will be strikingly in favor of the foil.

Braising pots should always be heavy iron or enameled cast iron. In France women braise in a *cocotte*, a round or oval pot made of cast iron or enameled cast iron.

Bread crumbs: In French cuisine, fresh bread crumbs are always made from the center crumbs of unsweetened French bread. If dry bread crumbs are desired, the bread is dried in a slow oven before being crumbled in a blender or food processor. Bread crumbs can be flavored with herbs and/or garlic, or even cheese.

Breading: Breading a food (fillets of fish, thin slivers of meat, etc.) has three phases: 1. the food is floured; 2. it is brushed with the egg mixture known as *anglaise* (see this word); 3. it is coated with either dry or fresh bread crumbs. Brushing the egg wash on the food instead of dipping the food into the wash results in a thin and crisp breading.

Brisket of pork: The cut of pork that is salted and smoked to make what is known as "bacon" (see this word) in the English-speaking world. Unsalted brisket of pork is known in French as *lard frais*.

Brunoise: see AROMATICS.

Butter: In French cuisine the freshest *unsalted* butter is used. Only the province of Brittany uses salted butter known as *beurre demi-sel*.

Butter heated and cooked until the solids turn golden brown will acquire a delicious hazelnut flavor and color. This is called "hazelnut butter" *(beurre noisette)*.

Butter that is melted, cleaned of its solids and of its liquid whey, is called "clarified butter." Clarified butter is best for panfrying breaded items for it gives a golden, clean appearance as well as the best taste.

Calvados: In Normandy the brandy distilled from cider is called Calvados. It is aged in oak casks and acquires its color from the wood. If you have no Calvados, you can replace it by applejack, an American apple brandy. It must be reduced or ignited for flambéing. See FLAMBAGE.

Caramel: When sugar is cooked, it progressively loses its moisture. When only the sugar or sucrose is left, it cooks and becomes darker and darker. As it darkens, it becomes "caramel." Caramel may be light or dark; the darker it becomes the more flavor it will have. Stop cooking any caramel as soon as you see tiny wisps of smoke coming off the surface of the sugar. If caramel cooks too long it becomes bitter, turns black, and eventually turns to carbon dust. Caramel is often used to coat baking pans in which puddings and upside-down custards will be baked. Adding a single drop of lemon juice to a cooking caramel will help to ensure that the pan full of sugar does not turn to crystals.

Crystals in caramel cooking are often due to fat in the pan, so wash your pot before cooking the sugar and dry it well with a paper towel.

Chicken livers: They are excellent in forcemeats. When you buy whole chickens, freeze three to five livers in small plastic bags. You can open the bag and add the livers one by one, then reseal the bag well after each addition.

Chopping board, chopping: Make sure that you own a chopping board of wood or plastic that is washable. Do not cross-contaminate your cooked foods by cutting them on a board which you have used previously to cut and trim raw meat or vegetables. The scrubbing and washing of a chopping board is a serious matter for the health of your family.

To chop, grab hold of the knife handle with your working hand. Block the tip of the blade with your other hand, fingers well extended, and chop from front to back of the board in one straight line. Do not "fan out" and do not hold the tip of the blade between your fingertips; it is dangerous.

Cocotte: The name used in France for a round or oval iron or enameled cast-iron pot used to braise stews and birds.

Cognac: The name of a brandy distilled from wine in the area surrounding the city of Cognac in western France. Cognac is aged in oak casks which give the brandy its color. There are several different types. The best of all Cognacs, called Grande Fine Champagne, should be used for desserts and special dishes only after you have become a crackerjack in the kitchen. Otherwise, three-star Cognac or V.S.O.P. (very superior old pale) Cognac will be adequate. Cog-

nac finishes a sauce beautifully for chicken, veal, beef, game or venison. It must be reduced or ignited for flambéing. See FLAMBAGE.

Condiments: These include any spicy sauce or relish eaten with meats or vegetables to perk up their natural taste, such as mustards, relishes, ketchup, steak sauces and horseradish.

Conical strainer: A small wire strainer with a plastic handle and wire mesh approximately ⅛-inch square is a must for careful cooks who want a sauce free of unwanted flour lumps and overcooked aromatics. The best investment is a strainer made of stainless steel, which will last almost 25 years.

Court-bouillon: This is the name given to a large water bath flavored with varied aromatics but mostly carrots, onions, a bouquet garni and white-wine vinegar or lemon juice, in which whole fish or fish steaks are poached. To be flavorful enough, the aromatics must be simmered in the water before the fish is added for at least 20 minutes. Adding enough salt to the court-bouillon is important to balance the acid of the vinegar.

Lamb's or calf's brains are also poached in a wine vinegar court-bouillon. Often some of the court-bouillon is reduced (see REDUCE) and butter is whipped into it to make a sauce for the fish or brains.

Court-bouillon freezes well and can be reused and "rejuvenated" by adding more wine and aromatics. The more a court-bouillon cooks, the better it tastes.

Cream: In French cuisine, cream for cooking always means heavy cream and is called crème fraîche. You can use your local heavy cream to replace it. Since French heavy cream has a slightly sour taste, add a bit of sour cream if you want. The few attempts that have been made in the United States to prepare *crème fraîche* have had various degrees of success and have always been fairly expensive in the end. Unfortunately, French *crème fraîche* cannot really be made.

Creams: A dessert cream in French cuisine is a pudding or an egg dessert sauce. Creams thickened with both egg yolks and a starch (flour, cornstarch or potato starch) must show three or four good boils before you remove them from the heat. Failure to see these boils may mean that the egg yolks have not cooked enough. If such is the case, you will soon see the cream liquefy and become "soupy." If this happens, put the cream back on the heat and recook until you can see those boils, and stir well so that the temperature is uniform all through the pot.

Do not hesitate to boil egg yolks as long as they are mixed with flour or other starch. The important thing to remember is that the temperature of the egg/starch mixture must rise very gradually and very slowly.

Custards made with egg yolks and milk only and with no starch *should never boil.*

Crêpe pan: Crêpe pans are made of cast iron or steel. Those of cast iron are better since they are more porous and retain more fat. French crêpe pans are best in sizes 18 through 22. (The number written on the handle represents the diameter of the pan in centimeters.) These pans should be seasoned in exactly the same way as an omelet pan (see OMELET for the proper way to season the pan). Like an omelet pan, a crêpe pan is never washed. It is sterile due to the high temperature it must reach in order to cook with it.

Curry: Curries vary with the taste of the person who composes them. They are always made of several spices, the most common being cuminseed, coriander, fenugreek, turmeric and cardamom. Since these spices contain starches, curry should always be cooked in butter before being added to liquid. If you prepare a curry sauce, it is best to cook the spice mixture in the butter before you add the flour to make the *roux.*

Deciliter: A deciliter is one tenth of a liter and it measures between $\frac{1}{3}$ and $\frac{1}{2}$ cup liquid in the American AVP system and $\frac{1}{2}$ cup in the BSI system.

Deglazing: The present participle of "to deglaze" is turned substantive to express the action of dissolving the concentrated and caramelized cooking juices of a meat or a gravy. You can deglaze with water, wine, plain broth or excellent stock. It is always better to discard any fat in a pan before deglazing, especially if you decide to deglaze with wines or spirits.

Deglazing is also done for roasts of all meats. You can add herbs, mustard, butter or cream to a deglazing to change the taste of the basic gravy.

Doneness: There are several ways to check the doneness of a meat:

Chickens are done when the juice runs clear from the cavity or from a hole left in the meat by a skewer inserted at the thickest part of the leg.

Ducks are done when the juices run clear from the cavity.

Braised red meats are done when a skewer inserted into the meat comes out without difficulty.

Panfried steaks and chops are rare when a finger can be pushed $\frac{1}{4}$ inch into the meat; medium rare when a finger can be pushed $\frac{1}{8}$ inch into the meat; well done when a finger meets resistance and cannot go into the meat.

Roasted joints are rare when a skewer inserted at the center, then pulled out, feels barely lukewarm when applied to the top of the hand; medium rare when the skewer feels warm; well done when the skewer feels very warm.

Cakes and breads are fully baked when a skewer inserted at the center comes out dry and feels too hot to be bearable to the top of the hand.

Baked custards are done when a skewer inserted two thirds of the way to the center of the custard comes out clean and hot. Cool the custard in its water bath.

Poached fruits are done when a darning needle pierces them and comes out freely.

Duck: French duck taste is not the preferred duck taste of the English-speaking world. French people like their ducks rare; as a result they slaughter them young before they have time to develop toughness and fat. If you can find true ducklings, barely 3 pounds in weight, try the French roasting method at a high temperature for about 45 minutes. But if you can find only larger ducks 4 pounds and over, the good old delicious English-style roasting in a slow oven is still the best to obtain soft meat and crisp skin.

Eggs: Large eggs are used in all recipes, although jumbo eggs give plumper omelets. A large egg weighs 2 ounces or approximately 60 grams. The best grade is AA fresh fancy quality.

The freshness of an egg can be readily seen from the size of its air pocket. If the air pocket is the size of a dime, then the egg is 3 to 8 days old; if it is the size of a penny, then the egg is 1 to 3 weeks old.

Eggs have the potential to coagulate and to foam, and both of these capacities are used in cooking and baking.

Fatback: The unsalted thick layer of fat removed from the back of porkers and used in the making of forcemeats for pâtés, terrines and stuffing.

Flambage, flamber: This refers to the action of igniting and burning the alcohol in wines and spirits. Besides being at-tractive to look at, the *flambage* of an alcohol or wine is necessary so that the alcohol burns off and does not act aggressively on the palate. To *flamber*, heat the alcohol in a small pan, ignite it with a match, and pour it flaming over a dessert or into a sauce.

Flours: Flours vary with the grain they are made of. Some are soft, some are hard. The more starch a flour contains, the softer it is; the more proteins a flour contains, the harder it is.

European flours are softer than American flours. It is up to the cook to learn to work with the flour at her disposal. Read the labels on your flour packages. If a flour appears to be too strong to make a pastry with, remove approximately 1 ounce per pound and replace it by cornstarch.

Basically soft flours make better, softer pastries and hard flours make better breads, but you can work with anything you have.

Folding: This refers to the action of introducing an egg-white foam into an egg-yolk foam or a flour batter, without deflating the egg-white foam so it retains its leavening power. To fold, always start by mixing one quarter of the total volume of the whites into the receiving batter, then empty the remaining bulk of the whites over the lightened batter. Using a large rubber spatula, cut down to the bottom of the batter at dead center. Bring the batter on top of the whites by turning your wrist toward the center of the bowl. Do not turn the spatula handle, but twist your wrist so that it ends up facing away from you. As you do so turn the bowl regularly from left to right with your left hand. The faster the folding the better.

For cakes and mousses, fold until the batter is homogenous. For soufflés, overfold a little; it will not hurt.

Food processor: This is the best friend of

the modern housewife. Many models are made in the United States. The best remains the Cuisinart, originally designed in France. A food processor does everything from chopping to puréeing, cutting vegetables, and grinding cheese and nuts, thanks to diverse blades and cutters.

Forcemeat: This is a mixture of ground meats and pork fatback used in the composition of stuffings, terrines and pâtés. There is always twice as much meat as fatback in a forcemeat and the binders are bread crumbs and eggs. Note that salt pork or bacon cannot replace fresh fatback in a forcemeat or the forcemeat will be too dry.

To handle a forcemeat after it is finished, wet your hands in cold water so that the forcemeat does not stick to them while you are building your dish.

To taste the seasoning of the forcemeat, shape the meat into a patty and cook it in a frying pan, as for a hamburger patty, until well done. Refrigerate the cooked patty in the freezer so you can taste it chilled. Forcemeats always need a lot of salt since the cold diminishes the taste of the salt.

Garlic: *To peel* garlic cloves for chopping, crush them with the flat side of a knife blade. The skin will come off easily. *To chop* garlic, sprinkle a pinch of salt over the pulp and garlic will not stick to the blade. *To mash* garlic, flatten already chopped garlic with the tip of the knife blade until the garlic is reduced to a purée.

Glaze: When applied to meats, this refers to the reduction of an excellent broth which becomes very thick by cooking down or reducing. It also refers to the deglazing of a cooked meat which is reduced further so that it becomes syrupy and thick.

When applied to cakes, this refers to any sugar syrup or icing-type mixture that will give the top of a cake, pie or candy a smooth, shiny appearance.

Gluten: This is a strong protein that develops when you handle flour in the presence of a liquid (water, milk, etc.); it has so much elasticity that it is undesirable in pastries, but very desirable in breads. Gluten will also develop if you add flour to a cake batter by stirring. Your cake will have "tunnels " and feel rubbery. In "butter cakes" started by creaming the butter, sugar and egg yolks, the flour should be flattened into the butter, while in those cakes started by "ribboning," flour should be folded into the egg/sugar mixture.

Gram: The basic metric weight measure is the gram. There are 100 grams in a hectogram, 500 grams in a European pound, and 2 pounds or 1000 grams in a kilogram.

The American avoirdupois ounce is just a little over 28 grams and can be rounded off in recipes as weighing 30 grams. An American pound is 454 grams.

Gratin, gratiner: A gratin is any dish allowed to bake in the oven or brown under the broiler to develop a crispy, delicious top. The verb *gratiner* expresses the action of browning and developing that brown top. The brown top can be made with butter and crumbs, with cheese, or with plain heavy cream.

Gravy: A gravy is not a sauce, although the words are often used interchangeably. A gravy is made of the cooking juices of a meat which are deglazed and defatted, and then bound with a little starch. To make a good gravy, pour the cooking juices into a glass cup. Let fat and lean separate. Extract the lean part with a baster. Mix a bit of cornstarch or potato starch with a drop of cold water and stir into the simmering gravy. You can, if you want, add a pat of butter.

In the case of a roast, you may think that there is no gravy because the meat juices are all hardened (caramelized) on the bottom of the roasting pan. Dissolve these hardened juices with hot water, bouillon or wine.

Ham: Ham comes from the legs of porkers usually cured in salt and sugar, then smoked or air-dried, or simply boiled after curing.

Air-dried and *cured:* Europeans are fond of all air-dried hams such as prosciutto from Italy, Bayonne ham from France and Serrano ham from Spain. In German countries ham is often smoked. The chances are that in any cookbook translated from French you will see Italian prosciutto as a replacement for the "mountain or Bayonne ham" of France, which cannot be found in America. You can use any air-dried and local ham that you may have and like.

Boiled ham is universally known as such and exists all over the world. You must remember, though, to taste it before cooking. If the ham is highly salted, soak it in milk before using it so that the excess salt leaches into the milk. This will also prevent your dish being ruined by excess salt.

Hazelnuts: These are known in French as *avelines* when they come from wild trees or as *filberts.* Buy them already shelled. *To peel* them, put them on a jelly-roll pan in a medium oven. As soon as you see the skin begin to crack and shred, remove nuts to a tea towel and rub them firmly. The skin will come off easily. *To grind* them, remember always to add a bit of sugar to prevent caking in the blender or food processor.

Hazelnut butter, brown butter: see BUTTER.

Herbs: The leaves and stems of aromatic plants are used to flavor foods, as well as medicinal teas and compounds. The best herbs are always fresh and come in "taste families" such as mint-basil; anise-fennel-tarragon; rosemary-savory-marjoram-thyme. When no fresh herbs are available, you can use dried herbs in lesser amounts but you must revive them in a small amount of hot water first.

Julienne: This is a style of cutting vegetables. See AROMATICS.

Knives: A good home cook needs only two knives: a paring knife and a chef's knife. The size of the chef's knife will depend on the size of your hand. An 8-inch blade is a good average. There are many brands and styles to choose from. Whichever you choose, consider that it will be an expensive investment but that it will last a lifetime. See SHARPENER.

Lettuce, salad greens: Greens require a great deal of care. First wash the head of lettuce under cold, running water to dislodge gravel from between the leaves. Remove each leaf separately and wash it again. Remove the lettuce ribs and tear each leaf into three or four bite-size pieces. Put the lettuce on tea towels and roll each towel loosely. Store in the refrigerator until you are ready to use.

Liaison: This is the French word for "binding" and it is applied usually to the following mixtures:

Egg yolks and cream: 3 egg yolks and ½ cup cream for each 2 cups of a white sauce. The way to add the *liaison* to the sauce is crucial. First add some of the hot sauce gradually to the *liaison* until half of the volume of the sauce is mixed with the *liaison.* Then reverse the process and gradually add the *liaison* to the other half of the sauce. Heat until you can see one or two small boils. Do not continue boiling or the sauce, rich in fat, will separate. To fix a sauce that separates, add hot stock, whisking well as you do so.

Liver and stock: Brown sauces for venison and game are often finished with liver puréed in stock. It is essential that this type of *liaison* never shows a trace of boiling or the liver will harden and discolor from pink to green! Bring the sauce to a high boil, then remove the pot from the heat. Proceed in the same manner as for the egg and cream *liaison*. When the liver *liaison* is combined with the sauce, you will not need to reheat the mixture and the sauce will retain the rose color it should have.

Macerate: Another word for marinate, but one that is applied especially to fruits soaking in a liqueur or spirit.

Marinade, marinate: A mixture of wine, or wines, or wine and vinegar, flavored with aromatics in which meats are steeped and allowed to soak for hours or days before being cooked so as to give additional flavor to the meats. Marinades flavor meats, they do not tenderize them for the effect is too superficial. Marinades may be cooked or uncooked. To obtain a cooked marinade, simmer the aromatics in the chosen wine for 20 minutes, but let this cool completely before pouring the liquid over the meat. Large pieces of meat must be turned in their marinade at regular intervals.

Meat extract: This is a semisolid commercial product sold in glass jars to replace homemade meat glaze. Add it in very small amounts to a finished sauce to correct the final taste, or to stews cooked exclusively in wine mixed with water to supply the lacking meat taste. Be aware that meat extract is very salty, very pungent, and can ruin a good dish. Therefore, add it little by little until you reach the desired meat flavor. Several brands of meat extract exist, so you should choose your favorite brand only after you have tried them all.

Melon baller: This is the down-to-earth name of the French potato cutter known as *cuillère parisienne*. It is used in France to cut potatoes as well as melon balls. A sturdy French one will last a lifetime and has two sizes of cutters, one is ¾ inch wide; the other is ½ inch wide.

Mirepoix: A style of cutting vegetables. See AROMATICS.

Mushrooms: By nature mushrooms are very spongy; if soaked in water, they will soak up almost all of the water and consequently lose a lot of their taste. It is, therefore, not a good idea to wash mushrooms too much. Wash them only if they are extremely dirty. Otherwise, wipe off the excess dirt with a paper towel. Also trim off the stem ends. Wild mushrooms, on the other hand, will invariably need to be washed because of dirt and slugs. Slugs will fall off if a bit of vinegar is added to the washing water.

To cook mushrooms for a garnish and use their juices in a sauce, heat some butter, add the mushrooms, and season with salt and pepper. Toss the mushrooms in the hot butter and cover them. The juices will run out of them within 3 to 7 minutes. Separate juices from mushrooms.

To sauté mushrooms as a vegetable proceed as above, but let the juices evaporate completely and continue sautéing until the mushrooms brown in the butter. Add whatever herb you like.

Mussels: Mussels always contain a certain amount of sand; the way to remove it is to soak the mussels in salted water. They will believe that they are in the sea again, especially if you use sea salt, and they will open up their shells to release the sand. Do not soak mussels in plain water since they will lose all their tang.

To clean mussels, scrub them with a knife or a clean plastic pot scrubber. Next squeeze the shells between your thumb and finger from right to left. This is extremely important since dead mussels will fall apart and healthy ones will let out a "phftt" as the air is squeezed out of their shells. When you steam the mussels, any that remain closed after steaming should be discarded.

Mussel juices are always used in sauces because of the marvelous flavor. But the juices are sandy and they should be strained either through a paper coffee filter or several layers of cheesecloth.

Mustard: Mustard comes dry as a powder or prepared in jars. In French cuisine the mustard used is mostly prepared Dijon mustard which contains wine and vinegar. Dijon mustard comes plain, strong and yellow, or flavored with purées of herbs such as tarragon, in which case the mustard takes on a greenish tinge and an added delicious flavor.

Needle test: This is used to test the doneness of poached fruit such as pears and peaches. The fruit is done when a needle inserted in the body of the fruit goes in and comes out freely.

Olives: Olives are either green or black. Green olives are unripe, black olives are ripe. Both are soaked in brine to remove the strong bitterness contributed by the tannic acid contained in the skin. As the olives stay in the brine, they acquire a strong, salty taste. To prevent the salt permeating any dish prepared with olives, the olives must be pitted, then blanched in plain boiling water for a few minutes.

Black oil-cured olives are ripe olives cured in olive oil. They need not be blanched and are mostly used in salads.

Omelet pan: A good omelet pan is made of cast iron and must be conditioned before use. Wash the pan well before beginning. Sauté an onion in some oil in the pan. Discard the onion and rub the oil all over the inside of the pan with a paper towel. Fill the pan with oil to within ⅓ inch of the rim. Heat the oil well and let the pan soak overnight. You may reuse the oil to brown meats. After you have conditioned your pan *never*

wash it. The high heat at which it must be heated to cook the omelet keeps it always sterile. If your pan starts "sticking" add a tablespoon or so of oil to it and a tablespoon of coarse salt and rub vigorously. Wipe dry; your pan is reconditioned.

The same treatment may be applied to crêpe pans.

Omelet pans are best in sizes 20 (2 eggs), 22 (3 eggs), 24 (4 eggs) and 26 (6 eggs). An omelet made with 2 eggs is a reasonable portion for one.

Onions: There are onions and onions ...For cooking use ordinary yellow onions, chopped or sliced. They are excellent in stews, broth, soups and onion soup. For a side dish use either white boiling onions or their tiny little brothers, the silverskin onions. For a garnish in a stew, only silverskin onions look "French." Before cooking them you should cut a tiny cross in the root end to prevent them separating into layers. Red Spanish onions and large sweet Bermuda onions are excellent when thinly sliced in salads. Should they be pungent, soak the slices in salted water.

Ounce: The basic liquid and solid measure of the avoirdupois system is the ounce. There are 16 liquid ounces in a pint and 32 in a quart in the United States, while there are 20 liquid ounces in a pint and 40 in a quart in Britain.

There are 16 solid ounces in a pound and each ounce is the equivalent to 28 generous grams, most of the time rounded off to 30 grams.

Parisian spoon: see MELON BALLER.

Pastry bag: A bag made of plastic material or denim that can be fitted with a nozzle or a tip for decorating cakes or desserts with cream stiff enough to be piped. Pastry bags must be scrupulously washed, rinsed, and dried after each use or they will become unsanitary and dangerous.

Pastry tips or nozzles: These are diverse conical tubes that fit into a pastry bag. Piping cream through each nozzle results in different designs, such as rosettes, leaves, flowers, etc. Plain tubes may be fitted for piping éclairs, *choux* (cream puffs) and *profiteroles* (tiny cream puffs).

Pàté: A pâté consists of a pastry casing containing a forcemeat. Both are baked together and eaten either hot or cold. Pâtés come in all shapes: round; loaf shaped; etc. At home they are best made in a pie plate. See also TERRINE.

Persillade: This is a mixture of finely chopped garlic and parsley widely used in French cuisine, especially in the provinces south of the Loire. The cooks of Provence prefer the *persillade* browned whereas those of the Languedoc and Aquitaine provinces prefer it plain.

Poaching: To poach means to cook in liquid without boiling. Fish is mostly poached in *court-bouillon* or in the oven in a small amount of fish stock and wine. The term also applies to white meat of chicken cooked extremely fast in a very high oven to obtain a "super tender" texture.

Pots and pans: If you can afford good expensive pots and pans, fine and all the better. But if you cannot, please do not worry, but relax, since one can really cook in anything. It is the cook who has the intelligence and the pot which has to follow the cook. If you are going to buy pots and pans, make sure that they are thick and heavy for good heat conduction rather than thin and more liable to warp under high heat. Heavy aluminum and enameled cast iron are the best. Only three types of pans must be specialized; you must have: a braising pot, nice and heavy, preferably of enameled cast iron; an omelet pan, made of cast iron; and a crêpe pan, made of cast iron. In any case, try to work with what you have. If your pots are thin, start cooking over lower heat so that your foods will not burn.

Copper pots for all their beauty and appeal should be considered a thing of the past in a home. They cost too much and are difficult to maintain. The only ones that you should consider are those pots coated with copper on the outside and with heavy stainless steel on the inside.

Pressure cooker: This is one of the best friends of working cooks. Read the directions carefully and observe them with care. However, remember that French cuisine prepared in a pressure cooker does not measure up to French cuisine prepared in those good old slow-cooking pots.

Prosciutto: This is air-dried Italian ham used in this book to replace the Mountain and Bayonne hams of France.

Provençale herbs: In Provence, herbs grow naturally on the *garrigues*. The three main ones are rosemary, savory and thyme. These are often sold in jars or bags labeled "Provençale herbs." Often the blend will also include mint and orégano.

Reduce, reduction: In culinary terms, the verb *reduce* is used to express the action of cooking down a liquid to evaporate moisture and concentrate taste. A *reduction* is the result of reducing a mixture. The best example of a reduction can be found in the base of a Béarnaise sauce where wine, vinegar and aromatics are reduced together, before the eggs and the butter are added to finish the sauce.

Ribbon, ribboning: This is the translation from the French *ruban* or *faire le ruban*. This technique refers to the building of the foam which results when egg yolks and sugar are whipped together. Many writers use the expression "beat the yolks until thick and lemon-colored," but since egg yolks beaten with sugar very quickly turn lemon-colored this is no guarantee that the mixture is stiff enough. The French have a way of checking this: they lift the beaters out of the egg-yolk foam and if the batter folds heavily back upon itself in slow folds reminiscent of those of a heavy silk ribbon, then the egg-yolk foam is ready for the completion of the next step. Pay great attention to the "ribbon" when you are making cakes or creams since their success depends on it.

Roux: A roux is a thickener or binder made of a mixture of melted butter and flour cooked together to give a better taste to the flour by starting the cooking of the starches. The more one cooks a roux, the more the thickening power of the flour diminishes. There are basically two types of roux: the "white roux" which is really straw yellow and cooks for 3 to 5 minutes, and the "brown roux" which is hazelnut brown and cooks for 10 to 15 minutes.

Salpicon: This is a style of cutting vegetables. See AROMATICS.

Salt pork: This is the salted fatback of pork. It can never replace the French salted pork called demi-sel, nor can it replace the fresh fatback used in forcemeats since it contains too much salt and has been kept too long in storage.

Sauce: A sauce is not a gravy, although the words are often used interchangeably. As stated under GRAVY, a gravy is made from the drippings or cooking juices of a piece of meat. A sauce, on the contrary, can be made with a white roux and milk (Béchamel, p.55); a white roux and white stock (Velouté, p. 56); a brown roux and brown stock (Brown Sauce, p. 58). To create a tie between the sauce and the meat, the deglazing of the meat can be added to a basic sauce.

There are also sauces prepared with a reduction of acid, poached egg yolks and melted butter. These are called "emulsified sauces," and they include Béarnaise and Hollandaise (see p. 63).

There are also cold emulsified sauces which include Mayonnaise and Vinaigrette (see p. 62 and p. 65).

Modern sauces are made by simply adding butter to a reduction of broth, a gravy or a reduction of white wine or vinegar. These sauces are also emulsified sauces but are often called butter sauces.

Sauceboat: The best sauceboat is the French type built with a gravy separator. It has two spouts with M (maigre = lean) which will let only lean gravy pass through, and the other with G (gras = fat) which will allow both lean and fat to pour onto food.

Sauce spoon: This is the large oval spoon usually part of the basic kitchen spoon-sets.

Sauter: Sauter means "to jump" in French, thus it conveys the idea that the food is tossed into the pan and "jumps" above its bottom. However, the word has acquired diverse meanings. It also means panfrying when a scallop of veal, for example, is cooked quickly in hot butter in a skillet. For vegetables it can also mean panfrying or tossing the vegetables in hot fat until they are crisp and tender and have lost all their moisture. Sautéed potatoes will become crisp and turn golden as will tiny onions. Finally, a sautéed chicken is first browned in butter or olive oil. Then you add a cupful or so of liquid to the pan, and you may also add a garnish of vegetables. The chicken then cooks until it is tender.

Seasonings: Seasonings are those ingredients that are added to foods to modify their basic taste and to make them more palatable. Sugar, salt, pepper, celery salt, spices, herbs and condiments are all seasonings. Note that *cold* deadens the effect of seasonings and that more salt or more sugar should be added to foods that will be served cold, deep-chilled or frozen.

Sharpener, sharpening: Your knives are just as good as your sharpener. Buy a good stone or a good steel and sharpen your blades by rubbing them on the stone or sharpener at a 20-degree angle. There is a sharpener made of hard carbon material which is expensive, but will last a lifetime.

Skewer test: see also DONENESS. The skewer test is used for meats that have been pot-roasted or braised. If a skewer inserted at the center of a piece of meat goes in and comes out freely, then the meat is done. As long as the meat lifts with the skewer, it needs longer cooking.

Skimming: Bouillons, soups, boiled dinners and sauces are skimmed, which means that the impurities coming to their surface can and must be removed with a spoon. Use a large sauce spoon to bring the scum from the center of the pot to its edge. Use the "belly" of the spoon, not its tip, and lift off the scum or fat. Discard the scum.

Skins: Skins build on sauces, creams and custards while they cool due to superficial dehydration. To prevent this happening, proceed as follows: cover sauces in saucepans with clear plastic wrap stretched over the pan; brush the top of creams of the pudding type with a pat of very cold butter stuck on the tines of a fork, or sprinkle with a thin layer of sugar; stir *crème anglaise* (stirred custard) constantly until it has cooled.

Slurry: A slurry is a mixture of pure starch (cornstarch or potato starch) and a cold liquid. It is usually added to a simmering gravy to turn it into a sauce by thickening it. It is essential that the gravy simmer and not boil, for excess mechanical action prevents the starch thickening, and excess heat provokes the hydrolyzation of the starch. Hydrolyzation is the liquefaction of the sauce so that the thickening does not take place.

Spatulas: There are several types of spatulas: turners are spatulas for turning over meats; folding is best done with a rubber spatula of a large size, approximately 3½ x 2½ inches, with a plastic or wooden handle; frostings and icings are best spread on cakes with long stainless-steel spatulas approximately 10 inches long and 1 inch wide.

Spices: Herbs are chiefly plant leaves used freshly chopped, or dried and revived; spices are seeds, dried or ground, roots, twigs or even barks. Allspice berries, for example, are dried, and they can be used whole for some preparations, but they are more often ground, as are cinnamon bark, nutmeg seeds, and white and black peppercorns.

Spirits: A spirit is any brandy at least 90 proof which is distilled from wine or fruit. Applejack and Calvados are both distilled from apple cider, Cognac and Armagnac are distilled from wines. Whisky and Bourbon are distilled from grains. All of these are used in cooking to give foods a special aroma, but if added to sauces they must be flambéed to burn off their alcohol.

Stir-frying: This is a Chinese technique for cooking vegetables adapted in France by the modern cooks. It consists of tossing finely cut vegetables (¼-inch-wide julienne strips) in hot oil until they are tender and crisp. The French "doneness" is one tiny stage beyond the "grassy" Chinese taste.

Stock: the technical word for BOUILLON.

Strainer: see CONICAL STRAINER.

Terrine: An earthenware dish in which the French bake forcemeats; these preparations then take on the name of the container in which they are baked. A terrine refers both to the container and its contents. Some of the best terrines (containers) are made of enameled cast iron and are fitted with lids. Terrines (the contents) are baked in a hot-water bath and left to cool in the bath until cold. A weight is then put on the meat to insure the proper texture.

Thickeners: see BINDERS. *Beurre manié, roux,* slurry and *liaison* are the most common thickeners.

Tomatoes: Fresh tomatoes good enough to eat or to make sauces with are only available at tomato season from July (in hot climates) or August (in cold climates) until the end of October. It is useless to try to make a sauce with the "vine" tomatoes "manufactured" for shipping rather than for eating, so in the winter use canned tomatoes. All those coming from the Mediterranean Basin (Israel, Greece, Italy, Spain) are excellent. Most of them are the "pear-shaped" tomatoes which the Italians label *pelati.* All countries with a national tomato canning industry can use their own product. Remember that the hotter the climate, the better the fruit.

Peeling tomatoes is easy: Bring a pot of water to a boil. Remove the stem and immerse the tomato in the boiling water for 2 minutes. Lift the tomato with a slotted spoon, rinse it under cold running water, and peel it.

Trussing: This is the tying of a bird so that it cooks evenly. Here is an easy method that does not require a trussing needle: Use a 20-inch length of kitchen string. Tie a knot around the "parson's nose" (the tail of the chicken) with half of the string in each of your hands. Then tie the string over the two drumstick ends. Pass the string on each side between the leg and the breast, pushing down. Turn the chicken or bird upside down and finally tie across the wings folded akimbo.

Vanilla: Use only pure vanilla, whether it is vanilla extract or vanilla bean. Vanilla extract is always added to desserts containing eggs to temper the egg taste, whatever the final flavoring of the dessert might be. When using a vanilla bean, cut it or use a small portion of it, and scrape the seeds into your dessert preparation.

To make vanilla sugar: bury the used or unused beans in a jar of granulated sugar.

Vinegars: Vinegars are made with many things: red and white wines; cider; pineapple wine; raspberries; etc. Use the vinegar you prefer; also think of flavoring basic vinegars by adding fresh sprigs of herbs to them, such as tarragon, chives and basil. White alcohol vinegar is not used in French cuisine for cooking purposes, but it used to pickle such vegetables as tiny gherkins and onions. Sherry vinegar is excellent but very potent; use it sparingly.

Water: Water for boiling pasta or rice should be salted at the very last minute, just before adding the noodles or rice, to prevent off-tastes from developing in combination with the starches.

Water bath (bain-marie): This is the *ban maria* of the Italians, who invented it before the Renaissance. It was brought to France by the cooks of the Medici princesses. It then became rebaptized *bain-marie.*

Remember always to proceed this way: Bring a kettle of water to a rolling boil. It is important that the water boils so that when you pour it into a baking dish it stabilizes at about 190°F. to help poach the food. Put the baking dish on the oven rack and set the container of food to be cooked in the dish. Pour the boiling water into the baking dish until the water comes up to ¾ inch from the rim of the container in which the food is cooking. When the cooking is completed, cool the food in the water bath.

A hot-water bath is also used to keep sauces hot.

Whisks: Small sauce whisks are a *must* in any kitchen, home or professional. The whisk is the best friend you will ever have in the kitchen. It allows you to gain time by adding hot liquids to hot *roux*. It breaks any lumps that form instantly. Stainless-steel whisks are the best.

Wines: There are two types of wine used in cooking: Natural red and white wines with 10 to 13% alcohol content; remember always to cook these wines down by at least 50% of their original volume so that they completely lose their alcohol by reducing. Fortified wines with 18 to 25% alcohol; these are Madeira, Sherry, Port, Marsala, etc. You may reduce these wines by adding them to a sauce while it cooks, or if you prefer you can add 1 or 2 tablespoons (US) or 1 tablespoon (UK) to each cup of finished sauce. All fortified wines come both dry and sweet. The dry ones are best for savory dishes, and the sweet ones for desserts.

INDEX

Recipes are listed under both English and French titles; under menu category (First Courses, Soup); under type of preparation (Aspic Dishes, Custards); under the chief ingredient (Apple, Beef, Leeks). Also listed are the suggestions and cooking hints. Advice can be found at the head of each recipe; *Notes* are at the end of recipes.